Walking With Your Ancestors

WALKING WITH YOUR ANCESTORS

A GENEALOGIST'S GUIDE TO USING MAPS AND GEOGRAPHY

MELINDA KASHUBA

FAMILY TREE BOOKS
CINCINNATI, OH
www.familytreemagazine.com

09 08 07 06 05   5 4 3 2 1

Library of Congress Cataloging-in-Publication Data

Kashuba, Melinda
    Walking with your ancestors : a genealogist's guide to using maps and geography / by Melinda Kashuba.
        p.   cm.
    Includes index.
    ISBN 1-55870-730-1
    1. Cartography—Handbooks, manuals, etc. 2. United States—Genealogy—Handbooks, manuals, etc. 3. United States—Genealogy—Maps. I. Title.
CS49.K37   2005
929′.1′072073—dc22   2005007209
                                                                              CIP

Editor: Sharon DeBartolo Carmack, CG
Associate editor: Erin Nevius
Production coordinator: Robin Richie
Interior designer: Sandy Conopeotis Kent
Cover design by David Mill, Design Mill
Icon designer: Cindy Beckmeyer

About the Author

Melinda Kashuba is a genealogical researcher, writer, and speaker with a Ph.D in geography. She writes for several periodicals. Her research specialty is nineteenth- and twentieth-century American maps and records. Visit her Web site at www.kashubaresearch.com.

DEDICATION

To my friend, husband, and fellow lover of old maps,
Timothy John Kashuba,
with grateful thanks for enduring many months of household
chaos and maps inhabiting almost every room of the house.

In memory of my uncle, Clarence Joseph Sweet Jr.
who loved books. His gentle nature, telephone conversations,
and sincere interest in this book are greatly missed.

Acknowledgments

Thank you to the numerous librarians and archivists nationwide who patiently answered my inquiries via e-mail and telephone. Michael Klein and Diane Schug-O'Neill of the Library of Congress, Kathleen Correia of the California History Section of the California State Library, and David Deckelbaum of the Henry J. Bruman Map Library at UCLA were particularly helpful. Joe Kreski, a geographer with the USGS, also took time away from his busy schedule to answer my persistent questions. My appreciation is sent to Bill Forsythe of HeritageQuest who provided me with a trial access to ProQuest's Historical Sanborn Collection.

A special thank you to the staff of The Newberry Library, who were gracious and accommodating at every turn during my participation in the "Reading Popular Cartography Institute" during the summer of 2004, especially Dr. Robert Karrow Jr., Patrick Morris, John Long, Peggy Tuck Simko, Jack Simpson, Grace Dumelle, and Susan Hanf. No words can express my gratitude to Dr. James Akermann, the director of the Herman Dunlap Smith Center for the History of Cartography at The Newberry Library, for inviting me to take part in that invaluable Institute that forever changed the way I look at maps. This book would not have been half as valuable without the benefit of the workshop lectures and resulting class discussions. My thanks also to my fellow Institute participants, seminar instructors, and fellow Newberry map pal, Art Holzheimer, who was gracious with his time and always knew "just the map I needed to see." My appreciation is also extended to the National Endowment for the Humanities for providing partial assistance for my participation in this Institute.

My thanks are given to John P. Wilson of Safety on Sight for his review of the chapter on GPS and John Kashuba for providing me with a scan of map-related material used in this book.

Special acknowledgments to Sharon DeBartolo Carmack and Erin Nevius, my editors at Family Tree Books, without whose help and encouragement this book would never have come to press.

Table of Contents
At a Glance

1   Maps in Genealogical Research, *1*

2   Finding Information about Places, *16*

3   Determining Boundaries and Jurisdictions, *41*

4   The Secrets of Map Reading, *64*

5   Topographic Maps, *96*

6   Land Division and County Maps and Atlases, *116*

7   Migration Trails Across America, *143*

8   Military Maps, *158*

9   Fire Insurance and Other Urban Maps, *183*

10   Using Global Positioning Systems, *196*

Appendix
      Major Map Collections in the United States, *210*

Index, *220*

Table of Contents

1   Maps in Genealogical Research, *1*
- *What is geography?*
- *What is a map and what is an atlas?*
- *How are maps and geography used in genealogical research?*
- *What does this book cover?*

2   Finding Information About Places, *16*
- *Why should I start with a gazetteer rather than a map?*
- *Where are gazetteers found?*
- *What is the best way to search in print or online gazetteers?*
- *Is there a way to locate old place-names?*

3   Determining Boundaries and Jurisdictions, *41*
- *Why are jurisdictional boundaries important in genealogical research?*
- *How do the definitions of* county *and* township *differ across regions in the United States, and does this affect where records are found?*
- *Where can I locate information about present and historical jurisdictions within a country?*
- *Where do I find political administrative maps that detail jurisdictional boundaries?*
- *Can census enumeration district maps help me locate someone I can't find in a census index?*

4   The Secrets of Map Reading, *64*
- *Are people born with the ability to create and read maps?*
- *How can reading a map help me in my research?*
- *Are maps like any other source of evidence?*
- *What is more important to genealogical research—knowing the absolute location or understanding the relative location of a place?*
- *What are the basic components of a map?*
- *How do you cite maps and atlases in your research?*

5   Topographic Maps, *96*
- *What is a topographic map?*
- *Why are topographic maps considered to be the mother of all maps?*
- *How do genealogists use topographic maps?*
- *Where do I find topographic maps for my personal use?*
- *Are the topographic maps on CD and online the same as the topographic maps on paper?*

6   Land Division and County Maps and
    Atlases, *116*
    - *How is property represented on a map?*
    - *Where do you find property maps?*
    - *How can I locate my ancestor's property?*

7   Migration Trails Across America, *143*
    - *What kinds of maps show migration information?*
    - *What kinds of maps did migrants use?*
    - *Where can I find a map that shows how my ancestor traveled from point*
      A to point B?
    - *Are there maps of railroad networks?*

8   Military Maps, *158*
    - *How has war influenced the way we draw maps?*
    - *What types of maps produced by military agencies are helpful to*
      genealogical research?
    - *Where can I find military maps; aren't they all top secret?*

9   Fire Insurance and Other Urban Maps, *183*
    - *What types of maps are available for towns and cities?*
    - *What are panoramic or bird's-eye-view maps?*
    - *How are fire insurance maps useful in genealogical research?*
    - *Where do I locate historical maps of towns and cities?*

10 Using Global Positioning Systems, *196*
    - *What is GPS navigation and how can it aid genealogical research?*
    - *Why do we still need to use maps if we have GPS technology?*
    - *What are the "rules" of using GPS?*
    - *What is GIS and how does it relate to GPS?*

APPENDIX
    Major Map Collections in the
    United States, *210*

Index, *220*

CHAPTER 1

Maps in Genealogical Research

Overview

- What is geography?
- What is a map and what is an atlas?
- How are maps and geography used in genealogical research?
- What does this book cover?

I f you picked up this book, chances are you belong to one of two categories of genealogists: (1) You love maps and use maps already in your research, and you are interested in learning more about them; or (2) Someone suggested that you should use more maps in your research because maps can help you find "the really good stuff." To a genealogist, the phrase "the really good stuff" is code for "records on my family back to Adam and Eve." Well, maybe not that far back, but I think you know what I mean. To the latter group, being told to use more maps is something akin to being told that you should eat more vegetables or lower your cholesterol level. Good advice—but rather vague. You might not know where or how to begin to access the rich world of maps. Fear not: This book will show you what to do. If you are a veteran map user, this book will help you by introducing you to different types of maps you may not have used before and by providing tips on how to search for them in libraries, archives, and on the Internet.

This book is designed to provide assistance to both types of genealogists: those who enjoy maps and live to pick up the latest edition of the *AAA North American Road Atlas*, and those who haven't had serious face time

WHAT IS A MAP?

A map is the basic tool of geography. All maps have the following characteristics:

- a description, representation, mirror, resemblance, or delineation, either of the world or some part of the earth or other body (including celestial).

- generally drawn on a flat surface or plane.

- contains selected features or characteristics that are culturally recognizable or are meaningful symbols depicted in spatial relation to one another.

- a product of creative human effort and choices designed to tell other people about the places or spaces they have experienced.

Maps have been drawn on many types of material, including stone, wood, metal, parchment, animal and fish skins, cloth, paper, vellum, and film. The computer screen is the latest medium that cartographers use to create their maps.

The words *map* and *chart* are sometimes confusing in their usage. In today's parlance, *chart* generally refers to maps that sailors or aviators use for navigation. Maps have a much broader meaning today and also include some types of imagery, such as pictures that represent the location of things, processes, and events on earth.

Important

with a map since eighth-grade geography class. And, of course, all the other genealogists who fall somewhere between these two extremes can also benefit from reading this book.

The truth about genealogy is that, although you might believe that it has something to do with *history*, it actually has something more to do with *geography*. Genealogy is a geographically driven subject. There's no question that history and historical events are important to tracing family trees; those names and dates are vital. But let's face facts: Records are made and kept by location. That makes geography *as* important if not *more* important than history to the genealogist. Knowing where your ancestors lived is the key to finding "the really good stuff" in those records.

What is geography? According to the etymological information in the eleventh edition of *Merriam-Webster's Collegiate Dictionary*, the word *geography* comes from the Greek word *geographia*, which means "to describe the earth's surface." The word has been in use since the third century B.C.E., when the Greek scholar Eratosthenes first used *geographia* in his writings about faraway places in the ancient world. That is probably the most easily understood meaning of the subject, though truth be told, geography is such a broad discipline even modern geographers have a tough time defining it. It is a much bigger subject than memorizing all the world's capitals or studying latitude and longitude, archipelagos, and permafrost. Geography has to do with *everything and anything that can be mapped*. It is a place-based or spatial science. Geographers not only describe the earth and study the distribution of things on the earth's surface, but also research the complex interactions between people (culture), the natural world (biology), and the physical world (geology, soils, hydrology, oceanography, climatology). Geographers see themselves as no less than heirs of the "Mother Science" that bridges the gap between the human and natural sciences, and maps are their primary tools.

You probably remember hearing schoolmates or your own children (or even yourself) lamenting, "Why do I have to learn this stuff? I'll never use it!" Maybe you were one of the lucky ones who really loved history and geography from your earliest school days, but most genealogists tell me that they came to love history and geography later in life—years after the last school bell rang for them. It was after experiencing life for a few more years that they discovered the role history plays in current events. Geography is much the same: The experience of traveling to other places is often the first taste of the role geography plays in our lives. Understanding geography not only makes us better people but opens up our genealogical research to new frontiers.

What are some of the ways maps can help you in your research?

Notes

The word *atlas* comes from the name of a figure in Greek mythology, *Atlas*. Punished by the gods for siding with the Titans, he was condemned to hold the earth and all the heavens for eternity on his shoulders. Atlas became a generic term used to described a book comprised mostly of maps, charts, and plans bound together in one or more volumes.

Maps identify the location of specific places.

Probably the premier function of maps is to help us answer specific locality questions, like "Where is the courthouse located?" or "Where is Park City, Illinois?" or "Where is Quebec?" Most of the time when genealogists reach for a map it is to answer a narrow question about location. "Where are such and such located?" Depending on the level of detail of the map (refer to the discussion on scale in the next chapter), really small places can be depicted on a local map, or only major and capital cities on a larger scale map that shows less detail but a bigger area (see Figure 1-3 on page 7).

Maps tell us how far specific places are from one another.

Not only do maps show us where specific places are located, they can also help us estimate distances between locations and show us the quickest route between them. Genealogists can answer questions such as "How far was it from my ancestor's farm to the nearest town?" or "How do I get from the courthouse to the library?" by looking at a map. The better constructed a map is, the more accurately we can measure or "scale off" (there is that pesky word *scale* again) distance. A map can save you the time and hassle

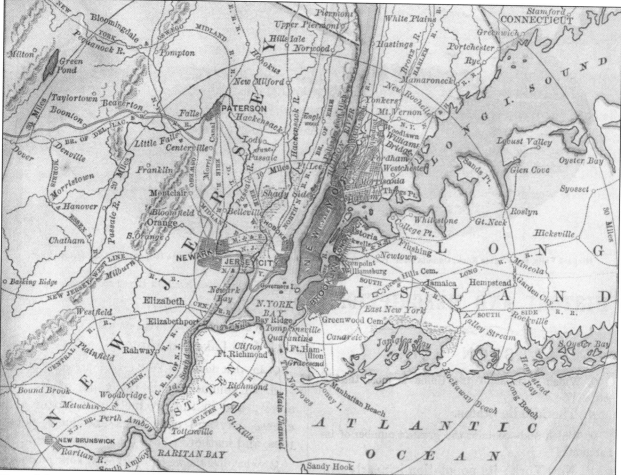

Figure 1-1
A map from a nineteenth century school book proclaiming "New York, the largest city on the Western Continent. Its vicinity for twenty miles around." Maps not only communicate the location of specific places, but also their context—in this case, topography, rivers, canals, roads, railroads, and cemeteries around New York City. *Source: James Monteith*, Manual of Geography Combined with History and Astronomy, *New York: A.S. Barnes & Company, 1868. Private collection.*

of writing down directions. The adage "a picture is worth a thousand words" can be modified to "a map is worth ten thousand words." Consider all the information a typical road map shows. What if you had to write all that information out by hand? Maps can reduce complicated reality into simple visual pictures.

People relate to the visual imagery of maps in an almost magical way. Whenever we have guests over for dinner, people are drawn to our "map wall," a collection of topographic maps showing the vicinity of where we live stuck to the wall with push pins (not a home decorator tip unless you like pin holes on your wallboard). More animated conversations take place next to this wall than anywhere else in the house (except around the kitchen table).

Maps can depict the relationship of a place to the region around it.
No place exists in complete isolation. Even an island in the middle of an ocean is affected by ocean currents and weather. Maps can show us the relationship of a place to its surroundings. Early towns were established in places specifically because of protection or defense offered by topographic barriers or the availability of a specific resource such as water, food, iron, or coal. In the eastern United States, there exists a "line of the falls" which separates the Piedmont or Upper Country region from the broad, sandy coastal plain of the East Coast. Towns grew up along this line that separated lower reaches of major rivers from the small falls and rapids of the hilly, upland region. These rivers served as both early sources of power generation and as heads of navigation on a number of rivers between Massachusetts and Georgia in the American southeast (see Figure 1-2 on page 6).

Maps capture the changes in the landscape over time. Towns grow, flourish, and die. Rivers shift their course (which sometimes changes boundaries). Some places are hard to find because their names have changed one or more times. Maps are good sources to document those name changes over time.

Maps help us visualize the places where our ancestors lived and died.
With the advent of modern map production in the nineteenth century, maps became cheaper both to produce and purchase. Mapmaking flew into high gear as the market for them grew. Depending on the country you are researching, chances are good that you can find a historical map of the locality your ancestor is from—perhaps even several over a given time period. One of the purposes of this book is to acquaint you with the incredible diversity of map resources available to the genealogist and local historian. **Maps are "cartofacts" (the combination of the French word *carte* meaning "card or map" and the word *artifact*) that contain historical place-names, boundaries, and locations of cultural features such as villages, schools, churches, fields, and cemeteries.** Like no other source, maps preserve these historical features and spatial relationships.

Maps enhance the background reading of historical places and eras. Whether the map covers a neighborhood (such as a fire insurance map) or a specific area (a topographic map or battlefield map), it can help us imagine what a place was like during a particular event in the past in much greater detail than even a photograph can.

Maps suggest migration routes as well as barriers to migration.
Typical questions that maps can answer include: "Where is the river, trail, or railroad nearest to my ancestor's land?" "How did my ancestors get from Boston to Ashtabula County, Ohio, in 1840?" "How difficult was it to travel from St. Louis, Missouri, to Sacramento, California, during the Gold

\di'fin\ *vb*

Definitions

PAWTUCKET FALLS.

Figure 1-2
A historic photo of the falls and rapids near Lowell, Massachusetts, a fall line city. The falls were created from resistant bedrock and exploited in the region as a source of power for textile mills. *Source:* Illustrated History of Lowell and Vicinity, Massachusetts. *Lowell, Massachusetts: Courier-Citizen Company, 1897.*

Rush?" "Did my ancestor's ship make any other stops in Europe between the time she embarked from Hamburg, Germany, and arrived in New York City in 1899?"

A topographic map that shows the shape of the hills and mountains, the depth of the valleys and gullies, and the network of creeks and rivers through a region can assist our understanding of the physical opportunities and constraints to migration our ancestors faced. Some of the earliest survey maps of an area attempted to portray animal migration routes, native hunting traces, and trading paths. Rivers were common migration routes during the formative years of our country. For that reason and others, the earliest accurate mapping in North America focused on coastlines and navigable streams and rivers. A map depicting North Atlantic shipping routes would provide insight into the passage between Europe and New York City and possibly even the volume of passenger traffic between ports (see Figure 1-3 below).

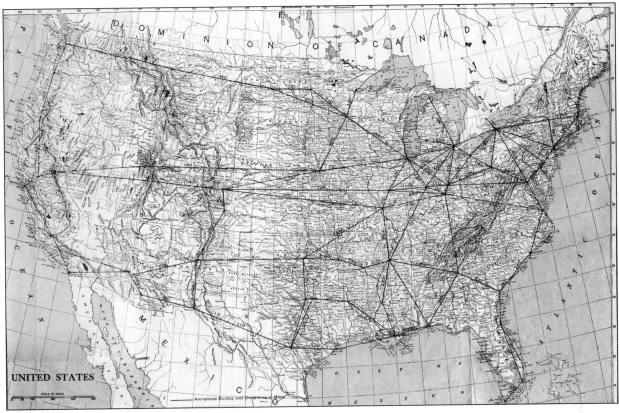

Figure 1-3
Old atlases often include at least one map showing shipping lines, major highways, and railroad routes. Modern highways and railroads often use or parallel earlier trails. *Source:* The New World Atlas and Gazetteer, *New York: Collier, 1921.*

Barriers to early migration into the hinterland included dense stands of forests, rough mountainous terrain, rivers, large bodies of water, and the presence of hostile native groups and representatives of competing European powers.

Maps provide us with insight into the culture of our ancestors.

The types of ornamentation used, the way patterns and distributions were represented, and all the little details found on historical maps give us a sense of what our ancestors considered important and what they were told about places distant from their homes (see Figure 1-4 on page 8). Mapmaking is not a "value-free" operation: All maps present a particular worldview. The mapmaker often reflected the tastes, perceptions, prejudices, pride, biases, and beliefs of the era. Maps were and still are used as propaganda tools. For instance, eighteenth-century maps portrayed North America as a

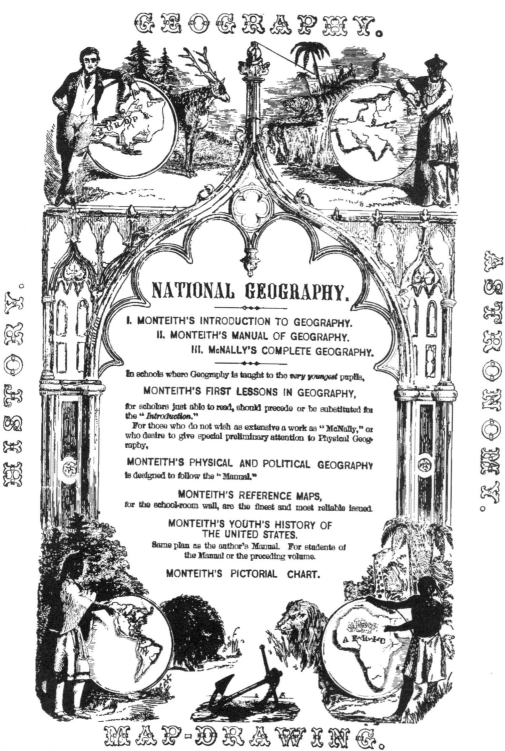

Figure 1-4

The symbols used on old maps give us insight into the culture of our ancestors. This advertisement found in a geography school book combines images of exotic animals and people, gothic architecture, and an anchor placed above the word "map drawing" symbolizing trust and confidence in the material presented to shape young minds. *Source: James Monteith,* Manual of Geography Combined with History and Astronomy, *New York: A.S. Barnes & Company, 1868. Private collection.*

BEGINNING A LOCALITY FILE

Your first step to becoming a committed map collector was probably the purchase of this book, or perhaps you are already a "closet geographer" and hoard maps in boxes, shoehorn them into your research files, or stuff them under your bed. Throughout this book are tips on creating your own library of maps or organizing a locality file that is personalized to your research interests.

Your first step should be to obtain current road maps of each area you research. It does not matter whether you start with a nationwide map or a state map. Gathering maps for each area you research educates you on the localities where your ancestors resided—the arrangement of natural and cultural features, place-names, and migration networks such as roads and railroads that pass through the area. You might want to start with where you live and work backward in time to the places where you lived or where your parents and grandparents lived.

Rather than squeeze these maps into family surname files, create a separate file folder or binder to house maps for a given location. That way you don't need to remember which family file folder you stuffed that map of San Francisco into (especially if you have several families that relate to San Francisco).

When I start researching a new place I use a hanging box-bottomed file (the kind that can hold several file folders and that you get from an office supply store) and give it the name of a country or state—"the big area." Within that box-bottomed file I have folders for regions or parts of the big area, such as county road maps, topographic maps, or Civil War battle maps.

Never punch holes in a map to hold it in a binder. Instead, use an archival, top-loading sheet protector also available from office supply stores. For larger maps that can't be folded or that you do not want to fold, purchase a freestanding cardboard map holder from the office supply store. You can note the location of the rolled map on a separate piece of paper and file it in the front of your "big area" file.

In her article "Building a Locality File," Juliana Smith suggests adding to your locality file a section that pertains to specific resources available in your research locality, such as the names, addresses, telephone numbers, Web sites, and hours of operation of libraries, archives, and historical societies. (See *The Family History Compass* online at <www.ancestry.com/library/view/columns/compass/5456.asp>.) Juliana further personalizes her locality file to include a brief history of the area, a synopsis of the various types of records available, a chronology of county formations, and beginning dates for vital, land, probate, and court records.

colony of the British Empire. The selection of place-names and wording depicted a successful transplantation of English culture in the New World. Likewise, nineteenth-century immigrant maps painted North American real estate in glowing colors and prose for landless European audiences.

Maps help direct us to records.

Of course, maps can show us where the courthouse is located. Maps can also give the boundaries of the local and regional governmental administrative units—the parishes, villages, towns, townships, and counties—where records were created and, possibly, are still stored today. I say "possibly" stored because many records have been destroyed, either by accident or on purpose. Some records may have been transferred from a "parent county" to a newly minted county or from local custody to the state archives. To begin to track records, you need to find out what the jurisdictional boundaries were at the time you believe the record was created. There is no guarantee that our ancestors respected boundaries. If a courthouse in an adjacent county was easier to get to than the courthouse in the county your ancestor resided in, chances are records for the ancestor may be found in both courthouses. People did not always behave rationally when it came to their travel habits.

As mentioned previously, old maps are terrific repositories for historical boundary information and are good places to start asking where records might be found (see Figure 1-5 on page 11).

Maps can be used to analyze the information we have on our families and help us see that information from a different perspective.

These are some of the questions you can use a map to help answer: "Can I identify where all of the families of the same surname lived in a particular county in a specific census year?" "Can I place a dot on a map where each family lived and then 'step back' and look for a pattern of residence?" "Are they scattered all over the county or concentrated in a few townships or villages?" "How would this information assist me in going forward with my research?"

You can map the prevalence of surnames by township, by county, and by state. For example, **you can go to the Hamrick Software's U.S. Surname Distribution Web site <www.hamrick.com/names> and request a map showing the distribution of a particular surname for the census years 1850, 1880, 1920, and 1990.** For each census year, you can observe the spread of a particular surname across the United States and see the relative concentration of the surname by state population (depicted by various colors).

Internet Source

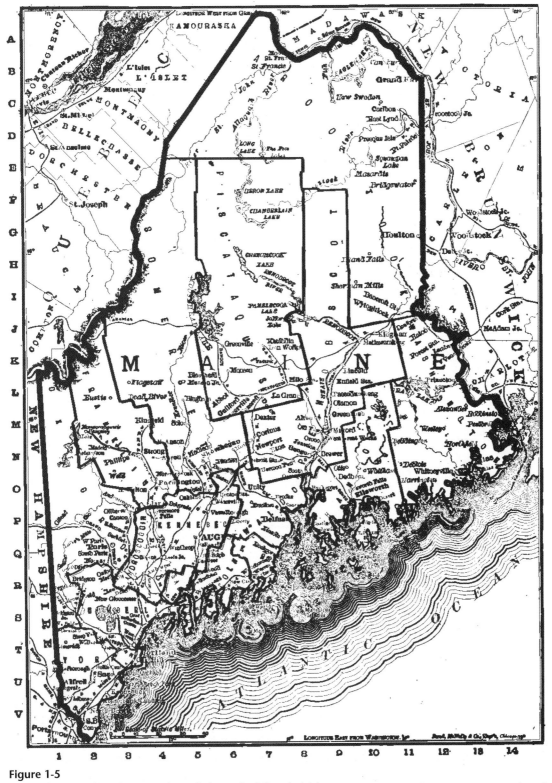

Figure 1-5
A map depicting historic county boundaries and rail lines in Maine. *Source: Rand, McNally & Company.* New Pocket Atlas. *Chicago: Rand, McNally & Company, 1893. Private collection.*

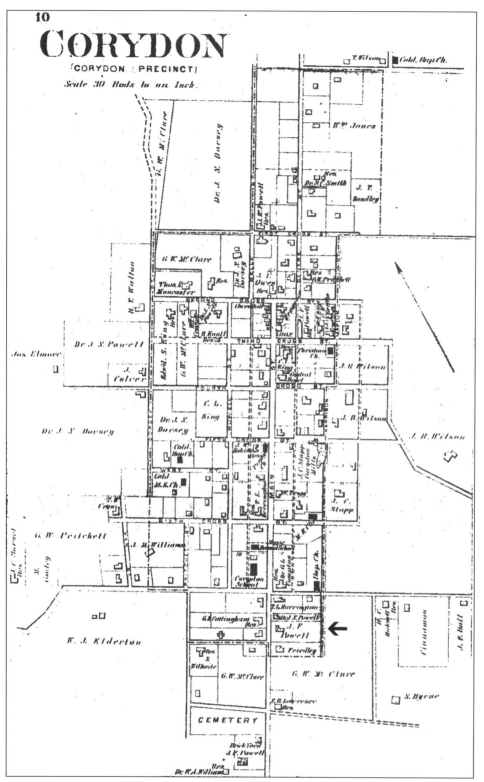

Figure 1-6A

A portion of Corydon, Kentucky, from a nineteenth-century county atlas map that lists the names of property owners on parcels they own. Although subject to some inaccuracies, county atlas maps are useful tools showing the relative locations of property owned by individuals. *Source:* An Illustrated Historical Atlas of Henderson and Union Counties, Kentucky. *Philadelphia: D.J. Lake & Company, 1880.*

Figure 1-6B
Powell children in front of their home in Corydon, Kentucky. *Source: Author's collection.*

Maps help us remember information about places.

Maps are tangible memories (see Figures 1-6A and 1-6B on pages 12-13). Our early ancestors recognized that maps scratched in the dirt communicated where water, food, or shelter could be found. Some geographers theorize that maps even predate written language, although none of these early maps survived, given that they were created on ephemeral materials such as animal skins or bark.

With maps, we don't have to clutter up our minds and remember the details of how to get to a relative's house located two states away. We are a culture awash in maps, with many sources of geographic information available to us: a paper map that captures the route, a virtual map from Web sites such as MapQuest <www.mapquest.com>, or an onboard navigational system in our car to show us the way to go.

Maps are also great storytelling tools and memory prompts. Next time you interview an elderly relative, bring along a map of the same era showing the place where he or she grew up—and watch the stories come out! The things you will learn! For example, I showed my mother a map of the San Francisco neighborhood she lived in during the 1930s and found out where she shopped for groceries, what streetcar she caught to go to school, and even where she received her first kiss from a boy! The last item was probably more than I wanted to know, but it made for a great story to add to the family history.

What is the best map for genealogical research? There is no one answer to that question. The best map is the one that answers your research question. One of the purposes of this book is to introduce you to the variety of maps available and help you formulate a research question that will enable you to locate the map you need. But in the most general sense, to repeat the advice given by the U.S. Geological Survey (USGS) in its descriptive pamphlet "Using Maps in Genealogy" (fact sheet 099-02, September 2002, <http://erg.usgs.gov/isb/pubs/factsheets/fs09902.html>), the best map is the one that:

- shows you the most detail of the area around where your ancestor lived;
- shows you the location of the place within a certain county or other jurisdiction;
- shows you the relationship of that place to the borders of adjacent governmental jurisdictions.

WHAT THIS BOOK COVERS

Maps are so basic to our modern culture that they often pass without notice. This book will be able to touch on only some of the maps available to us—those primarily relevant to genealogists—and it focuses only on U.S. maps. Obviously, you'll be able to uncover maps for foreign countries, as well, both in print and online. As the geographers Arthur H. Robinson and Barbara Bartz Petchenik elegantly state in *The Nature of Maps: Essays Toward Understanding Maps and Mapping* (Chicago: University of Chicago Press, 1976, page 15):

> There are specific maps and general maps, maps for the historian, for the meteorologist, for the sociologist, and so on without limit. Anything that can be spatially conceived can be mapped—and probably has been. Maps range in size from those on billboards or projection screens to postage stamps, and they may be monochrome or multicolored, simple or complex. They need not be flat—a globe is a map; they need not be of the earth—there are maps of Mars and the moon; or for that matter, they need not be of any place real—there have been numerous maps made of imaginary "places" such as Utopia and even of the "Territory of Love."

Summary Points

★ Geography is a wide-ranging spatial discipline that studies anything that can be mapped.

★ Maps have probably been around at least as long as written language, if not predating written communication.

★ Geography is important to your research in many ways beyond just locating a specific place on a map. It is as important if not more important than history when it comes to locating genealogical records.

★ Consider creating a separate locality file for each ancestral state or region.

★ With so many different kinds of maps available, the use of maps in your family history research is only limited by your imagination and time.

CHAPTER 2

Finding Information About Places

There is no part of the world where nomenclature is so rich, poetical, humorous, and picturesque as in the United States of America.

Quote attributed to Robert Louis Stevenson
by H.L. Mencken, "Geographical Names" in
The American Language, *rev. ed. (New York: Alfred A. Knopf, 1921).*

Overview

◆ *Why should I start with a gazetteer rather than a map?*

◆ *Where are gazetteers found?*

◆ *What is the best way to search print or online gazetteers?*

◆ *Is there a way to locate old place-names?*

Robert Louis Stevenson may have exaggerated his point a bit; every culture has named physical and cultural features colorfully and fancifully. H.L. Mencken, in his lively and monumental study *The American Language*, paid homage to the passage of a historic American landscape "besprinkled with place-names from at least half a hundred languages, living and dead." He particularly mourned the havoc and cultural destruction created by the U.S. Board on Geographic Names' eliminating or changing place-names of American Indian or foreign origin to please federal bureaucrats. He published his study at the end of World War I, when the United States was feeling the effects of its transition from a rural economy to one dominated by an urban and industrial economy. The older place-names were quickly disappearing from the landscape as people moved from the country to the city to follow employment opportunities.

As genealogists, we love to find these colorful old place-names amidst our families' records. However, we can become frustrated when we cannot locate them on a modern map. So what's a family historian to do? Make a dash for the nearest map collection? Perhaps. But simpler and easier tools are available that might bring faster results and point us toward the best map to answer our research question.

LOOKING IN ALL THE RIGHT PLACES

If map-collection librarians had one wish regarding their genealogical patrons (and contrary to what you might think, it's not that pesky genealogists would just go away), it would be that people searching for a map showing the location of their ancestor's village would begin their quest on the reference shelves of the library among the gazetteers and topographical dictionaries rather than in the drawers of the map room. Jumping into maps without adequate preparation more often than not leads to disappointment among novice researchers and a headache for the librarian. This chapter will describe the process of discovering information about specific locations in books and online before launching into a search for them on maps. This may seem counterintuitive, but the time spent researching an unfamiliar location through place-name dictionaries and gazetteers is well worth the preparation and will open doors to map resources you may not have considered using.

GAZETTEERS

If you have a U.S. road atlas at home, chances are you already own a gazetteer. Flip to the back of the road atlas and you will find a list of place-names in alphabetical order for the entire country. Some road atlases break the list up into smaller alphabetical lists by state. Sometimes these lists give a population figure and the page number where the place-name is found in the atlas. Location coordinates can be given either in latitude and longitude or by some internal system combining letters and numbers that represent grid squares on the map. As Global Positioning System (GPS) receivers have become popular with genealogists to locate features in the landscape, many genealogical software programs are able to accept latitude and longitude coordinates. Gazetteers often can provide you an approximation of latitude and longitude.

A gazetteer can be as simple as a list of place-names combined with a reference to where they are located by latitude and longitude, and the name of the county, state, or country where they are found today. Generally speaking, a gazetteer can be more elaborately described as a "place-name" or "topographical" dictionary. The entries can be encyclopedic in nature, giving lots of additional information besides the location of a place. It is not uncommon to find a brief history of a place-name, including who originally found it or named it and when. Older, archaic names for a place or a feature are also

Notes

sometimes given. If the entry is for a physical feature, such as a mountain or a river, additional information is usually given describing the height or length of the feature and when it may have been first discovered or described on a map and by whom.

A gazetteer might include a phonetic guide, just as in a word dictionary, to assist you in pronouncing the place-names. Sometimes a gazetteer combines features found in an almanac or encyclopedia and gives additional information that might include:

- a population count from the most recent census
- geographical descriptions beyond simple location
- brief historical information (e.g., famous battles or the birthplace of an important person)
- political divisions and jurisdictions (e.g., incorporated city, townland, manor, estate, county)
- economic development such as agriculture, industry, and services
- land use
- local religions
- educational institutions
- tourist attractions

Gazetteers as we recognize them today date back to the 1692 publication of the *Gazetteer's or Newsman's Interpreter* by Laurence Echard (London: John Salisbury). (See Figure 2-1 on page 19.) The need for a standardized list of place-names, political divisions, and geographic features grew out of the publishing industry. During the late eighteenth and early nineteenth centuries, place-name references became popular with businessmen, particularly those involved with the shipment of goods. During the nineteenth century the United States was undergoing tremendous expansion, and the hunger for the geographical information contained in gazetteers and maps was great. Early gazetteers were sometimes named "encyclopedias," so be sure to check library catalogs for all types of place-name compilations: gazetteers, topographical dictionaries, place-name dictionaries, geographical dictionaries, and encyclopedias.

The scope of a gazetteer can be international or national, and some focus only on a particular state, region, or even a single county. Place-name lists exist for empires long past, too. Just because you cannot find your particular location or physical feature listed in one gazetteer does not mean that it is not listed in another. As with any other reference, an important hint to using a place-name guide effectively is to read the introductory material to find out what sources were consulted to create the gazetteer and what may not have been included.

So why reach for a gazetteer first and a map second? Gazetteers can help

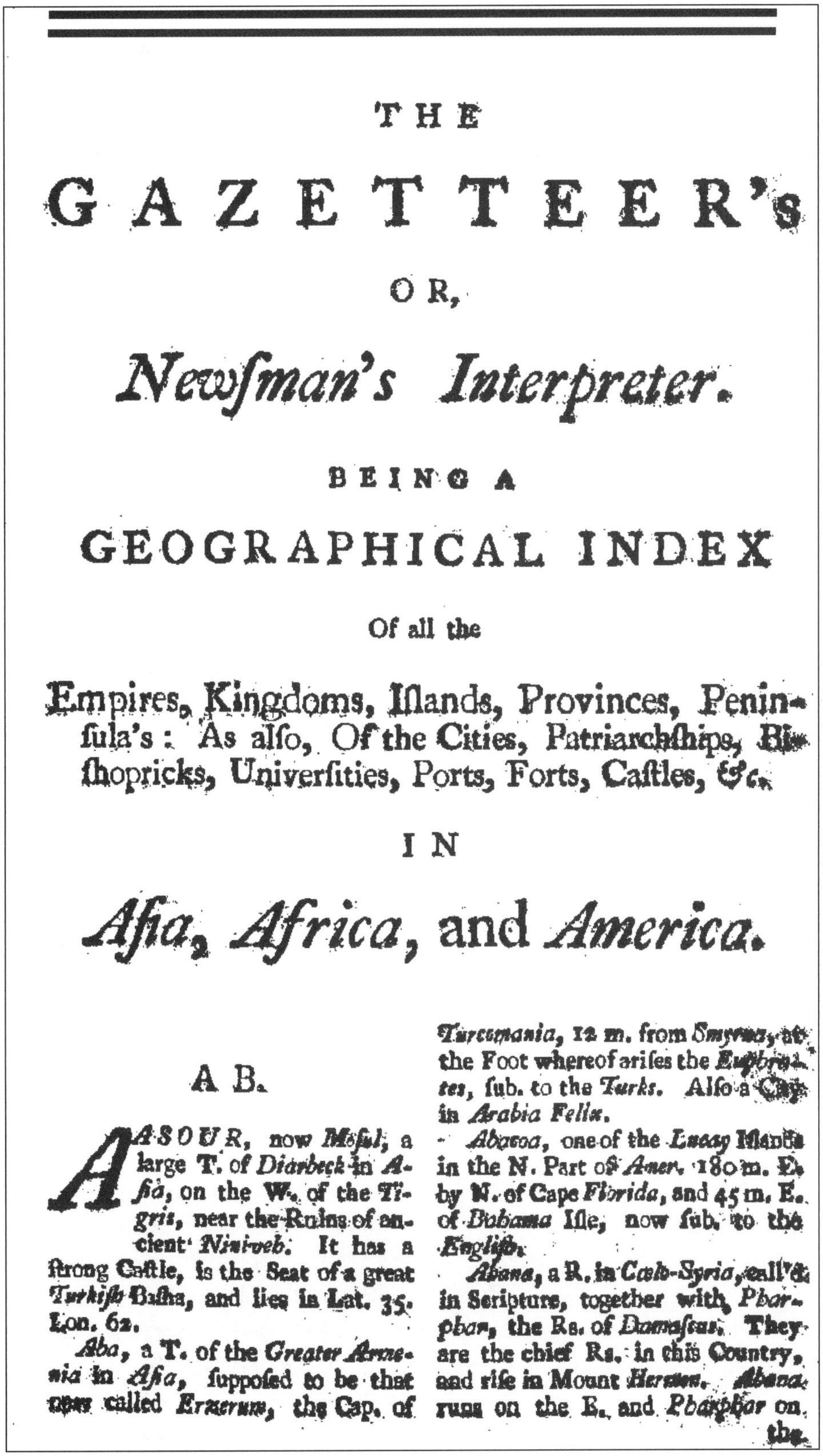

Figure 2-1
The Newsman's Interpreter was one of the first place-name gazetteers produced to assist writers and business-men with the standardization of place-names. *Source: Private collection.*

THE

GAZETTEER's

OR,

Newsman's Interpreter.

BEING A

GEOGRAPHICAL INDEX

Of all the

Empires, Kingdoms, Islands, Provinces, Penin-sula's : As also, Of the Cities, Patriarchships, Bi-shopricks, Universities, Ports, Forts, Castles, &c.

IN

Asia, Africa, and America.

A B.

A*ASOUR*, now *Mosul*, a large T. of *Diarbeck* in *A-sia*, on the W. of the *Ti-gris*, near the Ruins of an-cient *Niniveh*. It has a strong Castle, is the Seat of a great *Turkish* Basha, and lies in Lat. 35. Lon. 62.

Aba, a T. of the *Greater Arme-nia* in *Asia*, supposed to be that now called *Erzerum*, the Cap. of *Turcomania*, 12 m. from *Smyrna*, at the Foot whereof arises the *Euphra-tes*, sub. to the *Turks*. Also a City in *Arabia Felix*.

Abacoa, one of the *Lucay Islands* in the N. Part of *Amer.* 180 m. E. by N. of Cape *Florida*, and 45 m. E. of *Bahama* Isle, now sub. to the *English*.

Abana, a R. in *Cœlo-Syria*, call'd in Scripture, together with *Phar-phar*, the Rs. of *Damascus*. They are the chief Rs. in this Country, and rise in Mount *Hermon*. *Abana* runs on the E. and *Pharphar* on the solve several typical problems related to locating places or, just as important, head off incorrect assumptions that might lead you astray in your research.

One of the most common problems related to locating an ancestor's town is that you cannot find it on a modern map. Gazetteers can be thought of as reference documents created at a specific time in history that reflect the names used at that time period. Just as you might consult an old medical or law dictionary to research an archaic cause of death or an antiquated legal term, an old gazetteer can provide you with clues about places that have long dropped off the map. There is no such thing as a complete every-place-that-has-ever-graced-this-earth listing of modern and historical place-names, either in print or online.

Research Tip

The best bet for locating an old town name is to locate a gazetteer compiled around the time period of the document containing the place-name in question. In spite of H.L. Menchken's disappointment, the best gazetteers might be those published by the U.S. Board on Geographic Names (see "U.S. Government Gazetteer Resources" in this chapter) because of their long history of collecting place-names.

PLACE-NAME PROBLEMS

Another common situation encountered by the family historian is the place may exist today on a modern map, but the name has changed since the map was made. This might happen for many reasons, not the least of which is the problem hinted at by H.L. Mencken earlier in this chapter: Governments, for a variety of reasons, rename places. One popular reason is to establish dominance over the native population.

The place-names we encounter in our research can sometimes be ambiguous and difficult to identify based on local or vernacular use of names. A funny incident happened to me while I was documenting the location where my grandfather Richard Story Shackleford was buried. What I had written in my notes based on an interview with a cousin was that he was "buried on the family farm at sundown." Several years later when I visited the location of his grave on the ancestral farm in the company of another cousin who grew up in that section of northern Florida, I remarked to him in my straightforward Yankee manner that I thought it seemed peculiar to hold a funeral at sundown and wondered if that was a local custom. He looked at me in a puzzled way and said, "Why, honey, the name of that section of the farm was called 'Sundown' because it was located on a rise above the river and we used to go up there to watch the sun set." Oops.

Like surnames, place-name spellings can be recorded in wildly different ways. When using a gazetteer, a good strategy is to brainstorm all the possible ways a place-name can be spelled (or misspelled). Two ancestors of mine,

Preston Tucker Wilkins and Nancy Jane Coburn, were said to have been married in "Brown County, New York." I checked every resource I could find and never located a Brown County or even a town named Brown in the state of New York. Prior to their marriage, they resided in Chenango County. A map showing the county boundaries for 1820s-era New York suggested that the county might actually be Broome County, located just to the south of Chenango, and not the mythical "Brown County." I now have a new place-name to research because sometime in the past *Broome* may have sounded a lot like *Brown* to someone's ears.

A similar problem occurred while I was attempting to verify the residential locations of the sideshow performer Eli Bowen. One published biographical statement in *Very Special People* by F. Drimmer (New York: Bantam Books, 1973) indicated that Eli and his family had made their home in "Ogden, California." Repeated searches for an Ogden in every gazetteer and place-name list I could find turned up nothing in California. Out of frustration, I posted a message to a circus e-mail list, and eventually a response came that indicated that Bowen's wife and children had resided for a time in Alameda County, California. Meanwhile, Eli Bowen maintained a residence in Brooklyn, New York. With that small clue in hand, it was easy to locate his wife and children living in Oakland, California. Again, someone mishearing the name of *Oakland* and then publishing the incorrect information as *Ogden* sent me on a wild-goose chase for several months.

Another problem encountered by the family historian is jumping to the conclusion that the place found on the map with the name you are searching for is the correct location; many places in different states share a name. The geographer John Leighly studied colonial New England town names and traced their occurrence in the twelve Midwestern states immediately west of the original thirteen colonies ("Town Names of Colonial New England in the West," *Annals of the Association of American Geographers* 68 [June 1978]: 233-248). In this region alone he found forty-seven towns, counties, and other communities named Salem. Taking the United States in its entirety, at least eighty-eight Salems are in present use and it ranks as the ninth most common city name in the United States (see "The Name Game" on pages 22-23). Imagine if you were told that your ancestor came from Salem. Would you necessarily know which one?

Additional confusion can occur with places named after states and countries. My great-grandfather George Wilkins resided in Oregon for thirty years—Oregon in Dane County, Wisconsin! A whole host of communities share names with foreign places: Norway, Maine; Switzerland County, Indiana; Moscow, Idaho; Ontario, found in both Ohio and California; Cuba, inhabiting Illinois and New York; and Mexico, tucked away in Maine and Missouri.

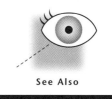

See Also

For more information, see Dan Tilque's article "Common Placenames" in *Word Ways* <http://wordways .com/commonp.htm>. For a ranking of the most common place-names in the United States, see Russell Ash's book *The Top 10 of Everything 2005* (New York: DK Publishing, 2004).

THE NAME GAME

Contrary to what you might think, the town of Springfield—which has been the fictional setting of popular television programs *The Simpsons*, *Guiding Light*, and *Father Knows Best*—is not the most common place-name in the United States. Springfield does not even make the list of top ten most common city names in the United States, according to the U.S. Geological Survey.

The Most Common Names of Incorporated Cities in the United States

RANKING	UNITED STATES
1	Fairview
2	Midway
3	Oak Grove
4	Franklin
5	Riverside
6	Centerville
7	Mt. Pleasant
8	Georgetown
9	Salem
10	Greenwood

Source: Ash, Russell. *The Top 10 of Everything 2005*. New York: DK Publishing, 2004.

The most common topographic feature name in the United States is Mill Creek (1,473 entries) <www.usgs.gov/public/press/public_affairs/press_releases/pr125m.html>. It is also much more common than you think to find two or more similar-sounding place-names existing in the same state or region.

The genealogist confronted with an ambiguous place-name has much in common with the family historian who has either no place information or the name of a place that is so vague (like a country or state) that it gives little direction where to look. What is the next step?

Indeed, the next step might be to "step back" into the records to look for additional place-name information. Certain records have a greater chance of yielding more specific place-name information. The problem is you have to know the location to find the records—a classic "chicken and egg" dilemma.

Examples of sources that often include clues to place-names are:

- Vital records (birth, marriage, and death)

- Obituaries and death notices

- Biographies

- Community histories

- Deeds

- Probate files

- Immigration and naturalization records

- Passenger lists (the port of departure and sometimes the last city of residence are recorded)

- Marriage announcements in newspapers

- Newspaper stories

- Personal papers, including insurance documents, Bible records, baby books, and anniversary books

- Gravestones

If all you have identified is the state or country, you will want to make sure that you search large databases such as census indexes, FamilySearch (see the section on the Family History Library in this chapter), International Genealogical Index (IGI), and the Social Security Death Master Index. You can also access large subscription databases for a fee at Ancestry.com, Genealogy.com, and Pro-Quest/HeritageQuest Online either through your public library or as part of your membership through several major genealogical societies.

If the surname you are researching is particularly uncommon, you can also search online at any of the national white pages directories to get a "snapshot" of where others with the surname presently reside. Hamrick Software's U.S. Surname Distribution Web site <www.hamrick.com/names>, mentioned in chapter one, can suggest states where common surnames can be found among the lower forty-eight states for the census years 1850, 1880, or 1920. The maps are displayed in color keyed to either the number of occurrences of a particular surname per so many thousands of population or direct count from a representative population sample. These maps can suggest states that may have a greater chance of yielding records on your family. Leland Meitzler's booklet *Locating Your Ancestor's Family When All You Know Is the State* (Elbe, Washington: Heritage Creations, 1997) is a quick overview to some of the major sources and databases to look at for each state. The International Genealogical Index (IGI) available online at <www.familysearch.org> is also another way to search on a particular surname and come up with a general idea of where it occurs throughout the world.

A gazetteer can help you identify many occurrences of a particular place-name. Using other documents and a bit of common sense, you can probably eliminate some communities and investigate a much shorter list. While trying to put together a chronology of my great-grandmother Sarah Addelaide Wilkins prior to her marriage to Nelson Sweet in Jackson County, Michigan, I was told that she came from Utica. From other family stories I knew that she had been born in Ohio, grew up in New York, and spent her young adulthood in Michigan. Checking my gazetteer, to my chagrin I found a city named Utica in Licking County, Ohio; Oneida County, New York; and Macomb County, Michigan. I knew that her grandparents were from Oneida County, New York, and after some digging found her living with her maternal grandparents in Oriskany Falls, a small town not too far away from the New York Utica. Had I not known where her grandparents were from, I would have had to check out all three possibilities and would probably have begun with the Utica in Macomb County, which is the closest to Jackson County, Michigan, where I had found her marriage record.

So, did my great-grandmother lie about where she lived? Yes and no. It is not uncommon to find that people who live in small towns will often reply to the question "Where are you from?" with the name of a large city nearby. It helps smooth social conversations by locating yourself in relation to a large, recognizable city that the person you are speaking to is familiar with—and Utica, New York, is a much bigger city than Oriskany Falls. I find myself doing the same thing when I travel and people ask me where I am from. Depending how geographically knowledgeable the person appears to be, sometimes I say "Redding" and sometimes I say "Northern California, north of Sacramento." If the name Sacramento draws a blank look, then I say that I am from a small town "north of San Francisco," and this usually suffices, because everyone has heard of San Francisco. But San Francisco is four and a half hours to the south by car from my home, and anyone overhearing my conversation might think that I was from San Francisco or Sacramento. It's easy to imagine how a misunderstanding can be formed and passed down through the generations.

This is an important point to keep in mind as you collect your own place-names to study: Until you have a document in hand with information given by someone close to the event depicted in the document, treat the stories about the places your ancestors are from with a grain of salt rather than accepting them as the absolute truth, especially if they involve large cities. The name of a large city may have been given as a reference location rather than an actual location of origin or of a particular event.

AVOIDING "CREEP"

A common pitfall in locating historical places is an encounter with "creep," a term coined by William H. Lamble in "Genealogical Geography: Place Identification in the Map Library" <www.ifla.org/IV/ifla65/papers/045-94e .htm>. Creep, in terms of maps, is not some scary-looking person who hangs around the map drawers or gazetteer shelves in the library's reference room, but **the phenomenon of naming a town and then calling a nearby town by the same name or some variation of it.** These communities may exist at the same time and in the same county. Creep can be frustrating. It requires that you check the records of all the possible candidate locations in order to ensure that you have found the right one.

\di'fin\ *vb*

Definitions

The obituary of my great-grandfather Nelson Maynard Sweet stated that he was born in Newport, Nova Scotia. Four communities in Hants County, Nova Scotia, located within six miles of each other include the word *Newport* in the name: Newport, Newport Corner, Newport Landing, and Newport Station. Aside from this obituary I have not been able to connect him with Newport proper, so I will need to check the three other nearby communities with similar-sounding names.

Place-names are not static. They change and they can "move" or creep along in the landscape with the migration of people. Consider how an older community can become less fashionable and a new one springs up with a similar-sounding name. To further add to the confusion, sometimes the older community or jurisdiction can disappear entirely, only to reappear years later in a new position with the same name in the same or adjacent county.

Never assume that the place you are looking for is where you think it is. Genealogists should not automatically assume that the historical place-name they find on the map or read in an old document is the same place in which their ancestor resided. You should read background information on local history and geography to confirm that there was not another place by the same name or that the name of the place has not changed over time. Consider the plight of the poor researcher working on ancestry from Kingsport, Tennessee. Since its settlement in the eighteenth century, Kingsport has been known by many names: The Island, Island Flat, Peace Island, Big Island, Fort Patrick Henry, Fort Robinson, Boat Yard, King's Port, Christianville, and finally, in 1822, officially Kingsport, according to Jack Cross's "Genealogical Tidbits" <www.tngenweb.org/sullivan/tid bits.htm>. Gazetteers are useful tools in scoping out some of these potential place-name hazards before you expend a lot of time, energy, and money pursuing the wrong location. This makes them an ideal first stop before consulting old maps.

GAZETTEER SEARCHING TIPS

A place-name is not that different from a surname when it comes to trying to find it in an alphabetized index in a printed book or in an online database. These few things to keep in mind will help you tease out a place-name, particularly if it is misspelled, incomplete, or incorrectly translated from another language into English. Laying aside the obvious problem of a place changing its name entirely, listed below are suggestions to assist you with locating a place-name entry.

- Read the introduction to the gazetteer, documentation, or the "most frequently asked questions (FAQs)" section of an online database. That information will tell you what has been included and what has not been included in the listings. Some gazetteers attempt comprehensive listings, while others may limit the entries to incorporated locations, to locations that are "officially" recognized by the government, or to a particular region or time period. It is so tempting to dive into the list and see what you find, but when you can't find your place-name you need to be disciplined and read the introductory material to make sure you are consulting the best list for your needs.

- Spelling variations account for many missed place-names in a list. You think you know the spelling based on what you have been told or have seen in a document, but in reality the place is not spelled that way today. Common consonant mix-ups include the letters *K* and *C*, *T* and *D*, *V* and *F*, *M* and *N*, *P* and *B*, *G* and *J*, and so on. Errors involving vowels are even more common—*I* and *E* or even *I* and *Y*. You can come up with more spelling variations by saying the place-name out loud and rhyming it with other sounds. I often ask my elementary-school-aged children to spell a name and come up with additional variations!

- Silent letters can also cause subtle problems. The letters *E, Y,* and *H* can appear and disappear in a place-name.

- The letter *S* can cause complications with its presence at the end of a place-name. Sometimes it, too, is dropped. Online indexes may or may not include an apostrophe for place-names that have one, such as Martha's Vineyard. Make sure you try *Martha's, Marthas,* and *Martha* in online databases. Some databases are more "forgiving" than others in performing searches.

- The same caution holds true for any place-name with apostrophes, as in the name O'Brien.

- Blank spaces between parts of a place-name are not always represented in both print and online databases. Just like with surnames, you should pay close attention and make sure you search using all the variations of place-names that include prefixes, such as *D', De, Du, El, Le, La,* and *Van,* with and without spaces between the words. Historically the U.S. Board on Geographic

Continued on next page

Names had a preference for combining two-word place-names into single-word place-names: For example, La Fayette becomes Lafayette.

- The same advice can be given with regard to place-names that include *Saint* or some variation: *Saint, Sainte, St., Ste., San, Santo,* and *Santa.*

- In your Locality File (discussed in chapter one), you should have a page of the most common misinterpretations of the spellings of your difficult place-names. The list should be alphabetized so you can use it while quickly reading through alphabetical gazetteer listings.

- The person who transcribed the name found on the map to a gazetteer index can also make a mistake. Yes, publishers double-check their entries, but mistakes happen, especially in the era before the use of computers to compile place-name dictionaries. Just like with surnames, you should be sensitive to the type of error created by typing a key that is close to the one intended to be typed: The letter *F* is substituted for a *D*, or an *M* for an *N*.

- You should be aware of another type of human error that can creep into a database when transcribing place-names from one source into another. One popular genealogy utility that analyzes place-names for standard spelling and composition requires the program creator to read and type each location into the database. Can errors creep in? Very possibly, because each list is a generation away from the original compilation and each generation introduces the potential for transcription errors. This is less the case with government databases that are downloaded and included in their entirety on some Web sites and CD gazetteer publications.

- Utilize the "wildcard" search if it is supported in the online database you are using. A wildcard search enables you to type in a portion of a name followed by an asterisk symbol (*) or a percent sign (%). For example, if you type in "Hunt*" you will get place-names that begin with those four letters in sequence:

   Hunt County, Hunter Mountain, Huntington, Hunts Peak, Huntsville . . .

   You should also notice if you can limit your search by type of geographic feature or entry. Again, read the FAQs portion or "help" section of the online database for tips on how to conduct an effective search. Learn how to use (if available) the advanced search features offered on some online place-name lists.

- Never disregard a place-name that appears to be the one you are looking for but is located in an adjacent country, state, or county. The next chapter will discuss shifts in borders and the implications to locating records. Be open to the possibility that the place-name that you are seeking was located in the past in a different county, state, province, or nation. The place may not have shifted, but the jurisdictional boundaries surrounding it did.

LOCATING GAZETTEERS

Today, gazetteers are available in many formats: in print, on microfilm or microfiche, on computer disks (although less so today than a decade ago), on CD, and online. Computer programs such as World Place Advisor by Progeny Software <www.progenysoftware.com> and U.S. Cities Galore by Frustration Solutions <www.uscitiesgalore.com> work with your genealogy database program to evaluate the names of locations contained in your data for completeness and correctness by comparing your information to their internal lists of place-names. Any variation between your information and the list's information is flagged for possible revision.

Several genealogical references contain excellent bibliographies of gazetteers. The eleventh edition of *The Handybook for Genealogists* (Draper, Utah: Everton Publishers, 2005) has a section entitled "Atlases, Maps, and Gazetteers" for each of the fifty states. The gazetteer entries listed in this section are for print versions of place-name compilations for each state. No entries for online or CD resources are given. The chapters on foreign nations completely omit the "Atlases, Maps, and Gazetteers" section.

The third edition of *Ancestry's Red Book: American State, County & Town Sources*, edited by Alice Eichholz (Provo, Utah: Ancestry, 2004), provides for each of the fifty states, under the section entitled "Maps," basic geographical references, including place-name lists and gazetteers. The state chapters vary in the amount of information given on place-name resources. As in the prior edition, this reference provides clean, black-and-white state maps showing present county boundaries, the names and locations of county seats, and major water courses. The names of counties in adjacent states are also included on these maps to assist the researcher in identifying potential research locations across state boundaries.

The Family Tree Resource Book for Genealogists, edited by Sharon DeBartolo Carmack and Erin Nevius (Cincinnati: Family Tree Books, 2005), also has sections in its state bibliographies, entitled "Maps," which contain books on maps, gazetteers, and place-names. The book also has maps for each state detailing every current county boundary and those counties immediately outside of the state.

Carol Mehr Schiffman's chapter "Geographic Tools: Maps, Atlases, and Gazetteers" in *Printed Sources: A Guide to Published Genealogical Records*, edited by Kory L. Meyerink (Salt Lake City: Ancestry, 1998), contains an excellent bibliography of maps and gazetteer resources for each of the U.S. states. Her list of gazetteer resources also includes entries for post office and shipping guides, which are valuable resources.

PLACE-NAME BIBLIOGRAPHIES

Here are several important bibliographies of gazetteers that will help you identify some of the larger printed resources:

Grim, Ronald E. *Historical Geography of the United States: A Guide to Information Sources.* Detroit: Gale Research, 1982.

Meynen, Emil. *Gazetteers and Glossaries of Geographical Names of the Member-Countries of the United Nations and the Agencies in Relationship with the United Nations: Bibliography 1946–1976.* Wiesbaden: Franz Steiner Verlag, 1984.

Sealock, Richard B., et al., eds. *Bibliography of Place-Name Literature: United States and Canada.* 3d ed. Chicago: American Library Association, 1982.

Gazetteers and place-name dictionaries are sometimes listed in guides to reference books or more general lists of published materials.

If you know the exact title of the book you're seeking, try the annual publication *Books in Print* (New Providence, N.J.: R.R. Bowker). If you want to browse by place or subject, try the annual *Subject Guide to Books in Print* (New Providence, N.J.: R.R. Bowker). This seven-volume subject guide is derived from the massive *Books in Print* and has been published annually since 1957. It uses Library of Congress subject headings, so you can check under gazetteers, place-names, or by the actual local name for which you're searching. An online database of the above two works is available by subscription, which may be available to you through your local public library's reference section. Larger bookstores might also subscribe to this database or even have copies of the above books behind the counter, which they might let you search if you ask nicely.

More general reference guides include "Gazetteers" and "Geographical Names and Terms" by Eugene P. Sheehy in the *Guide to Reference Books*, 10th ed. (Chicago: American Library Association, 1986). This is probably the edition you'll encounter in public libraries. A supplement edited by Robert Balay, *Guide to Reference Books: Supplement to Tenth Edition, Covering Materials from 1985–1990*, was also published by the American Library Association in 1992. A complete revision of the tenth edition was edited by Robert Balay and published in 1996 as the eleventh edition of *Guide to Reference Books*, and the publisher plans on revising it every ten years.

A yearly library industry publication, *American Reference Books Annual*, is published by Libraries Unlimited (Englewood, Colorado). Volume 35 was released in 2004. The compilers limit the entries to books published in the United States or Canada and do not include books that are less than forty-eight pages, books published by vanity presses, or self-published materials.

For a list of specific genealogical or local history materials that might be missed by standard references such as *American Reference Books Annual*, try Marian Hoffman's *Genealogical and Local History Books in Print: U.S. Sources and Resources*, 5th ed., 2 vols. (Baltimore: Genealogical Publishing Company, 1997) and *Genealogical and Local History Books in Print: General Reference and World Resources*, 5th ed. (Baltimore: Genealogical Publishing Company, 1997). This series includes smaller tomes, including those that were privately printed or published by a vanity press, as well as larger works in several formats, including works on computer disks. The fifth edition is the most recent and includes four separate volumes compiled by Marian Hoffman, three of which are of interest to someone looking for place-name resources; the fourth volume is confined to listing family histories. Two of the four volumes deal exclusively with U.S. materials, and a third lists source materials published on the rest of the world. The listings are a bit idiosyncratic and not complete. However, these volumes do manage to capture place-name guides published privately or by small presses overlooked by other references.

MAJOR GAZETTEER PUBLICATIONS

With nearly 1,500,000 entries, the *Omni Gazetteer of the United States of America*, 11 vols., edited by Frank R. Abate (Detroit: Omnigraphics, 1991) lists every place-name found on USGS topographic maps. The information given includes the place-name plus other names used for the feature, type of feature, population, zip code (when it is a locality), county, name of the USGS topographic sheet it is found on, latitude and longitude, elevation (if appropriate), and sources of information on the place-name. The source used to compile this massive list is the USGS's Geographic Names Information System (GNIS), which is now online (refer to "Researching Place Names Online" in this chapter).

The *Cambridge World Gazetteer: A Geographical Dictionary*, edited by David Munro (New York: Cambridge University Press, 1990), was originally published in 1988 under the title *Chambers World Gazetteer: An A-Z of Geographical Information* and contains more than 20,000 entries. Another work by the same publisher is *The Cambridge Gazetteer of the United States and Canada* by Archie Hobson (Cambridge University Press, 1995), which includes more than 12,000 entries on all incorporated municipalities with populations of more than 10,000 in the United States and more than 8,000 in Canada. An unusual feature of this work is the inclusion of many place-names of historical and contemporary interest, such as neighborhood names, landmarks, historic forts, Revolutionary and Civil War sites, and even popular fictional locations.

The Columbia Gazetteer of North America, edited by Saul B. Cohen (New York: Columbia University Press, 2000), covers more than 50,000 places—every incorporated place and county in the United States and several thousand unincorporated places, special-purpose districts, and physical features. It strives to be one of the most comprehensive encyclopedias of geographical places for the regions of North America, including Mexico and the Caribbean. This reference is also available online for free at Bartleby.com: Great Books Online <www.bartleby.com/69>.

Almost every public library has some edition of the popular annual U.S. atlas *Commercial Atlas & Marketing Guide*, 135th ed., 2 vols. (Chicago: Rand McNally, 2004.) The late nineteenth-century and early twentieth-century editions are particularly useful in identifying historical place-names. The 135th edition is published in two volumes. The second volume indexes 123,000 place-names, while the first volume contains the familiar maps and economic and population data. The gazetteer entries are in alphabetical order and include place-name, county seat designation, county name, map key, postal, banking, population, and zip code information.

The most recent edition of the venerable reference *The Columbia Gazetteer of the World* (New York: Columbia University Press, 1998) is captured in three volumes. It was published in 1952 as the *Columbia Lippincott Gazetteer of the World*, which was largely based on the work of an early gazetteer publisher, J.B. Lippincott, who had published world gazetteers since the beginning of the twentieth century. Lippincott's early volumes are worth seeking out for the historical snapshot they provide of communities one hundred years ago. Most libraries have some older edition of this classic general list of geographical places. The older editions are valuable sources for finding information about historical place-names or place-names that are not presently in use today. The current edition contains information on more than 165,000 global locations, arranged alphabetically by the most current name. The entries also list former names, a guide to pronunciation, latitude and longitude, population data, and geographical and historical information. An online version is available through subscription, but only to libraries. The online version is updated monthly with new names as well as essays on places of importance in the news.

Merriam-Webster's Geographical Dictionary, 3d ed. (Springfield, Mass.: Merriam-Webster, 1997), is a very popular geographical reference. It contains more than 48,000 entries and includes many place-names related to current events.

Although compiled to assist those interested in tracing their Jewish heritage, Gary Mokotoff and Sallyann Amdur Sack's *Where Once We Walked: A Guide to the Jewish Communities Destroyed in the Holocaust*, rev. ed. (Bergenfield, N.J.: Avotaynu, 2002) is useful to anyone trying to locate ancestral towns in central and eastern Europe. Among the listings contained in this gazetteer are the vernacular Yiddish place-names that never appeared on maps but nonetheless are found in records.

The Oxford Dictionary of the World, edited by David Munro (New York: Oxford University Press, 1995), draws 3,000 of its entries from *The Oxford English Dictionary* and includes 7,000 more place-names related to historical and contemporary events. The emphasis is on political and physical information, so it does not include latitude and longitude coordinates.

The two atlases listed below have good indexes to the maps and figures contained in their volumes. Although not written to function specifically as gazetteers, their alphabetical lists are quite good.

National Geographic Society. *Atlas of the World.* 8th ed. Washington, D.C.: National Geographic Society, 2004.

The Times Comprehensive Atlas of the World. 11th ed. London: Times Books, 2003.

U.S. GOVERNMENT GAZETTEER RESOURCES

The U.S. Board on Geographic Names (BGN) was founded on 4 September 1890 by executive order of the president of the United States. Initially, its mission was to resolve disputes that occurred when more than one name was used for the same locality or physical feature. In 1906 the BGN's name was changed to the U.S. Geographic Board, and its function was expanded to include the standardization of geographical names used in federal publications and topographic maps. Later that same year it was given advisory functions over the preparation of surveys and maps. In 1919, the map and survey functions were transferred to the Board of Surveys and Maps. In 1934 the U.S. Geographic Board was abolished and its functions transferred to the Department of the Interior. Its responsibilities were split between two new units: the Division of Geographic Names and the Advisory Committee on Geographic Names. In 1948, the agency reclaimed its original name: U.S. Board on Geographic Names. The BGN's records and publications are found in the National Archives and Records Administration in College Park, Maryland, under all four (or five if you count the original name twice) agency names in *Records of the Board on Geographic Names* (Record Group 324).

Only federal agencies are bound by the decisions of the BGN, but state and local governments as well as commercial mapmakers find it advantageous to use standardized names for localities and physical features. Most states have their own committees to evaluate proposed geographic names. Anyone can submit a name for a geographic location, including the state committees themselves. In states where these committees exist, the proposals are first submitted to the committee for consideration; if it approves the

For More Info

To find information about National Archives record groups, go to the online version of the *Guide to Federal Records in the National Archives of the United States* <www.archives.gov/research_room/federal_records_guide>. You can search the guide by keyword or enter a record group number for direct access. You can also search the Microfilm Publications Catalog <www.archives.gov/research_room/alic/research_tools/search_microfilm_catalog.html> by keyword, microfilm ID, or record group number.

petition, the committee then forwards the proposal to the BGN.

The BGN and its predecessor agencies published gazetteers of foreign countries in cooperation with several federal agencies, including the Central Intelligence Agency, the Army Map Service, and the Defense Mapping Agency. Copies of these gazetteers can be found in public and college libraries, as well as through the Geography and Map Reading Room at the Library of Congress and the Cartographic and Architectural Branch of the National Archives in College Park in Record Group 324. The BGN gazetteer publications first appeared in the mid-1950s and provide only basic information such as latitude and longitude. No geographical or historical information is given. These lists encompass the names of small and obscure places as well as variant and ethnic names not usually recognized by governments. The entries focus on geographical names approved by the U.S. government but also cross-reference variant names that are helpful in tracing older names in areas where boundaries have shifted.

A particularly useful reference for tracking down foreign gazetteers created by any of the above-mentioned federal agencies is Donald J. Orth and Elizabeth Unger Mangan's *Geographic Names and the Federal Government: A Bibliography* (Washington, D.C.: Geography and Map Division, Library of Congress, 1990).

You can also locate these gazetteers by searching in library subject catalogs under the following headings:

See Also

[Name of Federal Agency]	Country	Gazetteers
[Name of Country or State]	Gazetteers	
[Name of Country or State]	Description and Travel	Gazetteers

Place-name sources are less commonly found in library catalogs, but can be filed under:

| [Name of Place] | Names, Geographical |

For defunct or extinct locales such as ghost towns and ruins you can also try searching under:

| [Name of Place] | Cities and Towns, Ruined and Extinct, etc. |

FAMILY HISTORY LIBRARY GAZETTEER RESOURCES

The *Research Outline* series produced by the Family History Library (FHL) in Salt Lake City describes the many types of records available for each U.S. state, Canadian province, and many foreign countries. Each *Research Outline* follows a set format and summarizes the basic set of resources you need to start your research in a particular locality. Descriptions of different types of records include a brief explanation of their significance to family history research, as well as how to locate said records through governmental sources or through the microfilm, periodical, map, or book holdings of the Family History Library. Each *Research Outline* contains separate sections describing gazetteers and maps for the particular locality. Under the section on gazetteers is a brief discussion on how to find modern and historical place-names for the state, province, or country in question.

The outlines are available in several formats. You can purchase printed copies from your local Family History Center either in person or on the Web for a nominal fee. You can download versions of the outlines known as "Research Guidance" for free from the Church of Jesus Christ of Latter-day Saints' FamilySearch Web site <www.familysearch.org> by clicking on the "Library" tab, then clicking on the "Education" tab, and lastly, on the "Research Guidance" tab. Under "Research Guidance" you will find a long list of Canadian provinces, U.S. states, and many foreign nations and their subregional units. Click on a locality's name to see *Research Outline*.

The writers of the *Research Outline* series have included the microfilm or microfiche call numbers of the gazetteers and shipping guides found in the Family History Library catalog. Keyword search of the CD version of the Family History Library catalog produced the following numbers of entries:

Number of gazetteers:	more than 2,400
Number of entries with keyword "geographical names":	nearly 1,500
Number of topographical dictionaries:	close to 100

The online version of the Family History Library catalog also supports keyword searches. You can search in any field for the occurrence of a particular word. You can search both the CD and online versions of the catalog for author, title, and place.

Notes

You need to know two important things about this library's catalog in regards to place: **Places are listed only by their modern names and boundaries, and the catalog lists only names of places for which the library has material.** For example, to locate books about place-names you should look under these two topics:

[Name of Country or State]   Gazetteers
[Name of Country or State]   Names, Geographical

To look for place-names for a specific state or country, you should search on the name of the state or country using the "Place Search" capability on the Web site. Enter the name of the locale for which you are searching, which will give you a list of names. Click on your exact name and then select "gazetteers" or "geographical names."

The online version of the Family History Library catalog also functions as a big place-name list. Using "Place Search," type the name of the place and the search will return a list of places with that name and their locations (states and countries). You can also search on county names. The information returned will include the year the county was formed and the names of the parent counties. You can obtain a list of all the towns in a given county by searching on the county name and then clicking the "View Related Places" button on the screen; it will display a list of all the county's towns that are covered in the Family History Library's collection.

Other Repositories

The American Geographical Society Library collection, housed at the University of Wisconsin-Milwaukee, represents one of the largest university collections of geographic material in the United States. You can search its online catalog at <www.uwm.edu/Library/AGSL>.

RESEARCHING PLACE-NAMES ONLINE

You can use three search strategies to locate the best gazetteer to suit your needs. The first approach involves visiting several of the enormous megasites that have links to other Web sites with the information you are seeking. This approach works well if you are interested in finding an online source of place-names for a particular country or state. Two excellent sites to get started with are:

Cyndi's List: Maps, Gazetteers & Geographical Information
<www.cyndislist.com/maps.htm>

Cyndi Howell has created the largest list of geographical resources available on a Web site devoted to genealogy. It is updated regularly.

Oddens' Bookmarks
<http://oddens.geog.uu.nl/index.php>

This gigantic Web site maintains a list of online gazetteers that cover everything from locally focused lists to global coverage in many languages. It is frequently updated and can be thought of as the "Cyndi's List" of geography and maps.

Online reference sites are constantly springing up or disappearing, so no Web site is going to be completely current or without broken links. A second approach to locating place-name references would be to access your favorite

Web search engine, such as Google or Yahoo, and type in the name of the country or place followed by the word "gazetteer" or the phrase "place-names" and see what Web sites are returned.

A third approach to locating gazetteers is to access the many specific gazetteer resources that have been placed online. Literally hundreds of them are available. The list below represents several of the most popular ones. Try several, and read the database FAQs or other information associated with where the entries came from to determine what was included—they may only mention incorporated cities or require a certain population.

Worldwide Gazetteers
The National Geospatial-Intelligence Agency: GEOnet Names Server (GNS)
<http://earth-info.nga.mil/gns/html>

This site is maintained by the National Geospatial-Intelligence Agency of the U.S. government and provides complete files of geographic names from many countries worldwide. The files are not in gazetteer format, but in a special format allowing the user to input the information into geographic information systems, databases, and spreadsheets. Instructions to use this site are fairly straightforward, although it has lots of extra features available for you to experiment with beyond a simple search.

The Alexandria Digital Library Gazetteer Server
<http://middleware.alexandria.ucsb.edu/client/gaz/adl/index.jsp>

This online gazetteer boasts 5.9 million geographic names, making it one of the largest on the Web.

Getty Thesaurus of Geographic Names Online
<www.getty.edu/research/conducting_research/vocabularies/tgn>

This list includes about 1.3 million place-names and focuses on vernacular and historical names related to art and architecture. It is an excellent resource for ancient and historical place-names, but is limited to names related to items in the Getty Collection and its areas of research in the visual arts.

Global Gazetteer: Directory of Cities and Towns in World
<www.fallingrain.com/world>

This privately sponsored gazetteer searches for places by nation or by letter of the alphabet.

Heavens-Above
<www.heavens-above.com>

Here's another privately maintained place-name database that adds an unusual twist: It can list the nearest neighboring town to a given location. The site requests that you register, but you can use it anonymously. Once you have found your specific location in the database, request the nearest towns and the results will include the distance in kilometers, the name of the region they are in, the latitude and longitude, and the elevation. The place-names included in this database appear to be modern and officially recognized. This is a terrific little tool to use to locate nearby towns that might have vital, court, land, or church records for your ancestors.

United States Gazetteer Sources

The U.S. Geological Survey: Geographical Names Information System (GNIS)

<http://geonames.usgs.gov>

This is *the* site to search for places in the United States, its territories, or Antarctica (see Figures 2-2, 2-3, and 2-4 for some of its features). The site is easy to use, and the results link you to maps and aerial imagery available through the USGS, U.S. Environmental Protection Agency, U.S. Census Bureau, and TerraServer Web sites.

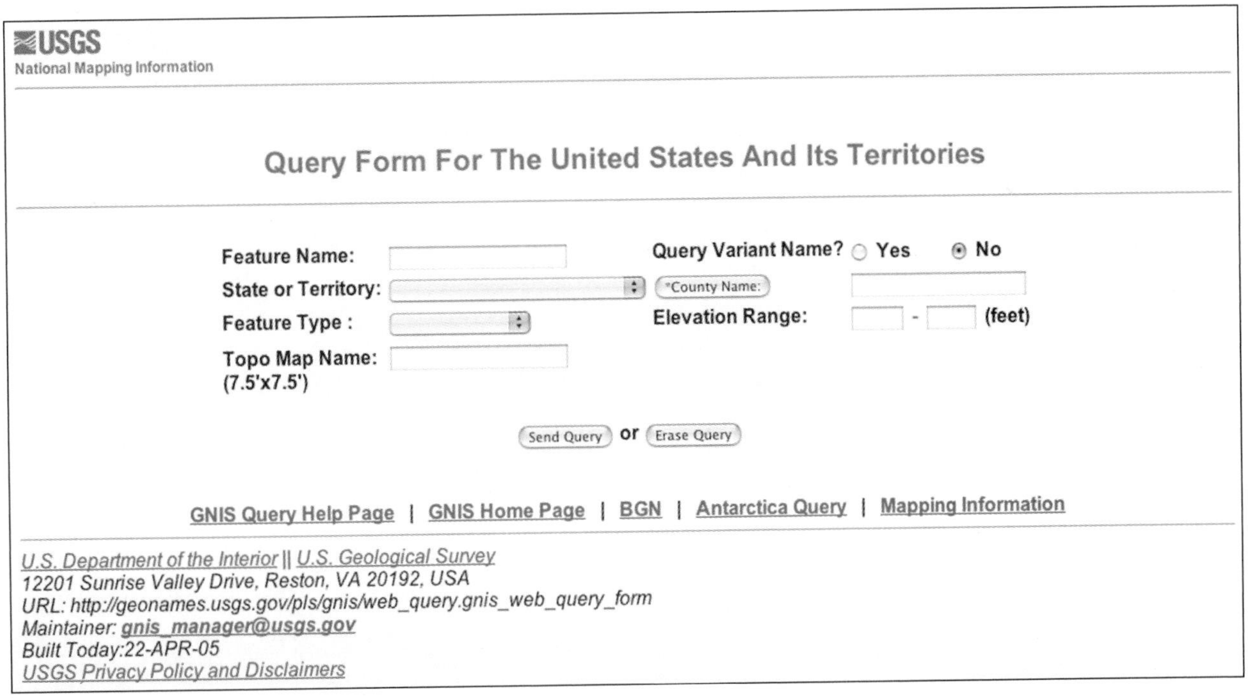

Figure 2-2
Query form available on the U.S. Geological Survey's Geographical Names Information System (GNIS). *Source: <http://geonames.usgs.gov>.*

National Geologic Map Database (for U.S. place-names)

<http://ngmdb.usgs.gov>

This site is not organized in the most straightforward manner, but the

≈USGS
National Mapping Information

1 feature records have been selected from GNIS.

Feature Name:	Freedom Lakes
Feature Type:	lake
Description:	Two lakes, 1 mi E of Atlas and 5 mi WSW of Frederic; NW lake is at 453830N0923315W

State	County
Wisconsin	Burnett
Wisconsin	Polk
Variant Name(s)	Negro Heel Lake
	Negro Heel Lakes
	Negro Hill Lakes
	Negrow Heel Lake
	Niger Heel Lake
	Nigger Heel Lake
USGS 7.5' x 7.5' Map:	Trade Lake
latitude (nn°nn'nn"):	453808N
Longitude (nnn°nn'nn"):	0923400W

Figure 2-3

When using the GNIS query form, make sure that you answer "yes" to the Query Variant Name? on the search screen in order to obtain from the database alternative or historical names. "Freedom Lakes" is an example of a place-name awarded to a location with a previously derogatory place-name. Certain racial epithets are disallowed on federal documents, including maps. Shocking by today's standards, our ancestors' prejudices and insensitivities nevertheless were transferred to maps as names of places and topographic features. As researchers we can choose not to include odious place-names in our work as long as they are properly identified by geographic coordinates or the new name is explained in a footnote with a proper source citation.

potential payoff for a little patience is worth it. Access the Geoscience Map Catalog on the left side of the screen and then press "Place Name Search." Fill in the box with the location you want to search for and then wait for the results. You will receive a list of the names of the USGS maps, including the scale of the map with your particular locality. You can further refine your search by selecting any of the bibliographic map citations listed. The next screen will show you the details about the map you selected, including a complete citation, if the map is still available for purchase, and where you can get it. This is a really nice shortcut to use before heading off to the map library or to a vendor to purchase a particular map.

U.S. Census Bureau: U.S. Gazetteer: 2000 and 1990

<www.census.gov/geo/www/gazetteer/gazette.html>

It is important to note that although you can download the 2000 census data, the place-names in the online search engine date from the 1990 census, and unincorporated places are not included. You can search by geographic name or by zip code. The search results link to 1998 TIGER®/Line data and

≋USGS
National Mapping Information

1 feature records have been selected from GNIS.

Feature Name:	Sweet Corners Post Office (historical)
Feature Type:	post office
History Notes:	Established in 1879. Discontinued in 1895.
State:	Massachusetts
County:	Berkshire
USGS 7.5' x 7.5' Map:	Williamstown
latitude (nn°nn'nn"):	UNKNOWN
Longitude (nnn°nn'nn"):	UNKNOWN

U.S. Department of the Interior || *U.S. Geological Survey*
12201 Sunrise Valley Drive, Reston, VA 20192, USA
URL: http://geonames.usgs.gov/pls/gnis/web_query.gnis_web_query_form
Maintainer: gnis_manager@usgs.gov
Built Today:22-APR-05
USGS Privacy Policy and Disclaimers

Figure 2-4
Sweet Corners is an example of a place-name that exists in the GNIS database that no longer appears on today's topographic maps. Although GNIS catalogs mostly contain names of present-day features and locations, some historic places are included. There is no such thing as a comprehensive place-name database on the Web. You might want to try several suggested in this chapter to locate an extinct place-name.

base maps via the TIGER® map server. The maps that are returned are simple, showing major transportation features and some topographic relief. Place-names created after 1990 are not included. For example, I searched on the City of Shasta Lake (created in 1993) and it was not there, but I was able to pull up a map of the area by using the name Central Valley, a town that was within the City of Shasta Lake boundaries.

CD Gazetteers and Computer Programs

A number of old gazetteer and atlas indexes have been scanned and republished on CD. For example, the New England Historic Genealogical Society (NEHGS) has reproduced early gazetteers covering several states and published them on CDs, available for purchase at <www.newenglandancestors .org>.

The software program AniMap Plus 2.5, available from Gold Bug <www .goldbug.com>, comes with a gazetteer of U.S. place-names called Site-Finder. This database lists 800,000 names, including more than 120,000 variations. These place-names come from a variety of sources, including GNIS, old postal guides, and atlas indexes. Just as in GNIS, cemeteries, schools, churches, and military installations are included in the database.

TIGER® MAP SERVICE AND GAZETTEER

TIGER® Map Service and Gazetteer were developed as a demonstration experiment in Web-based mapping in 1995 by the Bureau of Census. It was not intended to be a permanent source for the general public. The Bureau is currently perfecting its new American FactFinder (AFF) online mapping program that creates reference and thematic maps based upon 2000 census data. The TIGER® system has some limited mapping capabilities that can provide city and town locations and a place-name gazetteer based upon 1990 data. The zip code information is based upon 1999 data. The American FactFinder system when completed will have many more tools to offer the map user. You can view the American FactFinder at <http://factfinder.census.gov/home/saff/main.html?_lang=en>. There is a brief mapping tutorial accessible via the "Help" link on the main page that takes you through the creation and printing of maps.

Nearly all locations have latitude and longitude coordinates. You can transfer ("pluck") a location from SiteFinder and place it onto a map, then watch the county boundaries shift around the marked location.

Summary Points

★ A gazetteer, rather than a map, should be your first stop in trying to locate an unfamiliar place.

★ Gazetteers vary in scope and content, so be sure to read the introductory material of books or consult the FAQs if the list appears online.

★ Never assume that the place you are looking for is where you think it is.

★ Using gazetteers early in your research can help you locate modern and historical place-names, as well as head off incorrect assumptions—especially where common place-names are involved.

★ If you cannot find the place-name you are seeking, try another source. No database or reference is completely comprehensive.

★ Strive to identify at least one of these items: county name, jurisdictional description, or geographic location (latitude and longitude) for every geographic place listed in your pedigree charts and family group sheets.

CHAPTER 3

Determining Boundaries and Jurisdictions

Overview

⊕ Why are jurisdictional boundaries important in genealogical research?

⊕ How do the definitions of county and township differ across regions in the United States, and does this affect where records are found?

⊕ Where can I locate information about present and historical jurisdictions within a country?

⊕ Where do I find political administrative maps that detail jurisdictional boundaries?

⊕ Can census enumeration district maps help me locate someone I can't find in a census index?

One of my toys as a young child was a set of plastic "nesting dolls." A large doll contained a smaller doll, and that smaller doll contained yet a smaller doll inside it, and so on until five dolls could stand next to one another, each smaller than the next. The political units we call "jurisdictions" are a lot like those dolls. In our modern era, every place on earth can be claimed in some manner by some government entity. We can thank (or blame) maps for this situation. Cartography began to develop accurate tools and methods precise enough to describe legal territories in the seventeenth century, and that's when jurisdictions multiplied until all land and some of the sea fell under the jurisdiction of one nation or another.

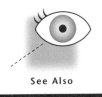

See Also

For more information on legal territory descriptions, see Richard T. Ford's article "Law's Territory" (*Michigan Law Review*, 97:4 <www.high beam.com>).

To be efficient and successful in the research of a specific locality, you need to know what jurisdiction that locality fell under during the time your ancestor or research subject lived there. Your ancestor may not have traveled any farther than from his cabin's porch to the well and back and spent his entire life in one place, but the territory he lived in became a county and that county became part of a state. Those county boundaries may have moved and shifted over time as new counties were added and old counties were abolished. It is important to be aware of these boundary shifts. Your ancestor may disappear from his county's records, when in actuality the boundary shifted and suddenly he and his family were recorded in the records of a different county. If they resided near a state or territorial border, you may need to check records in the adjacent state or territory.

Nations are subdivided into states or some other sort of subnational political entity. In the United States we have many different types of jurisdictions: territories, cities, townships, counties, the federal district, possessions, embassies and consulates, Indian reservations, military installations, and many (far too many to list) different districts for special functions, including schools, elections, census taking, libraries, mosquito abatement, utilities, and even trash collecting. In perspective, a major city the size of Chicago has more than one thousand local government entities that handle both specific functions and general administration within the metropolitan area.

One of the typical frustrations genealogists encounter is figuring out where to find records within these "nesting" jurisdictions. States, counties, parishes, and boroughs all have dates of origin that relate to the creation and collection of records.

COUNTIES

In the United States, most of our fifty states are subdivided into smaller administrative regions called counties. Exceptions to this are Alaska, which has boroughs, and Louisiana, which has parishes. Counties are further subdivided into smaller or "minor" civil divisions, such as townships, boroughs (not the same meaning as in Alaska), cities, municipalities, towns, and villages. At the lowest level, hamlets and crossroads serve to describe the locations where people are living in communities smaller than villages. In an urban setting, a neighborhood, ward, or precinct might also apply to a smaller geographical area within a town or city. Records are not usually kept at the neighborhood or ward level, although sometimes they are useful entities to describe geographical units for census taking. For the most part, people traveled to larger villages, towns, or cities to record their vital events, wills, or land transactions, or to participate in legal proceedings. In many states, records are kept primarily at the county level. Exceptions are Connecticut, Vermont, and Rhode Island, where the recording of documents takes place at the town or city level. The reason for this will be discussed shortly.

The United States has no rule regarding county formation or governance because of the way the nation developed from colonies along the eastern seaboard. The counties created in territories that were far away from the population centers sometimes tended to be larger than counties closer to the population centers, and were attached to another county for administrative purposes until there were enough people to sustain a government.

Several recurring themes appear in the literature concerning the formation of counties. The practice of *gerrymandering* by state legislators was prominent throughout the nineteenth century. Gerrymandering was the redrawing of county boundaries to swing votes a particular way by including or excluding certain populations. One of the most peculiar cases ever reported was the creation of bogus census returns for the 1857 Minnesota Special Census. Seven counties (Pipestone, Rock, Murray, Nobles, Cottonwood, Jackson, and Martin) were created by several Minnesota Democrats to stuff the ballot box in an election. Though the land had not yet been ceded by the American Indians, that didn't stop these politicians from creating census returns complete with names, ages, and occupations to swing the election.

Another common concern was land speculation. New counties were carved out of sparsely populated regions for the purpose of promoting settlement because being part of an established county rather than unorganized territory was thought to be an effective selling point. This was a common occurrence in North Dakota and other parts of the Great Plains southward into Texas.

Residents often promoted separating into a new county, particularly when the trip to their current county seat was especially onerous. The ideal trip from the outlying hinterland to the county seat and back would be about a day's time. Smaller counties were often created to satisfy these complaints by residents.

Genealogists can find local records more efficiently if they understand the way counties were formed in different U.S. regions. Geographer Ed Stephan postulated in his online book *The Division of Territory in Society* <www.ac.wwu.edu/~stephan/Book/contents.html> that the following three general models for county formation and governance were tied to the various cultures of the original thirteen colonies:

- The Southern County Model
- The New England County Model
- The "Mixed" County Model

For More Info

See William Dollarhide's article "The Old Boundary Line Blues" (*Genealogy Bulletin* 15 (January/February 1999): 1, 6-12).

The Southern County Model

The earliest counties in North America were created in Virginia. Although Stephan erroneously identified the start of counties as 1634, their formation actually began more than a decade before then and was not completed until March 1643, when Virginia burgesses enacted a law that renamed their colonial monthly courts "countie courts." Geography contributed to the type of government that eventually grew in Virginia. The mild climate and fertile soils formed the base of the development of the plantation settlement pattern. People were more dispersed in the Virginia colony owing to the need for large tracts of land to grow cotton and tobacco. They also established and administered their churches on a diocesan or regional basis. The early Virginia parishes encompassed large geographical areas.

Government power was initially centralized from Virginia's first charter in 1606 to its first legislative meeting in 1619 in a council, and then later it was embodied in a governor who administered law via a military regime. Gradually the administration shifted from governor-imposed martial law to an English civil law model. During this time period, plantations and "hundreds" (a geographic entity derived from English law that comprised one hundred families) existed but had no significant political or governing purpose. Over the next twenty-five years, cities began to incorporate, monthly courts were held outside of Jamestown to settle local disputes, and specific jurisdictional boundaries were defined for court proceedings and for the election of representatives to Virginia's House of Burgesses.

By 1643, counties formed the unit of representation; the House of Burgesses represented only counties and not plantations or hundreds. Counties had emerged as a unit of government that performed all the judicial and administrative functions familiar to us today, including the sheriff, clerk of court, surveyor, coroner, and constables. By 1700, counties in Virginia were performing most of their customary tasks, including the construction and maintenance of roads, regulation of various businesses such as taverns, pest control (wolves), public education, and the construction of public workhouses.

This model of county government eventually spread throughout the southern states and was replicated in the western states from Texas to the Pacific coast. It spread through migration westward and "hybridized" within territories that were also influenced by Spanish, French, and Mexican governments in Florida, Louisiana, Texas, Arizona, New Mexico, and California. Some exceptions to this model did exist: South Carolina abolished its counties and circuit court districts in 1800 and established twenty-five districts in their place. In 1868, during Reconstruction, South Carolina's new state constitution renamed the existing districts (which by then had expanded in number to thirty) as counties.

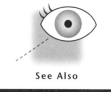

See Also

For more on Virginia counties, see Edgar MacDonald's article "The Myth of Virginia County Formation in 1634" (*National Genealogical Society Quarterly* 92 [March 2004]: 58-63).

The New England County Model

The New England colonies were governed on a town basis more than a county basis owing, in part, to the populace's familiarity with a congregational form of church government rather than the larger parish or diocesan type of government prevalent in the South. The geography of New England also starkly contrasted the South's. The climate was colder and the growing season shorter. The land was not nearly as arable, because the soil tended to be thin and rocky. Towns and villages grew up around smaller farms, fishing, and shipping. Quarter courts—held about four times a year—were established by 1635 in some New England towns. By 1639, these courts became known as "county courts" in spite of the fact that no county government existed. Local governance was through town council meetings. In 1643, counties functioned more as judicial units than as administrative bodies. Taxation on a county basis began in 1650, with towns electing representatives to serve on local governing boards. Countywide positions of treasurer (1654) and sheriff (1691) were added. With the exception of judicial proceedings, governance was focused on the local level. Town councils were charged with road maintenance and construction, tax collections, elections, public health, education, and social services such as poor relief.

This type of county model can be found in Massachusetts, Rhode Island, Vermont, New Hampshire, Maine, and Connecticut. The regional favoring of town administration over county government explains why documents are recorded at the town level rather than the county.

The "Mixed" County Model

The "mixed" county model developed in New York and Pennsylvania. To say it's a hybrid of the Southern and New England models is not entirely accurate. Both states have similarities to these models, but several distinct differences influence the way records are kept to this day.

New York was initially under the control of the Dutch West India Company. Large tracts of land were parceled into estates controlled by landholders. The governance of these parcels was largely decentralized. In 1665, the conquering English established towns as the basic form of local government. Judicial jurisdictions known as "ridings" were established that encompassed several towns and were presided over by a sheriff.

County establishment in New York began in 1683. It lost two of its original counties to Maine—Cornwall in 1686 and Dukes in 1692. The development of counties was slow because of ongoing disputes with Massachusetts over Columbia County, with Connecticut over Dutchess County, and with Vermont over the counties of Gloucester, Cumberland, and part of Charlotte. In 1691, representatives from each town were elected to serve on a Board of Supervisors for the purpose of local taxation.

The Reorganization Act of 7 March 1788 divided New York into 120 "towns." As Roger Joslyn correctly points out in the New York chapter in *Ancestry's Red Book: American State, County & Town Sources*, edited by Alice Eichholz (Provo, Utah: Ancestry, 2004), these towns are not to be confused with civil townships or geographic townships discussed in the next section, even though western New York was surveyed under the Public Land Survey System and has geographic townships. In New York, towns are the basic unit of governance, and records are kept at the town level. Cities and incorporated villages were not part of towns. A town could comprise several unincorporated villages and hamlets. Towns elected their own supervisors, clerks, assessors, surveyors, constables, and poor-relief administrators.

Pennsylvania presented an entirely different format. Pennsylvania governs at the county level through "commissioners" rather than "supervisors," as in New York. Counties were formed in 1682. Unlike New York, townships are the basic political units in the county. A township may include incorporated towns, boroughs, and cities. However, each may have its own government. In 1726, an elected board composed of three commissioners assumed the role of taxation from the county justices.

The "mixed" county model combines local town governance and county administrative functions. New York-type jurisdictions are found in states that received large numbers of New York migrants, such as New Jersey, Michigan, Wisconsin, and Illinois. States located in the Midwest that received a large number of Pennsylvania migrants were influenced by the Pennsylvania form: Ohio, Indiana, Minnesota, Iowa, North Dakota, South Dakota, Nebraska, Kansas, and Oklahoma.

EXCEPTIONS TO COUNTY RULE

Today there are 3,086 counties in the United States. This averages to about 62 counties per state, with Delaware having the fewest (3) and Texas having the most (254). A number of exceptions, however, are not included in this number, and if you include the exceptions, that number increases to 3,141. It is important for the genealogist to understand what these exceptions are, because they bear on where records will be recorded and located for research.

The exceptions are:

1. The District of Columbia is simultaneously governed by the U.S. Congress and the Washington city council. The boundaries of the city and the district are identical.

2. Alaska's situation is unique in the United States. Instead of counties, it has fifteen boroughs, three of which are unified "home rule" municipalities that combine borough and city government. It also has twelve

strictly home-rule cities. The state is also home to thirteen Alaska Native Claims Settlement Act corporations (ANCSA). Further demonstrating how tangled jurisdictions can become, the state is divided into four judicial districts. The judicial district boundaries may cross borough boundaries. Land records are filed in each judicial district office.

3. Independent cities are jurisdictions that belong to *no* county. The Census Bureau treats each one of them as if it is its own county. These cities have no intervening government levels between them and the state-level government. Since 1871, in the Commonwealth of Virginia, all municipalities incorporated as cities are independent cities—even if they are the county seat. Today, Virginia has forty-one independent cities. A table at <http://historical-county.newberry.org/website/Virginia/documents%5CVA_County_Index.htm> lists these cases.

Independent cities should not be confused with another type of jurisdiction known as the consolidated city-county, which merges city and county governments under the laws of a particular state. With concerns over state and local budgets, the merger of city and county governments into metropolitan governments is on the rise as cash-strapped cities and counties look to pool their resources.

EXTINCT COUNTIES

During the nineteenth century, county boundaries were in constant flux as larger counties were divided into smaller ones. On average, a given county might experience a dozen or more boundary shifts in the course of its lifetime. This is an important point to remember. Your ancestor may not even have had to move an inch from his homestead, but a jurisdictional boundary shift may have placed him in a new county. Original or parent counties break apart and new counties are created, appended, merged, or even abolished. Sometimes counties "reappear" in a similar location or elsewhere within the state years after they were abolished. It was not unheard of for the name of a long-extinct county to be revived decades after its initial disappearance.

Dates of creation or origin can sometimes be problematic to identify. Some state legislatures were more precise than others in citing when a particular county came into being. In the case where a creation date is not clear, the opening date of the legislative session is sometimes used. The same problem arises when selecting a date for when a county was abolished. Sometimes, both the population of a given defunct county and the census takers were unclear on this concept. The records include several instances of a defunct county showing up in the following federal census. Liberty County,

South Carolina, had been abolished prior to the 1800 census, but nevertheless shows up in the enumeration anyway.

THE GENEALOGY OF A COUNTY

Reminder

Given shifting boundaries and disappearing jurisdictions, locating records can become quite a challenge without an understanding of the history of a given county. **To be successful in your research, you have to consider researching the "genealogy" of the location itself: Was the county an original county?** Did it have a parent county or counties? Did it merge, split, dissolve, disappear, or become extinct? A genealogist needs to be aware of these changes and the outcomes of the splits, mergers, disorganizations, and reorganizations a county may have experienced; otherwise precious time, money, and effort will be spent searching for records in the wrong locations.

The third edition of *Ancestry's Red Book: American State, County & Town Sources*, edited by Alice Eichholz (Provo, Utah: Ancestry, 2004), gives a brief history of each state and a guide to record resources by type. Each state chapter includes an outline map and a table that shows when a county was created and identifies the parent county or territory from which it was carved. An excellent bibliography for each state includes a brief mention of map resources.

Published county histories often contain information related to specific boundary changes. P. William Filby's *A Bibliography of American County Histories* (Baltimore: Genealogical Publishing Company, 1985) provides a detailed bibliographic listing of all county histories of consequence up to the early 1980s. The bibliography is heavily weighted toward the collections of the Library of Congress and New York Public Library (which happen to be the best in the nation for these sources), but also draws on the collective knowledge of librarians throughout the country before the era of e-mail. He listed over five thousand such works in this bibliography. Although now a bit dated, his work stands as a monumental effort and is worth consulting to see if the county that you are researching has a published history. The county history may have been microfilmed and could be available through loan from the Family History Library.

Another great resource for state-by-state county information is *The Family Tree Resource Book for Genealogists*, edited by Sharon DeBartolo Carmack and Erin Nevius (Cincinnati: Family Tree Books, 2005). The resource listings include every county in the United States and cover date of formation, phone numbers, addresses, and Web sites for county courthouses, and the dates vital records originated and where to find them—all in easy-to-use tables. Each state section also includes a map detailing every county and bibliographies with information on maps.

The eleventh edition of George B. Everton's *The Handybook for Genealogists* (Draper, Utah: Everton Publishers, 2005) is yet another good source to consult. It describes county origins and formation. Each state chapter contains a bibliography that includes maps and gazetteers. Together, *Ancestry's Red Book*, *The Family Tree Resource Book for Genealogists*, and Everton's *Handybook* describe county origin, formation, changes, and extinction in general detail. It may seem like these books duplicate each other, but all three have distinct advantages. Consulting each is an excellent idea, and even small public libraries may have copies of one or all of these references.

Another source for county formation details is William Thorndale and William Dollarhide's *Map Guide to the U.S. Federal Censuses, 1790–1920* (Baltimore: Genealogical Publishing Company, 1987). These authors created a classic reference that depicts county boundaries for each decennial census year. Sidebar notes explain changes in county boundaries that took place in the intervening years between the censuses. The old county lines are superimposed over the modern lines so the reader can more easily observe the changes that have taken place since the prior census. Not all changes in between census years are explained, but it's still a fantastic reference. Consulting Thorndale and Dollarhide and the *Handybook*, *Family Tree Resource Book for Genealogists*, or *Ancestry's Red Book* together builds a fair picture of county boundary shifts and county creation and extinction every ten years between 1790 and 1920.

The Newberry Library of Chicago initiated a project through partial funding from the National Endowment for the Humanities to document every boundary change for each county in the United States. The Atlas of Historical County Boundaries project, the most detailed study of historical county boundaries ever mounted, is being worked on by the William M. Scholl Center for Family and Community History. The project editor, John Long, produced a five-volume reference work published in 1984 by G.K. Hall. The title of this work is *Historical Atlas and Chronology of County Boundaries 1788–1980*. The set covers fourteen states and nearly one third of the nation's counties, and is available on microfilm from the Family History Library:

Vol. 1: Delaware, Maryland, New Jersey, Pennsylvania

Vol. 2: Illinois, Indiana, Ohio

Vol. 3: Michigan, Wisconsin

Vol. 4: Iowa, Missouri

Vol. 5: Minnesota, North Dakota, South Dakota

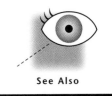

See Also

For further information or to view sample pages from the series of historical county-boundary atlases, see "Atlas of Historical County Boundaries" <www .newberry.org/ahcbp>.

Following the publication of these five volumes, the project continued and several new volumes were issued. Those published as part of the original five volumes were revised. However, the expense of them has limited their availability. Presently, all the volumes are out of print. Since the first volume of the new series appeared in 1992, eighteen volumes have been published through Charles Scribner's Sons (now Gale-Thomson Publishers):

New Hampshire, Vermont
Maine, Massachusetts, Rhode Island, Connecticut
Wisconsin
Florida
Iowa
Illinois
Michigan
North Carolina
Ohio
South Carolina
Alabama
Indiana
Kentucky
Mississippi
New York
Pennsylvania
Tennessee
Minnesota

The *Historical Atlas and Chronology of County Boundaries* series focuses on providing a chronology of boundary changes for each county, along with references describing those changes. A map is created for each new boundary configuration as described in the published laws of the state or state legislative proceedings. The maps are displayed at a scale of about eight miles to the inch and drawn on an underlying base map from the U.S. Geological Survey. The maps show watersheds and many smaller historical towns, making the atlases extremely useful for researchers using census and deed records. Unlike Thorndale and Dollarhide's reference, the maps are not tied to specific census years, but cover many years from county inception to the late twentieth century. John Long has paid special attention to providing information on the maps to match censuses of population and other sources of historical data of interest to genealogists and local historians.

The atlases include information on unorganized territories, as well as early counties or noncounty areas that were attached to organized counties for administration purposes. County name changes are also included, as are descriptions of other jurisdictions equivalent to counties, such as independent cities and Louisiana parishes. The atlases feature an index of place-names found on the county maps and a comprehensive bibliography of all material used to draw the maps. Each state has a consolidated chronology, and each county has an individual chronology that's linked to maps depicting boundary changes.

Since 2001, the project has shifted away from the creation of printed atlases and toward the production of cartographic files used in geographic information systems (GIS) and digitized maps and text, which are in the process of being placed on the Newberry Library's Web site. The first six states—California, Montana, New Jersey, Virginia, West Virginia, and Wyoming—have been uploaded, and it's planned for all the states to eventually be there, including the out-of-print volumes. Priority will be given to those states that have not been published in hard copy. You can view these states at <www.newberry.org/ahcbp/sitefiles/state_index.htm>. At present you can display the maps only by date, but you can select from several different layers to display both historical and modern county boundaries. Click on "Chronologies" to see chronologies of state and county boundaries merged into a single timeline, as well as individual county boundary-change chronologies.

One project undertaken by the Works Projects Administration (WPA) as part of the Historical Records Survey was to create a data set of every roll call vote by congressional district. Since districts often follow county boundary lines, attention was paid to creating maps that showed district and county boundaries between the years 1789 and 1941. Approximately 2,200 maps were created during this project, known as the Atlas of Congressional Roll Calls. Most of the maps are small outline maps of counties, and some maps of larger cities include municipal and ward boundaries in force at the time. The *Atlas of Congressional Rolls* project was discontinued during World War II. It is described in the Web-based version of *Guide to Federal Records in the National Archives of the United States* (compiled by Robert B. Matchette et al, Washington, D.C.: National Archives and Records Administration, 1995) at <www.archives.gov/research_room/federal_guide/work_projects_administration_rg069.html>. The geographer Ken Martis continued the original project and published it in this monumental work as editor, *The Historical Atlas of United States Congressional Districts: 1789–1983* (New York: Free Press, 1982). He compiled and published congressional district descriptions from original legal documents for all districts in each state. He also identified every person who served in Congress between 1788 and 1989 and associated them with their proper state and district locations.

More than 2,300 maps, covering the years prior to the creation of the United States up to the 1980s, are available in outline form from the com-

Microfilm Source

For More Info

For Melinda Shackelford
Kashuba's review of Ani-
map Plus 2.5, see *Genealogical Computing* 22 (July/
August/September 2002):
37–42.

Internet Source

puter program AniMap Plus 2.5. The program allows you to watch "ani-mated" maps of states that depict the formation of counties and the shifting of boundaries within states and territories. It displays county boundary changes for the continental United States and will show county boundaries for a given year or sequentially, allowing the viewer to see how the boundaries change from their creation to the late twentieth century. The program permits the user to set points to represent towns, land parcels, or other points of interest within the county, and then watch how the boundaries change around the given points. It has overlays of particular physical features such as river drainages and cultural features such as railroad lines that can help locate a town.

An unusual source concerning the origins of a county's name, year of creation, population by census year, and the name of the county seat is Joseph Nathan Kane's *The American Counties: Origins of County Names, Dates of Creation and Organization, Area, Population Including 1980 Census Figures, Historical Data, and Published Sources* (Metuchen, N.J.: Scarecrow Press, 1983). The book includes several useful lists: One list contains the names of every county that has changed names, and another supplies a list of counties by year of creation, starting in 1634. Clever use of the latter list might help your search for an ancestor who disappeared during a specific year. You could find which counties were created that year or the year after and get a broad sense of where opportunities for settlement might have lured a wayward ancestor.

Whenever you work in an unfamiliar state or county, one of the first Internet sources you should consider turning to is the USGenWeb Project <www.usgenweb.com>. The site contains pages for each county in the United States, with descriptions of whether a particular county was original or created later, the date of origin, name changes, and where records are retained for that county. The pages are managed by volunteers conversant in the local records and history of a given county. If you chance on a county that is not hosted, usually you can send a query to the state coordinator, who can put you in touch with someone in the county. The quality and detail contained in each county page varies considerably. Some sites include map collections depicting local historical boundaries of towns, cities, townships, and counties.

The Census Bureau maintains a Web site that traces recent boundary changes reported to it from the annual Boundary and Annexation Survey <www.census.gov/popest/geographic/boundary_changes/index.html>. As you can guess, keeping track of boundary changes between decennial census years is important for population estimates and the division of federal funds. Each state is represented by a table showing the area that has changed, the effective date of the change, and the nature of the boundary change (disincorporation, annexation, disorganization, merger, etc.). It should be noted that some of the changes reported in this survey date back to the early 1990s, so don't assume that the changes represented in these tables have occurred since the most recent census. This information is important if you are searching for late twentieth- or early twenty-first-century records.

The "Evolution of United States County Boundaries" <www.ac.wwu. edu/~stephan/Animation/us.html>, maintained by Ed Stephan, is an animated map of U.S. county formation that includes county boundaries for the years 1650, 1700, 1750, and the census years from 1790 forward. It is a large GIF image that can load slowly depending on your system's capabilities, but it's worth the wait.

THE TROUBLE WITH TOWNSHIPS

The word *township* is sometimes difficult to pin down. Different countries apply the term in different ways, and even within a single nation the term can be used disparately due to history and settlement patterns. Usually the term refers to a jurisdiction or area associated with a town. In rural or semirural counties, it can be a smaller political unit that, when put together with other townships, makes up the entire county. **It is important to realize that the term varies in meaning and as applied to different record groups.**

Warning

In the United States, two kinds of townships exist. One type is related to the survey of land prior to the federal government selling public property to private individuals. This is known as a "survey" or "geographic" township. This type of township was defined by the Land Ordinance of 1785. This legislation created a systematic cadastral survey (an official register of the quantity, value, and ownership of real estate used to determine taxes) that became known as the U.S. Public Land Survey (USPLS). The law required that all public land be surveyed prior to settlement, that survey lines have a specific orientation, and that land be divided into townships and then into smaller units known as sections to be oriented along cardinal directions.

Maps and township plats created by the General Land Office will be discussed in greater depth in chapter six, but here's a quick description of the method used. Land was subdivided into a basic unit known as a "township," measuring 6 miles square and numbered north, south, east, or west of named principal meridians (north-south) and baselines (east-west). Each section is 1 mile square and contains 640 acres. The township was subdivided further into 36 sections. The sections were further subdivided into property parcels. When you fly across the country and see these geometric squares stretching across the landscape, you gain an appreciation for the massive task of inventorying this vast country. You might also notice some irregularities in the rectilinear pattern. This is due to the need for "correction lines" (fitting a square land parcel into northward converging meridians) and the quality of survey instruments used in compass bearings (a chain and magnetic compass were the two instruments most commonly used when the USPLS was initiated in 1785).

The other type of township is known as a "civil township" and is related to local governance of an area. It is an intermediate civic jurisdiction between a city and county. A city may cross the border between counties, but a township never does. One way to tell the two different types of townships apart: A survey township is always numbered (Township 5), and a civil township is usually given a name (Cherry Valley Township).

In states where both of these types of townships exist, do not assume that their boundaries automatically coincide. To further add to the confusion, in the United States a state may have neither type of township, only one type, or both.

Locating the boundaries of modern townships is made easier by two publications. The first is Jay Andriot's *Township Atlas of the United States* (McLean, Va.: Documents Index, 1991). Unfortunately it is out of print, but its earlier editions are available on microfilm and microfiche and are rentable from the Family History Library in Salt Lake City and through its local branches, the Family History Centers. Larger libraries may have the *Township Atlas* as part of their reference collection.

The other excellent reference is the annual Rand McNally *Commercial Atlas & Marketing Guide*. This atlas is the oldest continuously published atlas in the United States and is available at many Family History Centers in print form. Its maps show some of the smallest places in the United States—anywhere someone might have the least amount of commercial or marketing interest. It shows minor subdivisions such as civil townships.

LOCATING COUNTY BOUNDARIES

The first order of research of political boundaries and subdivisions is to locate a modern map of the area in question. State transportation agencies and county road departments are excellent and often low-cost sources of county-level maps.

The Dollarhide and Thorndale reference previously discussed would be the first source you might want to search for a U.S. county during a census year. You may also want to visit the county or state Web site hosted on USGenWeb and follow links to maps of the area in question. You should confirm whether the county still exists by consulting *The Family Tree Resource Book for Genealogists*, Everton's *Handybook*, or *Ancestry's Red Book*. These references can also tell you if the county was an original county, if it was created from another county, or if it carved off portions of its historical jurisdiction to create other counties. Records could be in several county locations. Pity the poor researcher who has to research records in Clay County, West Virginia. Tracing just one area within Clay County, you discover that:

West Virginia was created from Virginia in 1863.
Clay County was created in 1858 in part from
Braxton County (other portions from Nicholas and Kanawha), which
    was created in 1836 from
Lewis County, which was created in 1816 from
Harrison County, which was created in 1784 from
Monongalia County, which was created in 1776 from
Augusta County, which was created in 1738 from
Orange County, which was created in 1734 from
Spotsylvania County, which was created in 1720 from
Essex County, which was created in 1692 from
Rappahannock County, which was created in 1656 from
Lancaster County, which was created in 1651 from
Northumberland County, which was created in 1645/1648 from
York County, an original shire.

For locations outside of the United States, you might want to consult the FHL's *Research Outline* series to identify how records are recorded (at what jurisdictional level) and review map resources outlined in these helpful summaries. Consulting Gwillim Law's *Administrative Subdivisions of Countries* (Jefferson, N.C.: McFarland, 1999) will also yield a quick snapshot of how a country is organized internally and yield the names and historical names (used during the last century) of these regions. Access to the Internet will provide you with any number of Web sites, particularly government and university sites, that have scanned historical maps.

ENUMERATION DISTRICT, PRECINCT, AND WARD MAPS

For obvious reasons, cities have been a popular subject for mapmakers for thousands of years. **Many different types of city or urban maps are available.** Ward, enumeration district, and precinct maps are a special category of urban maps that focus on depicting political and administrative units, and they can be particularly helpful in finding certain records. Fortuitously, several finding aids are available to locate these special maps.

Wards were used for administrative, electoral, and representational purposes. Many types of records incorporate ward information—death certifi-

Research Tip

cates, draft boards, voter registrations, and of course, census enumerations. These are just a few examples of the types of records that have ties to ward numbers. One difficulty associated with locating ward boundaries is the fact that they can shift frequently. Ward boundaries change as a city spreads geographically outward and the population increases. Wards and enumeration districts are areas familiar to genealogists who use census records to research their urban ancestors. A handy way for a census taker to describe a subjurisdiction in a city is to use a ward or an election precinct. Even rural areas use election precincts or townships to describe the boundaries of a particular census area. For example,

1920 Florida, Madison County, Election Precinct #5 Greenville

1910 California, Los Angeles County, Los Nielos Township (E. Whittier Precinct)

1870 California, San Francisco County, San Francisco, 11th Ward 1st District

The U.S. Census Bureau devised two other special districts to describe the geographic area assigned to a census taker. Wards and precincts are grouped together to form an enumeration district (ED), which represents the area a census taker can complete during the course of the time period allotted for the census. It is important to remember that enumeration boundaries changed from census to census, as did the route the census taker would walk. Never assume that boundaries or routes remained the same. EDs were grouped together to form "supervisor's districts," districts assigned to a census supervisor to oversee the work of the census takers.

The Census Bureau prepared maps that describe the boundaries of enumeration districts for censuses from 1880 to 1970. No census enumeration district maps exist for censuses prior to 1880. *A Century of Population Growth, from the First Census of the United States to the Twelfth, 1790–1900* (Bureau of the Census, 1909; reprint, Orting, Wash.: HeritageQuest Press, 1989) compares the growth of counties between the 1790 and 1900 censuses with reproductions of county boundary lines for states in 1790. Even in 1900, the Census Bureau despaired over the lack of accurate county boundary descriptions for some states in its attempts to reconstruct 1790-era counties. To compile the maps appearing in this publication, the Bureau had to visit a number of sources such as state statutes, maps that represented county boundaries, gazetteers, yearbooks, state histories, and manuals. The redrafting work must have been frustrating, as demonstrated by this statement from the book:

In most instances, however, the statutes in defining county lines refer to landmarks which have long since vanished, such as a "stick and stones," or "three trees," or to the property of persons long since deceased, which can not now be easily identified.

However, written descriptions exist for the ED boundaries for the censuses taken from 1830 through 1950. These have been published by the National Archives as microfilm publication series T1224, *Descriptions of Census Enumeration Districts, 1830–1890 and 1910–1950.* Series T1224 contains 155 rolls of microfilm. The 1900 census has its own special series entitled *Descriptions of Census Enumeration Districts, 1900* (T1210), comprised of 10 rolls of microfilm.

For the 1880 census, the following states have neither ED boundary descriptions nor maps: Alabama, Arizona, Arkansas, California, Colorado, Connecticut, Montana, Ohio, Oregon, Pennsylvania, and Wisconsin. These census maps were ephemeral working documents that were used for the completion of the census and oftentimes were discarded without a second thought. Probably for that reason, only three maps have survived for the 1880 census: Washington, D.C.; Rockwall County, Texas; and Atlanta, Fulton County, Georgia.

The written boundary descriptions for enumeration districts in the 1880 census are also incomplete for the following states and territories: Dakota, Delaware, District of Columbia, Florida, Georgia, Idaho, Illinois, Indiana, Iowa, Kansas, Kentucky, Louisiana, Maine, Maryland, Massachusetts, Michigan, Minnesota, Mississippi, Missouri, Nebraska, Nevada, New Hampshire, New Jersey, New Mexico, New York, North Carolina, Rhode Island, South Carolina, Tennessee, Texas, Utah, Vermont, Virginia, Washington, West Virginia, and Wyoming.

For all other states a written boundary description for an urban area can be quite detailed, but *it does not list all the streets within the ED*—only those streets that define the boundaries of the district. Figure 3-1 on page 58 shows an example from the 1920 census for Los Angeles.

For rural areas ED descriptions may refer to major geographical features that appear on maps, such as rivers, hills, post offices, Indian reservations, and villages. Institutions such as hospitals, schools, jails, orphanages, and asylums, depending on their size, were sometimes assigned their own ED number or identified as part of an ED description.

ED descriptions are arranged alphabetically by state. Within each state, each county is addressed in alphabetical order, and then the arrangement shifts to numerical order by supervisor's district, and is then further subdivided by enumeration district. Figure 3-1 shows the ED number displayed in the far left-hand column. You can also see references to "assembly district,"

See Also

For more information on censuses, see Kathleen W. Hinckley's *Your Guide to the Federal Census* (Cincinnati: Betterway Books, 2002).

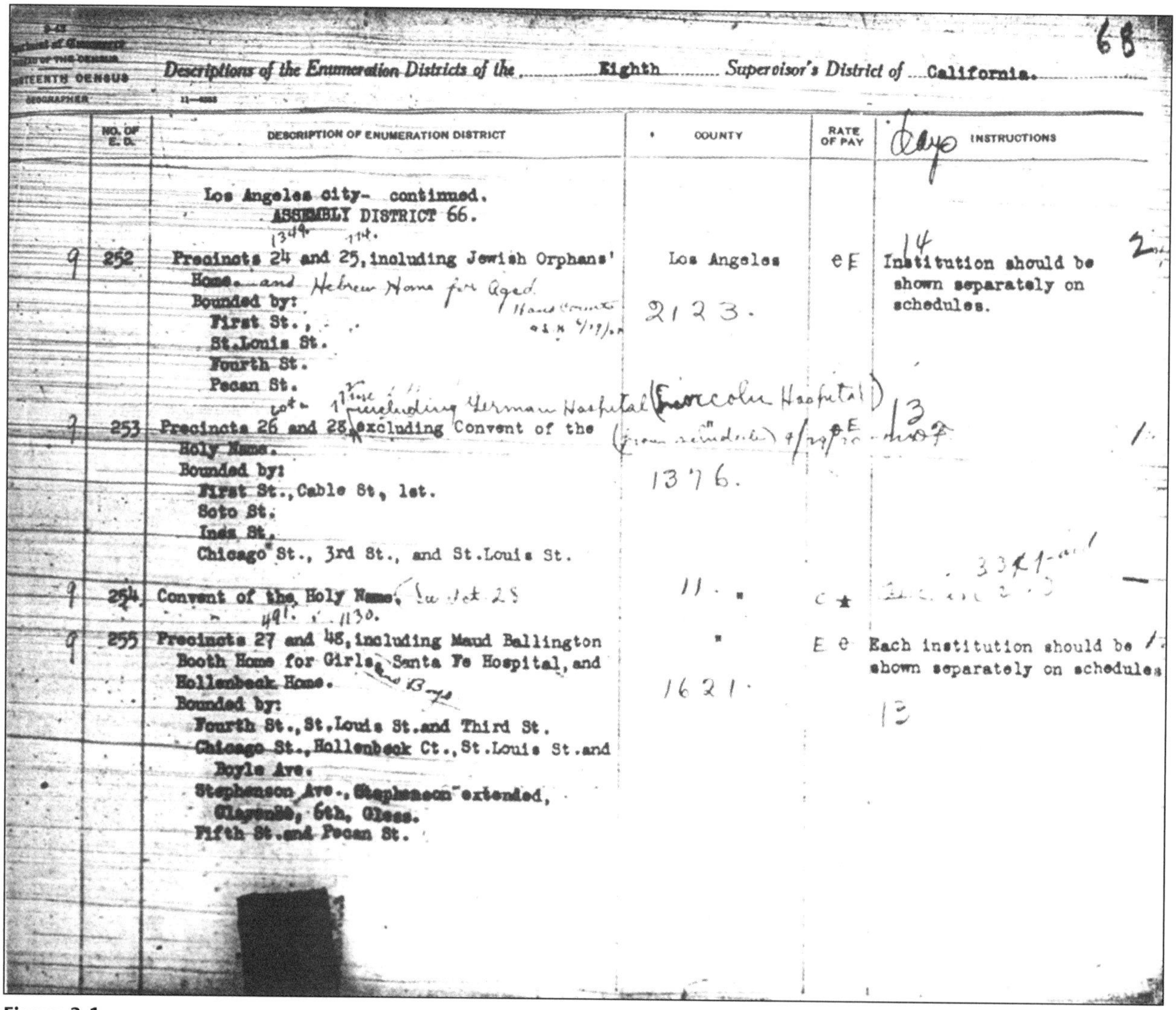

Descriptions of the Enumeration Districts of the Eighth Supervisor's District of California.

NO. OF E.D.	DESCRIPTION OF ENUMERATION DISTRICT	COUNTY	RATE OF PAY	INSTRUCTIONS
	Los Angeles city- continued. ASSEMBLY DISTRICT 66.			
252	Precincts 24 and 25, including Jewish Orphans' Home. Bounded by: First St., St.Louis St. Fourth St. Pecan St.	Los Angeles		Institution should be shown separately on schedules.
253	Precincts 26 and 28, excluding Convent of the Holy Name. Bounded by: First St., Cable St, 1st. Soto St. Inez St. Chicago St., 3rd St., and St.Louis St.			
254	Convent of the Holy Name.			
255	Precincts 27 and 48, including Maud Ballington Booth Home for Girls, Santa Fe Hospital, and Hollenbeck Home. Bounded by: Fourth St., St.Louis St. and Third St. Chicago St., Hollenbeck Ct., St.Louis St. and Boyle Ave. Stephenson Ave., Stephenson extended, Glavenso, 6th, Gless. Fifth St. and Pecan St.			Each institution should be shown separately on schedules

Figure 3-1
Sample page from a 1920 federal census enumeration district description for a portion of Los Angeles with instructions to census takers as to the boundaries of each enumeration district and the handling of various institutions such as hospitals, convents, orphan's homes, and homes for the elderly. *Source: National Archives and Records Administration.* Descriptions of Census Enumeration Districts, 1830–1890 and 1910–1950. *Series T1224, Roll, 42.*

which defines the census area. In creating census EDs, the Census Bureau relied on a combination of special districts, townships, wards, precincts, blocks, and streets to describe boundaries. No two cities were treated alike.

To use this source effectively, at the very least you need to know the county and an approximate street address or neighborhood the person resided in at the time of the census. ED descriptions also indicate what institutions were included within the boundaries of the district—hospitals, orphanages, poorhouses, jails, etc. The ED number is an important number to know because it will help you locate the portion of the census you want to search. Even with the advent of online census indexes that can speed the search for names, occasionally you have to dive into the census records and search page by page for a person's name because, for whatever reason, it does not appear in the index. Knowing which enumeration district the person lived in (by the person's street address) will accelerate the search of either the online or microfilm copies of census records.

Beginning in 1900, an increasing number of maps depicting cities, counties, minor civil units, and unincorporated areas are available for reference. The National Archives has collected these maps and boundary descriptions in the *Records of the Bureau of the Census* (Record Group 29), which is presently housed in the Cartographic and Architectural Research Room of the National Archives facility in College Park, Maryland. This collection contains approximately 110,000 printed, photocopied, and manuscript census maps. The maps are arranged alphabetically by the name of the state and then by the name of the county or locality.

The quality and value of information on these census maps varies from state to state and census to census. Census enumeration district maps showed boundaries for any election district, ward, precinct, civil division, township, unincorporated area, census supervisor's district, congressional district, or other subjurisdictional unit used in the execution of a census. Anne Bruner Eales and Robert M. Kvasnicka, in *Guide to Genealogical Research in the National Archives of the United States*, 3d ed. (Washington, D.C.: National Archives and Records Administration, 2000), report that, occasionally, even surnames of residents or property owners appear on some of these maps, particularly those in rural areas.

The major finding aid used to locate enumeration district maps for 1880 to 1940 and descriptions for 1850 to 1940 is James Berton Rhoads and Charlotte M. Ashby's *Preliminary Inventory of the Cartographic Records of the Bureau of the Census: Record Group 29* (Washington, D.C.: National Archives and Records Administration, 1958). It is available at the Family History Library.

1930 Census Maps

The recently released 1930 federal census has two finding aids to ED maps and boundary descriptions for selected cities. All of the ED maps have been microfilmed. They are available on thirty-six rolls of microfilm under the title *Enumeration District Maps for the Fifteenth Census of the United States, 1930* (microfilm series M1930). As was previously mentioned, the quality and condition of ED maps varies because they were used as working documents for the census enumerators. ED maps for American territories such as Alaska, Hawaii, Puerto Rico, Guam, and the Panama Canal Zone are found on the last roll of the series. These films can be ordered through the Family History Library, FHL US/CAN films 2339700–2339735.

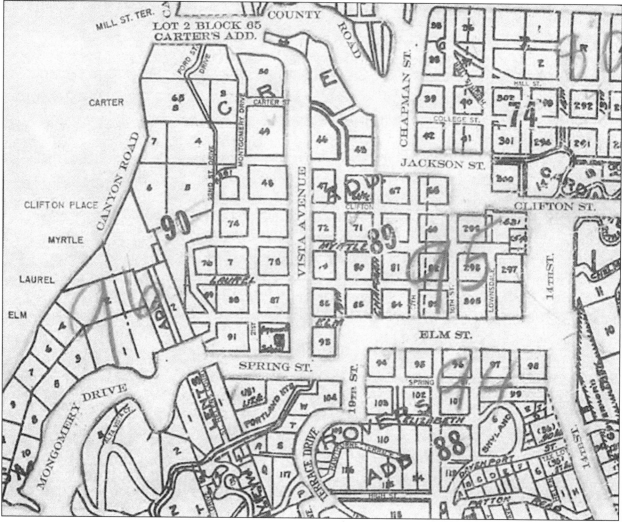

Figure 3-2
An example of a census enumeration district map of a portion of Portland, Oregon, showing the configuration of streets and numbered blocks with handwritten notations by census takers made during the 1930 federal census. *Source: National Archives and Records Administration <http://1930census.archives.gov/EDMapGraphicEnlarge.html>.*

An index to streets is included in the EDs of fifty cities, which can be found in National Archives Microfilm Publication Series M1931, *Index to Selected City Streets and Enumeration Districts, 1930 Census,* by Claire Prechtel-Kluskens (College Park, Md.: National Archives and Records Administration, 2001). The collection is made up of seven rolls of microfilm and available for loan from the Family History Library, FHL US/CAN films 2342403-2342409, or for viewing at any of the National Archives regional branches.

In *The 1930 Census: A Reference and Research Guide* (North Salt Lake, Utah: HeritageQuest, 2003), Thomas Jay Kemp reproduces the entire set of metropolitan district maps originally published by the Census Bureau for

1930. The maps show county lines and other census boundaries for ninety-six major cities. Kemp suggests using these maps in conjunction with the National Archives *1930 Census Microfilm Locator*, which is available online at <http://1930census.archives.gov/>. This site is cohosted by the National Archives and HeritageQuestOnline. You can perform a geographic search by selecting a state, then a county (or sometimes a city). Click on "Continue" and the site should provide you with a list of rolls of microfilm and enumeration districts associated with each film. Lastly, you can click on the small page numbers under the heading for the EDs and get a brief description of the boundaries for the EDs in the order they appear on the microfilm, which is not always numerical. The 1930 Census Microfilm Locator Web site provides an extensive description of the strategy to locate the appropriate film using geographic information.

Steve Morse has posted several census tools using ED information in "Overview of One-Step Census Forms" <http://stevemorse.org/census/intro.html> . You can use them to:

1. Obtain an ED number for either the 1910 or 1930 census based on the person's address.
2. Locate the appropriate roll of microfilm based on the ED number.
3. Convert between 1920 and 1930 census ED numbers.

This information can help you view the appropriate roll of microfilm at the National Archives or a regional branch of the National Archives, order a film from the FHL, or view online census pages at Ancestry.com or Genealogy.com.

More Ward Maps

A collection of ward maps for thirty-five cities is reproduced in Michael H. Shelley's *Ward Maps of United States Cities: Microfilm Reproduction of 232 Maps Described in Ward Maps of United States Cities* (Washington, D.C.: Library of Congress, 1975). These maps are microreproductions of maps found in the Geography and Map Division of the Library of Congress in Washington, D.C. These maps, although not created by the Census Bureau, are based on the 1880 federal census and represent the twenty-five most populated cities of the time, plus ten other cities that were frequently used by genealogists and other researchers to help make up for the missing 1880 ED maps. The microfiche collection encompasses 320 microfiches and is available through the FHL US/CAN fiches 6016554-6016787. These maps and more ward maps not reproduced in this collection are described in Michael H. Shelley's *Ward Maps of United States Cities: A Selective Checklist of Pre-1900 Maps in the Library of Congress* (Washington, D.C.: Library of Congress, 1975). This checklist is also reproduced on microfilm and is available through the Family History Library, FHL US/CAN film 0928120, item 16.

Another reference that may be helpful in identifying minor civil divisions, including wards in larger cities, is E. Kay Kirkham's *A Handy Guide to Record-Searching in the Larger Cities of the United States: Including a Guide to Their Vital Records and Some Maps, with Street Indexes with Other Information of Genealogical Value* (Logan, Utah: Everton Publishers, 1974).

City Directories

City directories are also useful finding aids for locating civil divisions within cities, such as wards or precincts. City directories are not only important sources for a person's address (especially useful for the 1930 census), but they also sometimes include maps dividing the city into its constituent districts. Not all city directory publishers were willing to reproduce maps in their guides, but many saw them as marketing tools for potential advertisers.

City directories sometimes reproduced ward, election district, or representational maps. My current telephone directory, which covers Shasta County, California, contains a map that divides the county by supervisor, state assembly, and congressional districts. Some city directory publishers did not bother including maps but reproduced written descriptions of ward or precinct boundaries, not unlike the ED boundaries discussed previously. For large urban areas you can use a contemporary city map to help plot these descriptions, focusing on the neighborhood or address where your ancestor resided.

City directories usually contain a separate index for street names, followed by a listing for each household that resided on that street. The street-directory section lists the address numbers on both sides of the street and at the corner intersections. A city directory published near the time of the census combined with the ED description will help reduce the number of census pages you need to search.

An eclectic collection of early city ward maps has been filmed and is available on two microfilm reels through the FHL, *Early Maps of Some of the Cities of the United States, ca. 1850–1877* (FHL US/CAN film 1548892 item 8 and film 1548893). The FHL film notes indicate that the maps were filmed from city directory sources. Not all major U.S. cities are represented, but most of the major post–Civil War American cities have at least one map. See the FHL film notes to discern which roll to order.

The Library of Congress has the largest collection of city directories in the nation. You can search the collection online at "Telephone and City Directories in the Library of Congress: Current Directories" <www.loc.gov/rr/genealogy/

Notes

bib_guid/telephon.html>. The Library of Congress also has a special online index to a huge microfilm collection of city directories published between 1861 and 1960 that can be searched at "U.S. City Directories on Microfilm in the Microform Reading Room" <www.loc.gov/rr/microform/uscity>. Scroll down to the bottom of the page and select a state. Many pre-1860 U.S. city and state directories have been copied onto microfiche from the Library of Congress and may be available through the Family History Library. Check the Family History Library catalog at <www.familysearch.org> to see if the directory for the city you're researching is available for loan from the FHL. For the widest variety of city directories available for a specific location, you should contact the public library, college library, or historical society closest to the place you are interested in researching.

Summary Points

★ Successful genealogical research requires a study of the history of the location of interest and includes the identification of historical boundaries and jurisdictions. Records are created and filed according to the location of these jurisdictions.

★ Do not assume that all states, provinces, or nations appear to define even simple geographic jurisdictions such as "county" or "township" in the same way. Make sure you check how each jurisdiction applies these concepts. Ignoring how they are used may mean you will not find the records where you think they should be.

★ If vital records are kept at the county level in one state, do not assume that they are kept at the county level in another. They could be kept at the town level or in some other jurisdiction.

★ You can go a long way toward identifying jurisdictions by using your local public library's reference collection or the resources of your local Family History Center. Online, try typing the name of the state or country followed by "+maps" into your favorite search engine (such as Google or Yahoo) to start you on your journey to obtaining jurisdictional information.

★ State Transportation Offices maps or County Public Works/ Road Department maps are inexpensive sources for county-level maps that often show minor civil subdivisions. You can obtain these by contacting the office directly.

CHAPTER 4

The Secrets of Map Reading

Maps organize wonder. Confronting a well-made map has all the fascination of opening an exciting novel.

—*George J. Demko,* Why in the World: Adventures in Geography *(New York: Anchor Books, 1992), 74.*

Overview

❖ *Are people born with the ability to create and read maps?*

❖ *How can reading a map help me in my research?*

❖ *Are maps like any other source of evidence?*

❖ *What is more important to genealogical research— knowing the absolute location or understanding the relative location of a place?*

❖ *What are the basic parts of a map?*

❖ *How do you cite maps and atlases in your research?*

R eading a map and reading a novel are more alike than you might think. Both require the reader to have experienced a few key things in life to appreciate the full benefits derived from understanding what a map tells you or what a fictional character may symbolize and resonate in a novel. One such experience in life is the *state of being lost.*

Nearly everyone can remember an episode in his or her life when that creeping realization takes over: *Where the heck am I?* You stop and look around and nothing looks familiar to you. Maybe this has happened to you while driving across unfamiliar territory and the landmarks and highway signs don't correspond with your intended destination. Maybe it's happened to you when you have temporarily forgotten where you parked your car at the mall. Or maybe it's happened while you were searching for a particular grave in an unfamiliar cemetery, and you look up and realize your preoccupation has caused you to become disoriented. Most of us can recall at least one moment of arriving in the completely uncomfortable, unhappy, universal state of being lost.

Our ancient ancestors made maps to relay information to one another long before written language even existed. They knew lost, and lost was a place you did not want to be. The state of being lost was serious business to a hunter-gatherer culture and had life-and-death implications. Whether scratching a map in the dust or incising a map on a cave wall or clay tablet, people made maps to communicate important information about where they were located in relation to something meaningful to them, such as water, food, shelter, or even a sacred site.

As people transitioned from wandering hunter-gatherers to settled agrarians, land ownership and the determination of property boundaries became important, as did the ability to represent a particular site in relation to other objects in the landscape. Maps are a fundamental means of communication, just like printed words on a page, spoken words, or a graphic such as a painting or photograph. And as in all means of communication, maps depict a simplified version or model of reality that reflects the author's (mapmaker's) and the sponsor's or publisher's view. An important point to remember about maps: **No two mapmakers will draw identical maps of the same environment, just like no two writers will write about the same subject in an identical way.** The maps may contain comparable information, but the style in which it's presented will differ. People see and process information differently. They notice landmarks depending on their individual interests, experience, and current state of mind (how fatigued, awake, anxious, relaxed they are, as well as their emotional state and degree of focus). It's important to remember that more than one map may be created and published during the same time period by different cartographers, and those maps will contain differing information. It's worth your time to seek out an additional map or two rather than relying on a single map.

Reminder

To a geographer, maps are more than useful tools for discovering where specific things are located. Geographers are also interested in finding out how things move and change over time. Phenomena that are here today may be gone tomorrow. Something that's not here at the present time might be here tomorrow.

Consider for a moment all the different types of maps you see every day but probably don't notice: weather maps on television, maps in newspapers, maps in commercials, maps used as decorations or backdrops in movies and television, maps incorporated into company logos, maps used as designs on postage stamps, and maps sold as art from framed prints to designs on mugs, coasters, and T-shirts. What about globes? How many times do you see the entire earth represented as a graphic? As an experiment, try keeping a diary for a week and note every time you see a map or globe and in what context. If you don't come up with a dozen or more in a week's time from just casual observation, you aren't paying attention! You will probably realize, like I did, that we are inundated with maps. Maps and globes signify knowledge, power, class, and—forgive the pun—worldliness. Their presence is designed to lend those qualities to whatever they are used in conjunction with.

\di'fin\ *vb*

Definitions

Map reading and mapmaking combine both art and science. They are dependent on a type of intelligence known as "graphicacy." **Graphicacy is to map reading as numeracy is to arithmetic or literacy is to reading; graphicacy is the ability to comprehend a visual object.** Just as some people have a talent in math or writing, others are able to understand and interpret images better.

You've probably heard of the term *math anxiety*—fear, mistrust, or dislike of anything related to using numbers. For several decades educators have poured money, time, and effort into treating the causes and societal effects of math anxiety. "Map anxiety" or "cartophobia" is every bit as real as math anxiety but far less acknowledged by society. You may know people who say they have no sense of direction or who shun maps altogether and declare "I rely on road signs to get me where I'm going." Map reading, like almost any other skill in life, relies on experience and practice. We are not born with the knowledge of direction. It comes with experience and observation and is communicated subtly to us during childhood by how the adults and peers around us used or didn't use maps in their lives.

Educators are concerned that map reading is falling by the wayside in our culture. I have heard more times than I can count from my adult geography and genealogy students that one of the reasons they became interested in maps is because, as a child, they were given one by their parents during a family road trip. With nothing better to do in the car (aside from tormenting a sibling in the backseat), they were forced to look out the window and keep track of where they were going on the map. Today, I wonder if children, with eyes riveted to built-in automobile DVD players and televisions, will have similar map-reading opportunities on car trips.

Our brains are divided into two hemispheres. Since the advent of modern brain-imaging techniques, little doubt remains that different parts of the brain process different types of information. The left side of the brain is associated with reason, logic, and analysis, and the right side is associated with intuition, creativity, and holistic thought. "Left-brained" people tend to be good at math, science, and language, and "right-brained" people excel in the visual-spatial arts and intuitive thinking. According to geographers Mark Monmonier and George Schnell in *Map Appreciation* (Englewood Cliffs, N.J.: Prentice-Hall, 1988), map reading and mapmaking are activities that require you to use both sides of your brain. The right side processes the visual graphics, and the left side works on the analysis of the information.

LOCATION MATTERS

The concept of location is a good example of how the study of geography combines an understanding of both science and art. The location of a place can be described in both *absolute* and *relative* terms. *Absolute location* describes the precise location of a place on the surface of the earth. For convenience sake, we invented several mathematically based reference systems to describe this position. The system of latitude and longitude is one means of finding and documenting the exact location of a point. Another example of this type of reference system is the township and range method used to describe property location in federal-land states. Absolute location is a unique place identifier that no other place on earth shares. It is useful for legal description, measuring distances between places, and finding directions between places—all left-brained scientific and mathematical activities.

When you look for a new place to live and your realtor tells you "location matters," he or she generally doesn't mean a place's absolute location but the relationship of that place to other places or things around it—that is, relative location. *Relative location* describes the interconnection and interdependence of places in the "big picture." Sites can be described according to their physical and cultural characteristics. Those characteristics differ from place to place. Sometimes these differences can best be understood only when that location is compared to or contrasted against the physical and cultural attributes of other places. This activity contains an element of left-brained analysis, but also has an artful, right-brained intuitive side when you look at a map of a particular place and ask questions about its relative location.

A genealogist may be more interested in the absolute location of an ancestral feature such as a house or a grave. More often than not, however, the more important leaps in genealogical research come from observing the relative location of a site—where it is in relation to physical features such as mountain ranges, rivers, or land that can be farmed, mined, or logged, and the cultural features such as forts, marketplaces, courthouses, cemeteries, churches, or migration and trade routes. The answers to questions about relative location may give family historians clues as to where to look for additional records on their ancestors.

Understanding the relative location of a place leads directly to understanding how a place interacts with other places. Geographers call this *spatial interaction*. Spatial interaction is often described in terms of the distance, accessibility, and connectivity between locations. This interaction between places can be described in a structured way.

Tip

Distance is more than the linear distance between places as measured on a map. It can also have a time component. Consider the months it took our ancestors to cross the Atlantic Ocean from Europe in the seventeenth century. Jump forward in time to improvements in ship mechanics during the nineteenth and twentieth centuries. The time it took for the same journey over the same distance was reduced to a week or two. With the advent of travel by airplane, the journey takes a few hours. The distance has not changed, but it has been overcome by technology. On a personal scale, think about where you shop, work, or dine out. Would you make the same choices if you had to walk rather than drive to them? Genealogists, for example, use this reasoning when searching for the families of their ancestors' wives. A rural ancestor's "courting distance" might have been limited to five miles away or a half day's journey from his farm, depending on whether he was walking, riding a horse, or traveling by wagon.

Distance also has a psychological component to it. Geographers have found that people consider known places to be closer than they actually are and little-known places to be farther than the real distance. The difference between perceived distance and actual distance is called *psychological distance*. Initially, when you move to a new neighborhood everything might seem far away. Later, when you've become accustomed to your commute to and from school, work, the library, or the grocery store, the distance might not seem very long at all. It's a strange trick that our minds play on us: Familiarity with a route or surroundings makes places seem nearer.

A discussion of distance requires a look at accessibility. How easy or difficult is it to travel between places? Our ancestors' "courting distance" might be longer or shorter depending on the terrain. Hilly topography would take longer to traverse than a flat road. A river or large body of water might act as a barrier to travel between places until a bridge is built or a ferry crossing created. On a larger scale, the Appalachians formed a barrier to settlement inland until passes were found through the mountains.

Connectivity is related to both distance (actual and psychological) and accessibility. The concept of connectivity refers to all the ways a place is bound to other places: telephone lines, cable television, sewers, roads, and even wireless networks. A location may also be connected to other places by patterns of global winds, ocean currents, or a river flowing toward the sea.

When you as a genealogist search for record sources, consider what the actual and perceived distances between places were. Given transportation technology of the period and the barriers to travel (topographic, limitations on time, etc.), how accessible was the local courthouse, the nearest church, or the cemetery to an ancestor's place of residence? Lastly, what were the connections between places during your ancestor's era? The answers to any of these questions may bring insight into an ancestor's pattern of daily life and suggest the location of additional information and new avenues of research.

THE ELEMENTS OF A MAP

One of the purposes of this chapter is to help those who have difficulty using maps or have avoided them in their research to become familiar and comfortable with them by dissecting maps into their components. If a map can be broken down into its elemental parts, then, hopefully, some of the dislike, confusion, and anxiety will evaporate and be replaced with the realization that maps are useful in many ways beyond helping you get from point A to point B. Maps are documents. A map is as much a source document as a vital record or a census enumeration. Like any other document, maps are created with the intention of satisfying a specific purpose. In the process of conveying information about the conditions of a given place at a given time, they also reveal something about their creator or creators—what they saw as important (included on the map) and what they saw as unimportant (left off the map).

While you read this next section, it might be helpful to have road map handy—any modern road map by any publisher of a place you are familiar with. A typical road map is designed to be user friendly and easily comprehended by the average driver, and it contains the components of a modern map:

- Title
- Mapmaker and publisher information
- Collar
- Date
- Legend
- Coordinate system
- Projection
- Orientation
- Scale
- Inset maps
- Symbols
- Place-names

Map Titles

Modern map publishers understand that in order to sell maps, the title, which tells the potential buyer or user what the map depicts, must be prominently displayed and easy to comprehend at a glance. The title is usually printed in a larger typeface than any other information. A potential map purchaser does not want to pick up a map of Portland, Oregon, when she really wanted a map of Portland, Maine. A successful title communicates the major theme of the map. One exception to this would be a map like a USGS quadrangle, which is part of a series. Each quadrangle is given a unique name that generally reflects a place-name of some prominent geographic feature on the map.

Modern maps tend to have shorter, more succinct titles than historical maps. Given the way road maps are folded for portability, the title has to fit on one of the small folded sections. Older maps may have elaborate titles that are part of a longer description, such as "Sketch of Routes of the 2nd Corps, Army of Northern Virginia, from Fredericksburg, Virginia, to Gettysburg, Pennsylvania, and Return June 4th to August 1st 1863." Some historical maps are untitled, which leaves map-library catalogers or the owner of the map the task of devising a title. When a title is created for a map after its creation, it's enclosed in brackets ([ ]) to indicate that it's a title that didn't originate with the mapmaker or publisher. You sometimes run across the abbreviation *sic* contained, italicized and in brackets in a title. This means "so" or "thus" and is used when a word is misspelled or incorrectly used. When citing a map as a source, you will want to copy the entire title with whatever brackets or abbreviations are associated with it.

Mapmaker and Publisher Information

A number of people are involved with the creation of a map. Sometimes, only the mapmaker is cited. Other times you can also find the names of one or more of the following individuals involved with the production of the map: the surveyor, the surveyor's assistant, the map editor, the engraver, and the publisher. On old maps, the name of the patron who contributed financially to the creation of the map is often given, along with a flowery tribute to his munificence. If the map was created by a military organization, you can sometimes find the name of the commanding officers in charge at the time the map was produced.

Citing Sources

You'll want to make note of who made the map (whether a single map-maker or a corporation) and who published the map. **"Citing Maps and Atlases" on page 90 shows examples of how to cite maps with single and corporate authorship.** Why should a genealogist care who made a map and why? The answer is the same for any source: Maps are sometimes created in a way that bends the truth of a situation to a particular viewpoint. Knowing why a document is made and by whom can help you understand the history, society, politics, economics, and even the basic veracity of the information contained in the document itself.

Collar

The *collar* of a map is the space between the line that frames the map (known as a *neat line*) and the edge of the paper. Sometimes this area is left blank, but more often than not it can contain information similar or supplementary to that found in a legend. A word of caution here: Collar information should never be overlooked by the map user. Often it contains information about how the map fits with adjacent maps, grid tick information (which contains coordinates) that helps you locate where you are on the map, provides new information on features included or left out, and source citations.

Date

While genealogists are trained to notice the date on a document, the date on a map can be elusive or nonexistent. A date may not necessarily reflect the day it was created. Map readers need to be aware that maps can depict several different types of dates—a date pertinent to the subject (in the example of the Virginia Army, the time that the expedition of the Army of Northern Virginia was operating between Fredericksburg and Gettysburg), a date when the map was drawn, a date when the map was last field-checked or verified by someone going out and looking at the landscape, a date of revision or publication, or a date when the map was deposited for copyright. A revision date is important when using topographic maps, so always check for one.

The placement of a date varies on different types of maps. On older maps you might find the date scrawled or printed in a corner or margin or prominently placed in the cartouche, the ornate frame that is sometimes used to surround a map's title, the name of the cartographer, or the legend. On road maps, the date can appear almost anywhere on the map—or not at all! "U.S. Road Maps" on page 72 describes the history of the road map and the intense competition between road map publishers. In order to lengthen the time period between revisions, road map publishers resorted to a complex system of date codes that represented the date of the map and subsequent revisions. These were understandable internally to the publisher but cryptic to all others—including the user. If you are curious about date codes, visit the Road Map Collectors Association's Web site <www.roadma ps.org>.

For example, a modern American Automobile Association (AAA) road map might indicate the date of its copyright as part of the legend: © AAA 2004/2005 Edition Heathrow, FL 32746. The date information reflects only the copyright date and not the age of the information on the map. Given the length of time a map might be in production, the actual age of the information might be a year or two older than the copyright date. Sometimes this information is represented for a map published in 2004 as: "Based in

U.S. ROAD MAPS

You may not be aware of it, but the heritage of that ordinary highway map stuffed into your car's glove compartment extends back to the late nineteenth century, when Americans fell in love with the bicycle. Here's a historical timeline of personal transportation and how it relates to U.S. road maps.

1877   Bicycles begin to be mass-produced in the United States.

1880   The first national organization, the League of American Wheelman, is founded and begins producing maps and handbooks of the eastern United States.

1893   First American automobiles produced.

1900   The United States has 8,000 registered automobiles.

1902   American Automobile Association (AAA) is founded. It begins issuing maps to its members before 1910.

1904   Rand McNally is one of the first commercial map publishers to publish a road map: "New Automobile Road Map of New York City and Vicinity." Later it invents its popular "Photo-Auto Guides." One of its first guides shows the best route from Chicago to New York using a picture of every corner or location where the road changes direction. Identifiable landmarks such as unusual trees, fence posts, houses, signs, and businesses are called out on each photo.

1908   Model T rolls off the production line and the first concrete highway is built.

1910   Almost one million cars are registered.

1912   Lincoln Highway Association is dedicated to marking an automobile route across the United States.

1915   Two million cars are registered.

1915   Rand McNally produces stencils showing a name, symbol, or marking to be associated with a particular route and distributes them to local organizations so they can stencil the route markers on light and power poles along the routes.

1920   Gulf Oil gives away 16 million maps of the eastern United States per year by this time.

1927   U.S. highway routes become uniformly marked and mapped.

1933   Color printing used in road maps.

Continued on next page

1952	AAA distributes 40 million state, regional, and city maps through its offices as free premiums to its members.
1956	Interstate Highway Act funds a new era of highway construction.
1972	More than 250 million road maps are printed just for the oil companies alone.
1973	Arab Oil embargo tightens profits for oil companies and free road maps become less available.
1974	AAA distributes 180 million maps.
1974–1984	Self-service stations become popular, replacing most "full service" stations and eliminating free road maps.

Sources: Akerman, James. "American Promotional Road Mapping in the Twentieth Century." *Cartography and Geographic Information Science* 29, no. 3 (July 2002): 175-191; Bay, Helmuth. "The Beginning of Modern Road Maps in the United States." *Surveying and Mapping* XII (July-September 1952): 413-416; Danzer, Gerald, and James Akerman. *Paper Trails: Geographic Literacy via American Highway Maps.* Chicago: The Newberry Library, 1996; Yagoda, Ben. "Unfolding the Nation." *American Heritage* 39 (1988): 34-41; Yorke, Douglas A., and John Margolies. *Hitting the Road: The Art of the American Road Map.* San Francisco: Chronicle Books, 1996.

part on copyright 2003. Navigation Technologies Corporation . . . Based in part on copyright 2002. Geographic Data Technology, Inc."

The two sources of information on the AAA map indicate that their copyrights date several years prior to the copyright on the AAA map. The user can assume that some of the information displayed on the map is at least two years old, if not older. Unlike the military maps discussed in chapter eight, road maps do not publish *reliability diagrams*—small illustrations generally appearing in the map collar area that show which parts of the map were based on another source and what that source was.

On USGS topographic maps, the date is printed in the lower left-hand corner. You should always check the date of any type of map before heading out into the field to find that old cemetery; otherwise, you might be surprised to find that the cemetery has been supplanted by a housing development or shopping mall. USGS maps will often list two dates: when the map was originally published and its most recent revision, as in "photo revised 1975" or "photo inspected 1975." These later dates are printed in bright, eye-catching red or purple on USGS maps to alert users to important new information. A photo revised map is a map that has been revised based on aerial

Figure 4-1
Early road map covers were designed to catch the eye and imagination of drivers. Old road maps sometimes contain inscriptions by family members memorializing vacations, significant locations, or merely the easiest route to the grocery store. Make sure you carefully examine old road maps found among family papers and treat them as heirlooms. *Source:* California Olympic Year Road Map. *San Francisco: Independent Pressroom, 1929.*

photography and maybe (but usually not) some cursory fieldwork. Statements like "photo inspected 1975" sometimes have companion statements such as "no major cultural or drainage changes observed." This means that aerial photos taken since the map was originally published were used to compare, and the conclusion was reached that nothing major had changed as of 1975. More detailed information related to topographic maps is presented in chapter five.

An older map may not have a date. If the map is part of a public or private collection, check the way the map is cataloged in the collection. Map curators often attempt to estimate the date of a historical map because it helps place the map in the broader context of knowledge about a place, the history of cartography, or the body of work created by a specific cartographer or publisher. In a library catalog entry, a map lacking an easily discernable date will have an estimated date written in brackets ([ ]) or be designated with a "c." (circa) in front of the date. If an old map is undated, you can estimate a date by researching what symbols, boundaries, place-names, and publisher information was included.

Legend

A legend functions like a map's users manual. It contains lots of important information, but no specific guidelines exist for what information is supposed to appear in a legend. The cartographer, the map editor, and the publisher decide what to include. Typically, a legend might include:

Tip

- Title
- Name of the mapmaker, publisher, sponsor, etc.
- Date of publication or copyright
- A copyright statement indicating who owns rights to the map
- A series number or reference connecting the map to a specific publication, report, article, or book
- Scale to measure or represent distance on the map
- Identification of prominent symbols, colors, and patterns
- A motto or some personalizing statement representing the company or sponsor of the map
- Source(s) of information used to compile the map
- An accuracy statement or a statement releasing the mapmaker and publisher from responsibility for changes that occur after publication

The legend information should never be overlooked. A well-designed legend will present its information clearly and without ambiguity, which will help the user understand the map and use it effectively (see Figure 4-2 on page 76). Not all map legends are created equally, however, and as you begin to read maps more carefully you will notice that not all symbols represented on a map are included in a legend. Whether due to lack of space in the legend or sloppy cartography, road maps are notorious for taking for granted the user's ability to figure out what a particular color, symbol, or pattern means. A poorly designed or incomplete legend can frustrate the user and could result in someone getting lost, or at the very least, not liking maps.

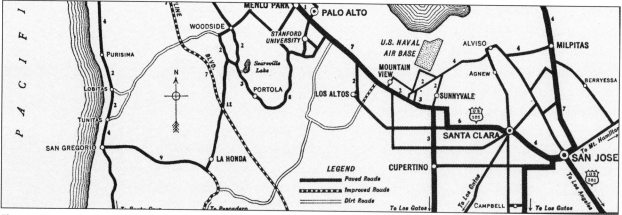

Figure 4-2
Plain or highly decorative, a map's legend ideally gives the reader the title or subject matter, date of publication, a scale, and a guide to the symbols used. This legend is on the plain side, being a road map, and only provides a guide to the condition of the roads. *Source: California Olympic Year Road Map. San Francisco: Independent Pressroom, 1929.*

Coordinate System

On road maps, collar information usually includes letters or numbers separated by arrows or lines that create a grid of squares. These letters and numbers comprise a method for locating features on a map. Since most road maps cover a local or regional area, using a larger system of location such as latitude and longitude gets complicated. Besides, the average road map reader usually doesn't care what the latitude and longitude of a given landmark or street is—they just want to find it—so road map publishers came up with their own localized grid system of describing where something is found on their maps. Road maps often have an *index*, which is a gazetteer that covers the names of the streets, cities, towns, cemeteries, churches, schools, colleges, features of interest, recreational facilities like parks, theaters, golf and country clubs, medical clinics and hospitals, and prominent physical features such as lakes, rivers, mountain peaks, and beaches.

The index works by assigning a feature listed in the gazetteer a corresponding letter-number combination that can be found on the map. For example, on a street map of Washington, D.C., the White House might be listed as "F-8" in the index. The map reader can find the White House by reading the letters that begin in the upper right- and left-hand corners and run vertically down the page, and the numerals in the upper and lower left-hand corners running horizontally across the map. "Square F-8" containing the White House is located eight squares from the left and six squares down. It's not certain when modern map publishers agreed on the convention of numbers running across the top and bottom of the map and letters running down the sides. Competition in the production of road maps, desire to create legible maps, and a familiar system of location probably drove the creation of this method. **Never assume that every cartographer or publisher follows the same indexing convention.** Cartographic license and different artistic traditions creep in from time to time. For example, "The Official San Francisco Street & Transit Map" has numerals running vertically and letters running horizontally, with lowercase letters *a-e* appearing in each grid square to further refine the location of features and streets.

Warning

On a larger scale, imagine looking at the earth from outer space. You'll see no grid lines, markings, or squares to help describe the exact location of a particular point on the earth's surface. A system of reference is required to describe a specific point. Several coordinate systems are in use today. Two types of coordinate systems usually encountered are *latitude* and *longitude* and the *Universal Transverse Mercator* (UTM) grid, which is also sometimes called the *Military Grid Reference System*. U.S. and Canadian topographic maps are marked with degrees of latitude and longitude. Canadian topographic maps and U.S. military maps may also use the UTM system because it's based on decimals. Global Positioning System (GPS) receivers can use either latitude-longitude or UTM coordinate systems. If a map does not have either one of these systems, it can't be used with a GPS; for example, a typical road map cannot be used with a GPS. If you are interested in using GPS for your research, it's explored in depth in chapter ten.

Why should a genealogist care about recording information such as latitude and longitude? Genealogical writer Dick Eastman makes a strong case for the recording of geographic coordinates in his article "Recording Longitudes and Latitudes" <www.ancestry.com/library/view/columns/eastman/5529.asp>. Now that GPS receivers are readily available, he advocates recording the exact latitude and longitude of each geographical location in your database for future genealogists and historians. Recording geographical coordinates ensures that, if an ancestor's grave or farmstead is abandoned, removed, or built over, future researchers will know the exact location of these places. Several genealogical software programs have specific database fields for geographic coordinates, such as The Master Genealogist <www.whollygenes.com> and Legacy Family Tree <www.legacyfamilytree.com>. Most other programs would allow the recording of geographic information as text notes.

If you lack a GPS receiver, you can always consult a topographic map and estimate the coordinates the old-fashioned way: Place a dot on the specific location and measure latitude and longitude with a ruler by estimating the degrees. Chapter five presents information on where to find topographic maps. Chapter two described how gazetteers, including the USGS's online GNIS gazetteer <http://geonames.usgs.gov>, can assist you in finding the geographic coordinates of locations.

Two clever uses of latitude and longitude as applied to genealogy include

Bob Maley's US GeoGen Project <http://geogen.org> and Matt Misbach's Web site <http://misbach.org>. The US GeoGen Project is a national database that is collecting the geographic coordinates of every cemetery and burial ground in the United States. This ambitious project accepts information from volunteers. Matt Misbach provides an example of how to link the latitude and longitude of a grave or house location recorded in a genealogical database to a MapQuest map. He has written a utility program, GED Browser, to create Web pages that contain links to MapQuest.

Probably the most familiar way to locate a point on a globe is the latitude and longitude coordinate system. Years ago, even road maps depicting large regions or states contained references to latitude and longitude. Today, these seem to have gone by the wayside in an effort to satisfy the seemingly contradictory goals of simultaneously supplying new information and streamlining older information to improve map legibility.

The main reference points in the latitude-longitude system are the North and South Poles, the equator, and the prime meridian. The North and South Poles are the end points of the axis on which the earth spins. The line that circles the globe halfway between the poles around the middle is the equator. The equator is perpendicular to the axis running between the North and South Poles. The equator is 0° latitude, and a point on the earth's surface can be described in terms of its distance north or south of the equator. The point on the surface is not entirely accurate until a second set of lines—meridians—is introduced to tell how far east or west the point is located from a designated central meridian. In 1884, by international agreement, the Prime Meridian was defined as passing through the Royal Observatory of Greenwich, England (see Figure 4-3 on page 79). **Prior to 1884, many countries established their own meridian system—keep that in mind when looking at old maps.**

Warning

Projection

For most research in genealogy or local history, the way the spherical earth is presented or "projected" in two dimensions on a map does not matter, because the area of interest is small. For this reason, many road maps don't even bother to indicate what projection was used to create the map. You probably recall from elementary school that flat maps distort the earth. Depending on the type of projection used, the earth is distorted in different ways; distances, directions, sizes, and shapes can be significantly changed. Globes are the obvious and preferred way to depict the earth. The earth is actually 30 million to 40 million times bigger than the globe you might find in a classroom or have at home. Globes give the truest possible view of the entire earth's surface. The drawback is that globes are not terribly easy to

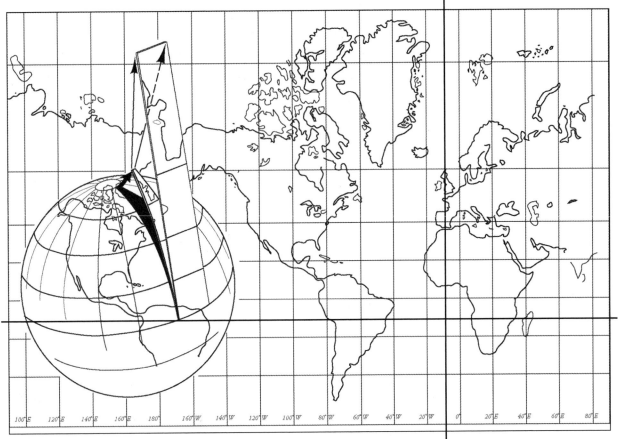

Figure 4-3
Transferring information from a three-dimensional sphere to a two-dimensional map surface can cause distortions in shape, size, and distance. The Mercator projection represented here has been the subject of controversy because of the way it makes high-latitude land masses such as Greenland appear to be larger than they actually are.

carry around or store. The compromise solution is a map, where portability and convenience are balanced against accuracy.

The bottom line is that no map can do everything, and the savvy map reader needs to be aware that the cartographer generally selects the best type of projection based on the ultimate purpose of the map.

Tip

Orientation

It's time to get back to our road map example. Is north always up? According to most contemporary road map publishers it's located at the top of the map, or very close to it. Our ancestors noticed that one star, Polaris, was always located in a constant position above the earth. It did not shift the way the sun and moon move throughout the seasons along the horizon when they rise and set. It became a special reference point, and so was born the special reverence for the direction of north. Many maps honor this tradition and usually place north at the top of the map, but historical maps

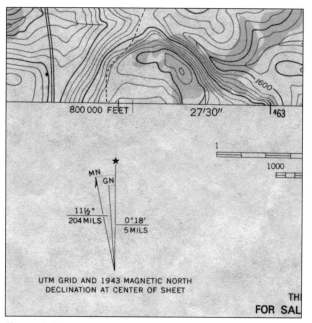

Figure 4-4
In this example from a USGS 7.5 minute topographic map, "MN" is used to indicate magnetic north.

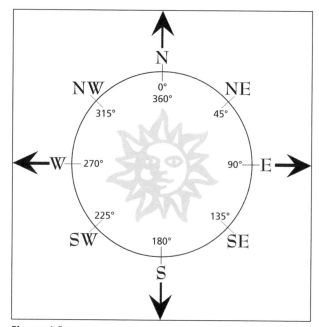

Figure 4-5
Wind rose or compass circle face showing the cardinal and intercardinal directions. A compass purchased from an outdoor or sporting goods store is a valuable tool in a genealogist's travel kit.

did not always follow this modern convention. It's important to make note of orientation.

In order to find yourself on a map you need to be aware of where north is located. Having north located at the top of the map enables the reader to find the four cardinal points quickly. A map's orientation can be shown in several ways. The simplest might be an arrow with the letter *N* pointing north. Another way is two crossed lines with arrowheads on each line with the cardinal points of direction: North (N), East (E), South (S), and West (W), similar to a weathervane. Older maps may include a "wind rose" or compass circle, which in its simplest form might be a circle with compass points with a long arrow drawn through the circle and pointing north (see Figure 4-5 above). More elaborate roses will have all the cardinal points plus four intercardinal points described in a clockwise direction: northeast (NE), southeast (SE), southwest (SW), and northwest (NW). Each of these four intercardinal points can be further subdivided into eight additional intercardinal points: north-northeast (NNE), east-northeast (ENE), east-southeast (ESE), south-southeast (SSE), south-southwest (SSW), west-southwest (WSW), west-northwest (WNW), and north-northwest (NNW). Though they vary from publisher to publisher, modern orientation symbols tend to be pretty simple and streamlined.

It is important to remember that the points on the rose sometimes mimic the face of a compass. North is located at the top of the circle and is equivalent to 0°. The rest of the circle is divided into 360 degrees. As you move clockwise, the position of 3 o'clock would be 90°, 6 o'clock would be 180°, and 9 o'clock would be 270°.

Scale

The single most important characteristic of a map is its scale. The scale of a map will ultimately guide you to determining how useful it will be in your research. A common mistake made by novice map users is to overlook scale and wind up finding that the map they purchased or found in the library will not answer their research question because the scale is too small to locate their ancestral village.

If you think of a map as "reality reduced to a manageable size," the scale is going to tell you how the map's size relates to the size of the real world. For example, my road map for the metropolitan area of Chicago has a scale of "1 inch equals approximately 2.60 miles or 4.18 kilometers." This means that 1 inch on the map represents 2.6 miles on the ground. At this scale, my map shows the major streets throughout the city of Chicago and important landmarks. If I want to know exactly where the courthouse or cemetery is located, this is probably the wrong map. I might try a map that has a scale of "1 inch equals 0.5 miles." A map scaled to "1 inch equals 1,000 feet" will show me lots of detail, including the streets and paths that wind through the cemetery. **A large scale gives you small details, and a small scale gives you large details.**

Notes

Scale can be represented in a variety of ways. It's usually either a ratio or representative fraction and/or a bar scale. A typical 7.5-minute USGS map has a scale of 1:24,000, meaning that 1 inch on the map is equal to 24,000 inches on the ground. (See "Series and Scale" in chapter five for more information about 7.5-minute maps.) When like units—in this case, inches—are used in a ratio, then the unit is dropped from the scale information. This ratio can also be expressed as the fraction 1/24,000. A ratio or fraction tells the map user how much smaller the map is compared to the actual

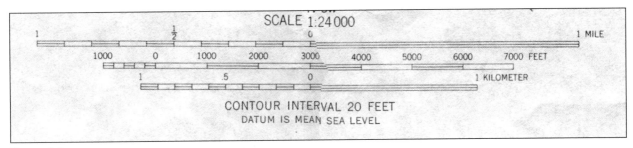

Figure 4-6
A bar scale as shown on a USGS 7.5-minute topographic map that gives distance in miles, feet, and kilometers.

---

size of the area. You can think of the map as ¹⁄₂₄,₀₀₀ the size of reality. Not to beat the subject to death, but a map with the scale of 1:1 would be life-size.

Another important way scale is shown on a map is with a bar scale—a line or set of parallel lines that are closed off at one end to create a long rectangle or "bar" shape, with alternating light and dark segments to help you measure distance. On a road map, typically the left side of the bar begins with "0" and distance is ticked off at a given interval—0.5 miles, 1 mile, and so on. On a 7.5-minute topographic map, the "0" point may be in the middle of the bar, with the right side of the bar showing a mile and the left side depicting increments of a mile divided by ticks equaling tenths. A bar scale is nice to have on a map because if the map is reduced or enlarged on a photocopier or scanner, the bar scale is reduced along with the copy. A reduced or enlarged map without a bar scale is no longer accurate to the scale originally drawn by the cartographer. The advantage of a graphic bar scale is that it is easy to use and understand for beginning map readers. The map reader places a ruler on the map and measures off a given distance, then measures the distance on the graphic scale.

When you hear the terms *large scale* or *small scale* in reference to a map, you should think about the size of the map's fractional representation. Just like in cooking, where ½ cup is larger than ¼ cup, a map's scale of ¹⁄₂₄,₀₀₀ is larger than ¹⁄₆₂,₅₀₀ or ¹⁄₂,₀₀₀,₀₀₀. A large-scale map tends to contain more detail but covers a smaller area than a small-scale map.

Inset Maps

Most road maps have an inset map that shows a specific locale in greater detail. For example, a map of Salt Lake City that shows all the streets might contain a smaller inset map divided by a border or enclosed in a box showing the location of specific buildings or points of interest. A map may even have an inset of a larger region containing less detail, such as Salt Lake City and communities adjacent to the Utah-Idaho border. Inset maps are great for orienting the reader, locating a specific place in the context of a larger area, or providing additional details. The scales will change between the main map and the inset map. Be sure to make note of what the scale is on the inset maps.

Maps scanned and placed online by the Library of Congress at the American Memory Web site <http://memory.loc.gov/ammem/gmdhtml/gmdhome.html> provide practice using an online atlas of historical maps, which can teach you how to maneuver between a regional view and a detailed view. Once you select a map and click on it you get two views: a "zoom view" and a "navigator view," which is the computer version of an inset map. You can select from six levels of "zoom" and can zoom in or out to get more or

\di'fin\ *vb*

Definitions

The earth is divided into 360° of longitude. Each north to south running line is equal to 1°. Each degree of longitude can be divided into 60 minutes and each minute into 60 seconds. Lines of latitude running east to west are divided into 180°. The distance between each line (all 180 of them) is a degree. Like longitude, these degrees can also be divided into minutes and seconds. A quadrangle is bounded by two lines of longitude A 7.5 minute quadrangle is a map that represents 7.5 minutes of latitude and 7.5 minutes of longitude.

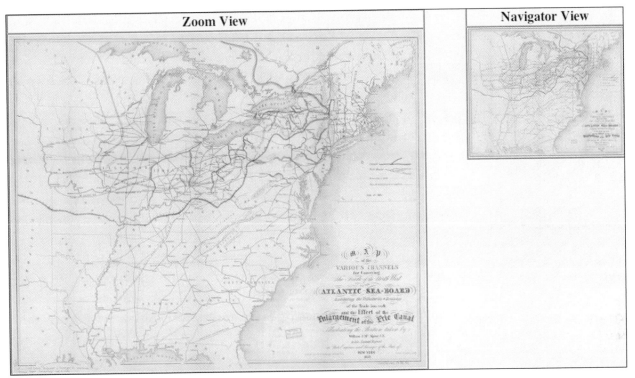

Figure 4-7
Two levels of detail are provided on many Web sites that host map collections. The Library of Congress' American Memory Web site presents a "zoom view" and a "navigator view." The Web site visitor is able to control the level of detail shown in the window on the left. The window on the right, known as the "navigator view," is always present and shows the position of the zoom view with reference to the entire scanned map.

less detail. Once you select a particular level of zoom, you can select an area on either the zoom view map or the navigator map by clicking on it once. A small red rectangle appears around the selected area. The zoom view will then display that selected portion of the map at a new scale. You can print the page after settling on the particular part of the map you want. It's a good idea to find and print the scale information (if it is on the map) at the same zoom level.

Symbols

Symbols are part of the language of a map. Through an array of lines, shapes, and colors, symbols create a visual representation of an environment. On a road map, symbols revolve around the type of information a driver needs: type and condition of roads and highways (freeway, toll road, unpaved dirt road, etc.), shapes and meaning of "shields" or numbered road signs (blue and red interstate, green business routes, round and oblong state routes, and square county roads), rest area symbols, and other symbols representing areas of interest such as airports, hospitals, schools, libraries, golf courses, and historical monuments. Depending on the map publisher, self-explanatory symbols are favored: A cemetery is depicted with a "⚲" or an airport with a "✦". Road maps use a variety of colors to depict specific land uses, such as green for parks, gray or pink for industry and education facilities such as college campuses, beige or yellow for urban areas, and so forth. The key to symbols on road maps is usually found in the legend.

U.S. topographic maps will have a brief legend on the map, but require you to be familiar with the various symbols, lines, and colors. You can request a free, separately produced key when you purchase your map. Old USGS maps reproduced a partial key in the collar or on the back of the map.

Warning

An important point to remember about symbols is that they are not drawn to the scale of the map. In order for them to be seen easily, map symbols are depicted at a slightly larger size. But the center of the symbol should be located at the geographic center of the object. In a similar fashion, small roads, streams, and trails may be drawn slightly larger than their scale would allow so they can be legible to the reader, but their center lines should be accurately depicted.

Place Names

Since the 1880s, commercial atlas publishers in America have had a fondness for creating dense maps filled with place-names. Compare a late nineteenth-century atlas by Rand McNally or an early twentieth-century map by the National Geographic Society to a European or British atlas from the same time period, and you easily see how much American mapmakers love to squeeze in as many names as possible. The geographer Susan Schulten wrote about the history of the atlas and its role in forming imagery and stereotypes in American and Western European culture in *The Geographical Imagination in America, 1880–1950* (Chicago: University of Chicago Press, 2001). She believes the tendency to crowd information on late nineteenth-century American maps stems from the "democratic practice of including as many towns as possible . . . regardless of size . . . suggesting that all areas were equally settled." That could well be true. By the 1890 census, the frontier period in America was declared to be officially over, and a map filled with place-names showing settlement from the Atlantic to the Pacific would certainly lend weight to that belief.

This preoccupation with place-names also had a practical side—marketing. Being able to advertise your atlas or map as a complete reference with more places listed than any other on the market was a strong selling point. Up until the 1940s, the National Geographic Society was particularly known for crowding lots of dense information into its maps. Since that time, American mapmakers have become more artful in the organization of information on their maps by communicating relative size of cities with type

Figure 4-8
An 1890s map of the United States showing an entirely settled United States crowded with place-names and transportation connections stretching from one side of the continent to the other. *Source: Rand McNally & Company.* New Pocket Atlas. *Chicago: Rand McNally & Company, 1893.*

size, underlining major cities, using color, and employing more creative placement of words by curving them to fit tight places. Some, like National Geographic, still communicate a sense of density of words or "busyness" in their atlases and maps.

Commercial road map publishers walk a fine line between creating a map that contains enough street names and landmarks to be useful and creating one that is easy to read. For this reason, all maps are edited to some degree. One method early road map publishers experimented with was to limit the area depicted to a strip map with a few cross streets and landmarks so tourists could negotiate the unfamiliar streets (see Figure 4-9 on page 86).

WHAT YOU SEE AND WHERE YOU'RE AT

One of the greatest experiences you can enjoy as a genealogist is using an old map of an ancestor's neighborhood and walking down the same streets

Figure 4-9
A "strip map" showing tour and major points of interest in Los Angeles that focus the visitor along a particular route including Warner Bros. Studios, Grauman's Chinese Theatre, and Charlie Chaplin's house. *Source:* Los Angeles Sightseeing Map Beverly Hills, Hollywood, Pasadena, *no publisher, no date.*

your ancestor walked. How do you relate what you see on a map to what you see in the landscape? One word: practice! First, find a landmark in the landscape that you can also locate on the map—a bridge, a building, an intersection of two roads, or where a road ends at the entrance to a cemetery. The landmark you select should be distinctive in the landscape and not easily confused with something else on the map.

TRIANGULATION WITHOUT A COMPASS

Another method to locate your approximate position on a map is called *triangulation* because you are using at least two landmarks in the landscape to help find a third unknown position (your location). Assuming that you do not have a compass but can turn the map so that it is oriented in a northerly direction (chapter 10 has a tip on how to find north using a wristwatch with hour and minute hands), first place your map on the ground after you have oriented it towards north. Find at least two or three landmarks in the distance such as a mountain top, a radio tower, or a bridge (this exercise works well if you are up high enough in elevation to have a nice view of a broad area). Locate these two or three distant landmarks on the map (these landmarks must be shown on the map).

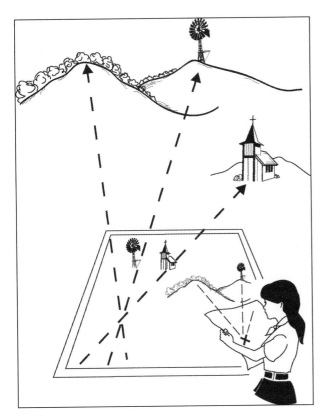

Figure 4-10
This image demonstrates how to establish your position using triangulation from three points selected in the landscape.

MAP ANALYSIS

Why does a genealogist need to analyze a map? Either the information is there or it's not there, right? Wrong. Maps, like any other source, need to be looked at with a critical eye. Looking at a map and understanding what's on it is the only way to decide if it answers your research question has been answered by a particular map. Genealogists have a reputation for not being critical about what they see on maps. No more! In short, map analysis forces you to *read the map*. It's always a source of amazement to me how many people can look at a map but not really see what's on it. This chapter introduces you to some of the basic concepts or mechanics of how a map is put together: title, projection, scale, symbols, etc. Now I want to prompt you to look deeper into the meaning of what is included on the map and, just as importantly, what is excluded from the map.

The following worksheet is designed partly as a "punch list" and partly as an outline where you can write down some of your observations about the map. The worksheet can be used with any kind of map, from a historical, handwritten, one-of-a-kind manuscript map to a commercially published road map or a computer-generated map available on a Web site. Not every map will display every component, so don't worry about leaving something blank. The important part of the exercise is to get you to *read the map* and think about what you see. Soon you'll be able to dispense with the outline and you'll be able to take notes on maps without it. Remember to file your map analyses with a copy of the map in your locality file.

If you're interested in reading further on map analysis, the following sources provide thought-provoking insights and examples of analytical methods used by geographers and cartographic historians:

Akerman, James, et al. *Two By Two, Twenty-two Pairs of Maps from the Newberry Library Illustrating 500 Years of Western Cartographic History.* Chicago: The Newberry Library, 1993.

Kaiser, Ward L., and Denis Wood. *Seeing Through Maps.* Amherst, Mass.: ODT, 2001.

Monmonier, Mark. *How to Lie with Maps.* 2d ed. Chicago: University of Chicago Press, 1996.

Wood, Denis. *The Power of Maps.* New York: Guilford Press, 1992.

Map Analysis Worksheet

Map Mechanics: Note the presence or absence of the following, plus any explanation that helps you understand this map.

- Title?

- Creator or publisher named?

- What is the domain of the map? Was it produced by a government agency, a commercial publisher, or a private individual?

- Legend?

- Scale: Bar graph, ratio, or fraction?

- Type size: Different sizes to show hierarchies?

- Orientation of the map: What direction is at the top of the map?

- Date of the map and/or the information the map is based on: Is there a difference between the dates?

- Has the map been revised? Is it an edition of a previous map?

- Grid lines: Latitude & longitude or other means of locating yourself on the map?

- Is the map part of a series, or is it a single map?

- Is the map part of an atlas, or does it appear in a book or journal article?

- Type of projection used?

- Symbols: Explained or unexplained?

- Colors used?

- Dedication to someone?

- Motto reflecting mapmaker, publisher, or sponsor?

- Imagery used to decorate the map's title or legend (the cartouche)?

- Index or gazetteer listing location names?

- Inset map to orient reader or provide additional details?

- What is the map's medium: Paper, parchment, microfiche/microfilm, computer atlas, online?

Map Meaning: Map reading considerations to assist you with understanding the mapmaker's/map publisher's purpose for the map.

- What was important to the mapmaker or his audience?

  —What did he include on the map?

  —What was excluded? Was there anything the mapmaker could have *reasonably* included but didn't? (For example, are native settlements or ethnic enclaves missing from the map that were known at the time but left off the map perhaps to make the land appear to be empty and habitable?)

- Who do you think the mapmaker had in mind when he created the map? Who was the map for?

- Is the map supposed to elicit a particular response or action from the viewer?

- What does the map appear to say?

- Was the mapmaker consistent in the symbols used across the map? (For example, were both picture symbols of hills used as well as contour lines to show topography?)

- What is at the center of the map? (Often the focus of the map is at the center and the less important items are relegated to the margins.)

- What is in the margins?

- What is the context of the map? Is it part of a larger series or a plate in an atlas or book? Does it fit within the larger work?

- If there are symbols or imagery in the map's design, how do they relate to the map's content?

- What was happening historically at the time this map was created?

After you have located one of the landmarks on the map, place a stick, pencil, ruler, or some straight object across it. Rotate the straight object until one end is pointing toward the landmark. The opposite end should be pointing toward your position. Draw a line across the map in the direction (also known as a bearing) created by the straight object. Follow the same procedure for the other landmarks. Where the lines converge should be a *rough approximation* of your position (see Figure 4-10 on page 87). Practice this technique in a place with familiar landmarks, and in time you can become adept at locating yourself. With the advent of GPS, the necessity of learning how to locate yourself this old-fashioned way has become less of an issue but it is good to know how to find your way without a compass or GPS receiver.

Using a compass in this same exercise would help you find your exact position because you would be able to measure the angles created between north and each landmark.

CITING MAPS AND ATLASES

Maps are documents that we spend time searching for, and therefore, they deserve the same attention as other sources we use during our research. The authoritative source that map librarians turn to is Suzanne M. Clark's circular published by the American Library Association (ALA), *Cartographic Citations: A Style Guide* (Chicago: American Library Association, 1992). An online version, "Guide to Citing Maps and Atlases," appears on the Lloyd Reeds Map Collection Web site in the McMaster University Libraries at <http://library.lib.mcmaster.ca/maps/mapcite.htm>.

The examples for historical maps and topographic maps found in Elizabeth Shown Mills's book *Evidence! Citation & Analysis for the Family Historian* (Baltimore, Md.: Genealogical Publishing Company, 1997) fall within the parameters for citations suggested by ALA. The world of maps and atlases is a vast one, with numerous permutations of maps in many formats. The examples on pages 91-94 list only bibliographic entries. You can consult Mills's book to obtain ideas for how to rework the examples into primary and subsequent citation formats for endnotes or footnotes. Her explanations are quite straightforward, so it's not difficult to take bibliographic entries and recast them into these other formats.

One of the suggestions made by Mills is the inclusion of the name of the collection and repository where a particular historical map is found. She also suggests that, in the case of other sources of a unique nature such as a family Bible, the chain of custody or provenance be included. This could certainly be applied to a manuscript map source if it were known. Although not specifically included in the examples on the Lloyd Reeds Web site, indicating the location of a rare or unique map source is a good practice that I have incorporated into several of the sample citations. It saves so much time in relocating that wonderful map you found in a particular archive. In your own notes, you should always note the call number, collection, and name of the repository where you found each map.

"Format" refers to what designation the original work is given, such as map, atlas, view, or aerial photography. Format can also pertain to reproductions on microfilm or production by computer software. If no scale information is available, then indicating "no scale" or "visual scale" is appropriate.

The guidelines for bibliographic citations are listed below. Not every map has each element of a citation. For example, USGS topographic maps do not have editions, whereas some foreign topographic maps do. If a map has no creator's name, it is appropriate to assume that the mapmaker is anonymous, unidentified, or unknown. You do not need to note "anonymous" in your bibliographic citation.

The guidelines are generalized to help you create consistent bibliographic citations. Genealogically related examples were created based on their application, as suggested at the Lloyd Reeds Map Collection Web site and in Mills's excellent guidebook.

Single-Sheet Map

Author. "Title" [format]. Edition. Scale. Place of publication: Publisher, date.

> The Everton Publishers, Inc. "Genealogical County Map of the United States of America" [map]. 1″ = approx. 125 miles. Logan, Utah: The Everton Publishers, no date.

Topographic Map in a Series

Author. "Sheet Title" [format]. Edition. Scale. Series, sheet number. Place of publication: Publisher, date.

> United States Department of the Interior, Geological Survey. "Redding, Calif." [map]. 1:24,000, 1″ = 2,000 feet. 7.5-minute series (topographic), Redding Quadrangle. Washington, D.C.: United States Geological Survey, 1957 photo revised 1969.

Map in a Series (not a topographic map)

Author. "Sheet Title" [format]. Edition. Scale. Series title and/or number. Place of publication: Publisher, date.

United States Department of Commerce, Bureau of Air Commerce. "Mt. Shasta Sectional Aeronautical Chart" [map]. 1:500,000, 1″ = 8 miles. 366/M. Washington, D.C.: Coast and Geodetic Survey, October 1936.

Facsimile or Reproduction Map

Author. "Title" [format]. Scale. Original place of publication: Original publisher, Original date of publication. As reproduced by publisher, place of publication, date.

L.J. Richards Company. "County Dublin" [map]. 1″ = approx. 1.4 miles. Philadelphia: L.J. Richards Company, 1901. As reproduced by Quintin Publications, Pawtucket, Rhode Island, no date.

Map in a Book

Map author. "Map Title" [format]. Scale. Place of publication: Publisher, date. In: book author. *Book Title*. Edition. Place of publication: Publisher, date, page.

Leyburn, James G. "The Valley of Virginia, with Adjacent Present-Day Counties" [map]. 1″ = 57 miles. In: James G. Leyburn. *The Scotch-Irish, A Social History*. Chapel Hill, North Carolina: University of North Carolina Press, 1962, 202.

Map in a Journal

Map author. "Map Title" [format]. Scale. In: Article author. "Article Title," *Journal Title*, Volume (Date): page.

Lennon, Rachal Mills, and Elizabeth Shown Mills. "Rivière aux Cannes" [map]. 0.5″ = 2 miles. In: Rachal Mills Lennon and Elizabeth Shown Mills. "Mother, Thy Name is Mystery! Finding the Slave Who Bore Philomene Daurat," *National Genealogical Society Quarterly*, Volume 88 (September 2000): 204.

Atlas

Author. *Title*. Edition. Place of publication: Publisher, date.

Stover, John F. *The Routledge Historical Atlas of the American Railroads*. New York: Routledge, 1999.

Map or Plate in an Atlas

Map author. "Map Title" [format]. Scale. In: Atlas author. *Atlas Title*. Edition. Place of publication: Publisher, date, page.

Braun, Molly. "Indian Territory and Oklahoma Land Openings: 1889–

1906" [map]. No scale. In: Alan Wexler. *Atlas of Westward Expansion*. New York: Facts on File, Inc., 1995, 211.

Map on CD

Author. "Map Title" [format]. Scale. *Computer Software Title* [format]. Edition. Place of production: Producer, date of copyright or production.

> "Map of Black Butte Lake" [map]. 1″ = 0.8 mile. *California Seamless USGS Topographic Maps on CD-ROM* [computer atlas]. San Francisco: National Geographic Maps, 2000.

Map Produced Using Software

Author. "Map Title" [format]. Scale. Computer database title [format]. Edition. Place of production: Producer, date of copyright or production. Using: Author. *Computer Software Title* [format]. Edition. Place of production: Producer, date of copyright or production.

> "California 1850" [map]. Visual scale. Using: *Animap Plus* [computer software]. Version 2.5. Alamo, California: The Gold Bug, 2002.

Map on the Web

Author (if known). "Map Title" [format]. Scale. "Title of the Complete Document or Site." Information date. URL, including the path and any directories necessary to access the document. (The date viewed or printed).

> Buckman, O.H. "Official Map of the County of Napa, California: Compiled from the Official Records and Latest Surveys" [map]. 1″ = 1 mile. "Library of Congress, Geography and Map Division—American Memory Collection." <http://memory.loc.gov/cgi-bin/map_item.pl?data=/home/www/data/gmd/gmd436/g4363/g . . .> (9 October 2004).

Manuscript Map as Part of Personal Papers Held Privately or in a Collection

Author. "Map Title" [format]. Scale. Date. Manuscript collection number (if appropriate). Manuscript Title (if appropriate). Repository Name or provenance (if appropriate).

> Shackleford, Oscar Cecil. "Map to My Cabin" [map]. No scale. No date. Original owned in 2004 by Melinda Kashuba, Redding, California. Pencil sketch map was passed from Oscar Cecil Shackleford to Betty Jane Shackleford, his wife, on his death. Betty Jane Shackleford gave it to Melinda (her daughter).

Interactive Reference Map

Author. *Title* [format]. Data date if known. Scale; Name of person who generated the map; Name of software used to create the map or name of the Web site. <URL> (date generated).

> Redding, California [map]. 2003. Scale unknown; generated by Melinda Kashuba; using MapQuest.com, Inc. <www.mapquest.com/maps . . .> (8 March 2005).

Interactive Thematic Map

Author or Organization. *Title* [format]. Data date if known. Scale; Name of person who generated the map; Name of software used to create the map or name of the Web site. <URL> (date generated).

> Harmick Software. Sweet Surname Distribution, 1920 [map]. 1999. Scale unknown; generated by Melinda Kashuba; Harmick Software. <www.harmick.com/names> (23 January 2005).

ADDITIONAL RESOURCES

Web Sites

Convert and translate coordinate systems from one type to another, such as latitude and longitude, UTM, degree decimals, and others at JeEep.com <http://jeeep.com/details/coord>.

"How Far Is It" measures the distances between locations by city name or latitude and longitude coordinates <www.indo.com/distance>.

"About Geography" by Matt T. Rosenberg is part of About.com, an award-winning megasite, and is devoted to everything having to do with geography, with hundreds of links to Web resources, at <http://geography.about.com>.

MapQuest is an interactive map creation program that is free on the Web <www.mapquest.com>. Google Maps is a similar program with additional features that allow you to identify categories of places (like cemeteries) with a given zip code <http://maps.google.com/>.

Books

Boardman, David. *Graphicacy and Geography Teaching*. London: Croom Helm, 1983.

Committee on Map Projections of the American Cartographic Association. *Which Map Is Best?* Falls Church, Va.: American Congress on Surveying and Mapping, 1986.

Dorling, Daniel, and David Fairbairn. *Mapping: Ways of Representing the World*. Harlow, Eng.: Longman, 1997.

Jacobson, Cliff. *Basic Essentials: Map and Compass.* Rev 2d ed. Old Saybrook, Conn.: Globe Pequot Press, 1999.

Muehrcke, Phillip C., and Juliana O. Muehrcke. *Map Use: Reading, Analysis, and Interpretation.* 3d ed. Madison, Wis.: JP Publications, 1992.

Schlereth, Thomas. "Twentieth-Century Highway Maps." In *From Sea Charts to Satellite Images.* David Buisseret, editor. Chicago: University of Chicago Press, 1990.

Thrower, Norman J.W. *Maps and Civilization.* Chicago: University of Chicago Press, 1996.

Summary Points

★ Maps depict a simplified version or model of reality that reflects someone's particular point of view.

★ No two mapmakers will draw identical maps of the same environment, just like no two writers will write about a subject in an identical way.

★ Map reading and mapmaking are dependent on a type of intelligence known as graphicacy. Even if you feel you were not born with this ability, you can learn to read maps with practice just like you can learn any other subject.

★ Maps are documents. Like any other document, maps are created to satisfy a specific purpose.

★ The single most important characteristic of a map is its scale. The scale of a map will ultimately guide you to determining how useful it will be in your research.

★ One of the greatest experiences you can enjoy is to use an old map and identify locations in an ancestor's neighborhood. Being able to read a map effectively will open up new opportunities for you to understand and appreciate your ancestors' lives.

CHAPTER 5

Topographic Maps

What is there on this richly endowed land of ours which may be dug, or gathered, or harvested, and made part of the wealth of America and the world, and how and where does it lie?

—Congressman A.S. Hewitt on the establishment of the Geological Survey in 1879, quoted by Morris M. Thompson in Maps for America, 3d ed. (Washington, D.C.: U.S. Government Printing Office, 1988).

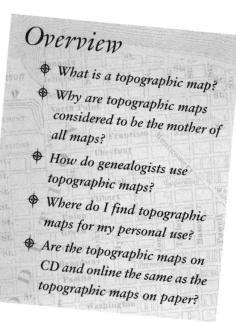

Overview

- What is a topographic map?
- Why are topographic maps considered to be the mother of all maps?
- How do genealogists use topographic maps?
- Where do I find topographic maps for my personal use?
- Are the topographic maps on CD and online the same as the topographic maps on paper?

WHAT IS A TOPOGRAPHIC MAP?

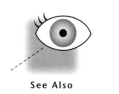

See Also

For more information, see Henry Gannett's, "The Mother Maps of the United States," *National Geographic Magazine* IV (March 31, 1892): 101-117.

Maps have mothers! As genealogists, we can relate to that statement in several ways. At the end of the nineteenth century the concept of "mother maps" was used by Henry Gannett, the U.S. government geographer in charge of mapping the 1880 federal census, to express the singular importance of topographic mapping to understanding all physical, cultural, and economic processes in the United States. Mother maps were great compiled maps made from direct measurements in the field by exploration parties. These were not like earlier compiled maps made from a mosaic of field observations and interviews with trappers, soldiers, Americans Indians, and other explorers. These were maps made with survey instruments, plane tables, copious field notes, and photography.

Topographic maps emphasize physical features on the surface of the earth. They are usually highly detailed, showing not only landforms but also vegetation. Their greatest value to genealogists is the degree to which they show cultural features. Topographic maps show not just large features such as towns, cities, highways, and some political boundaries, but sometimes detail down to some individual buildings, churches, cemeteries, and even fence lines between properties. To be particularly useful, topographic maps have to be at a large scale (a small area depicted in great detail) and accurate (resulting from scientific measurements).

Today, most topographic mapping in the United States is accomplished by the federal government through the U.S. Geological Survey (USGS). That has not always been the case. At one time a number of competing public agencies (the General Land Office, Corps of Topographical Engineers of the War Department, the Coast Survey), as well as private concerns such as the railroads and canal companies, were engaged in their own mapping programs. What developed was a hodgepodge of mapping, with some parts of the country depicted in great detail (1,600 feet to 1 inch in some parts of Pennsylvania) and other parts of the country where no mapping had taken place. Unlike some European countries, like England, who completed their mother maps by 1873 through the government-sponsored Ordinance Survey, the mapping of the entire United States was not easily accomplished. The sheer size of the country, coupled with its fast territorial expansion during the nineteenth century, created a logistical dilemma for the federal government. In 1892, when Gannett had issued his call for detailed, uniform "mother mapping" of the United States, the following areas were largely unsurveyed and true "blank spaces" on the map of the nation:

- Northern Maine
- Adirondack plateau of New York
- Southern Florida
- Most of Idaho and Montana
- Cascade and Coast ranges of Oregon and Washington
- Western North Dakota and South Dakota
- Western Texas
- Southeastern New Mexico
- All of Alaska (except the southeastern shoreline)

In 1879, more than a hundred years after our nation was founded, the USGS was established. Its mission was quite utilitarian—documenting the geography of the country so a base map could be created to show geological resources. Ultimately, USGS's charge was widened to include mapping other resources and cultural features, as well.

It was some decades before the USGS settled on a standard scale of topographic representation. The familiar topographic *quadrangle* (also known as a quad) that you see in sporting goods shops, bookstores, and libraries has a scale of about 2.5 inches to the mile (1:24,000, or 1:25,000 for recent metric versions). Mapping the United States at that scale takes more than 55,000 sheets to represent the entire nation. Up until about 1980, with the advent of computerized topographic mapping, it took the same amount of time that it took when Gannett was writing (late 1800s) to produce a finished topographic quadrangle—four years. Around 1900, it cost about $10 per square mile to map topography. It was little wonder then, from the very beginning, that the USGS was strapped for cash with the enormous task ahead made even more complicated by the fact that millions of people were enacting serious landscape modifications through their settling, clearing, logging, farming, mining, grazing, draining, dredging, and town building activities.

The areas that were initially mapped were the ones that were deemed most valuable and relevant to government programs: national defense areas (training sites, ports, borders), transportation, mining, land sales, and so forth. Not long into the 1880s, the USGS began seeking cooperative aid from states to assist in the actual mapping and help pay for the mapping of their state. Each state was approached: Some states, like New Jersey, turned over their entire topographic mapping to USGS, and others, like Massachusetts, chose to work cooperatively through their own state mapping agencies. Some states, like Indiana, elected to be mapped by default; they were initially depicted as part of quadrangles completed for adjacent states. By 1919, Indiana began cooperating with the federal government through its Office of the State Geologist. Western states, perhaps because they had more timber to harvest and mines to be dug, were quicker to pick up on the advantage of having USGS map their states. Between 1902 and 1904, 16,278 square miles of land east of the Mississippi was mapped by USGS, of which 84 percent was in states with cooperative mapping programs with the federal government.

The major drawback to the federal mapping program was the time it took to complete, even at small scales of 1:250,000 (1 inch = about 4 miles). Like an overoptimistic building contractor, the USGS continually underestimated the time it took to complete topographic mapping for a state. Smaller eastern states were completed quickly. By 1906, USGS had finished topographic maps for Connecticut, Massachusetts, New Jersey, and Rhode Island. West Virginia was added by 1907. It should come as no surprise, then, that the United States was finally completely mapped at 1:24,000 scale in 1990 just in time for the census that year—more than one hundred years after the founding of the USGS! **An online history of the USGS by Mary C. Rabbitt, *The United States Geological Survey: 1879–1989*, completed for its hundredth anniversary, is available at <http://pubs.usgs.gov/circ/c1050/index.htm>.**

Internet Source

It seemed that as soon as a state was completed it was time to revise the map. Some physical features disappeared—lakes drained, mountains mined away for building materials or coal, valleys filled—and many more towns, roads, railroads, and farms were created by people. New boundaries and place-names also needed to be depicted. What was a nuisance to mapmakers at USGS has proven to be a boon for the family historian: Successive revisions of topographic maps have given us insight into the evolution of the landscape in a way that few other sources could for the late nineteenth and early twentieth centuries. Topographic quadrangles that I have used to map my ancestors' properties in northern Florida have base mapping dates of the 1950s! Using one of those maps is like peering into the past; the fence lines, place-names, locations of farm buildings, churches, and graveyards depict the time my family was farming there. This is terrific for historical work but less than desirable for navigating roads today.

As discussed in chapter four, always make note of the date of the information contained on a map. On older USGS maps, the date is shown in the lower right-hand corner of the map (see Figure 5-1 below). Revision dates are often shown in pinkish purple below the date of the original quadrangle. Never rely completely on a topographic map for driving directions. Use it in conjunction with a modern road map.

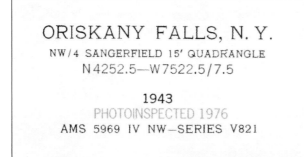

Figure 5-1

A typical title block from a USGS 7.5-minute quadrangle gives the name of the map, the location of the quadrangle, the year published, the year it was photoinspected and/or revised, military series identification, and an abbreviated identification of road symbols.

As mentioned earlier, states have cooperatively funded topographical surveys. Other federal agencies have also worked in conjunction with USGS to accelerate the mapping of a particular area. In the past, this has contributed to the scattering of topographic maps and geographic information throughout a number of agencies. USGS is the major federal agency that makes topographic maps today, but you can find topographic maps created by a number of other federal agencies or by agencies listed as coauthors with USGS.

Chapter eight discusses military mapping in the United States and the cooperative agreement that was signed during World War II to standardize maps prepared by a number of federal agencies involved in defense. Primarily, map scales, symbols, and geographic grids were of greatest concern when maps were shared between federal agencies.

When searching for any type of map in a library catalog, remember to look under the name of other federal and state agencies that may have had an interest or active part in the development of the region you are researching. While you might not find a topographic map made by USGS for a particular decade or time period, you might find a USGS base map that has been revised by another federal agency or a completely new base topographic map created by another agency that is closer to the time period you are researching.

Contour Lines

This may seem obvious, but one of the hallmarks of the topographic map is the way it shows topography. One of the terrific things USGS did in the nineteenth century was adopting the *contour line* to show the elevation and shape of the land surface. Contour lines are those light brown lines you see on quadrangles that snake, meander, and circle across the map. They are imaginary lines connecting all points of equal elevation that are above or below a particular surface (usually sea level, but not always). The biggest problem with contour lines is that they aren't as easy to understand as other ways to show landforms.

To make elevation more comprehensible, colors were added to create the familiar "school atlas"—*altitude-tint* or *hypsometric* maps. On these types of maps it's easy to discern the low and high places. The problem with them is that the same colors were used to show fertile areas on other maps. Schoolchildren and some adults looked at these maps and derived weird notions. For example, Death Valley, California, is lower than sea level and depicted as green, which makes it appear lush and fertile, but it's really a desert. To try to counteract this notion, tiny dots were added to maps to show arid conditions, but the tiny dots (sand?) only obscured the green tint underneath and made the map difficult to read.

Another way topography has been historically represented was depicting hills as "bread loaves" or "fish scales." People could relate to these hill-shaped features, but they were not terribly accurate for location or height. An alternate method that lasted up until the early twentieth century was the use of *hachures* on maps. Hachures are short strokes drawn down slope (see Figure 5-2 on page 101). The thickness of the stroke mark was determined by the relative steepness of the land feature. Relative elevation could only be inferred from hachures and not measured with any confidence. Sometimes hachures were combined with a visual trick mapmakers used that make them appear to cast a shadow as if illuminated from the northwest (which never happens in real life). This gave some nineteenth-century maps a three-dimensional quality that sometimes made them easier to read and lovely to look at, but not much more accurate.

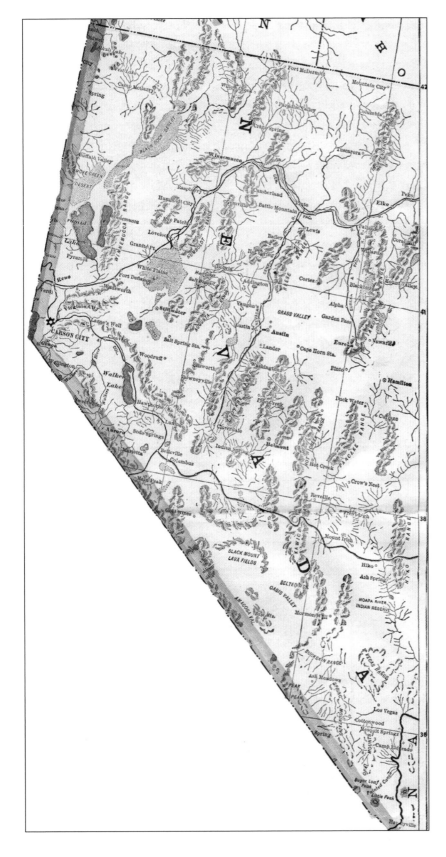

Figure 5-2
Hachures persisted on maps until the early twentieth century, when contour lines replaced them as a way to show elevation. This view from a late nineteenth-century atlas shows mountains in central Nevada that more closely resemble wooly bear caterpillars marching across the landscape than mountain ranges. *Source:* Cram's Family Atlas of the World. *Chicago: Geo. F. Cram, 1894. Private collection.*

\di'fin\ *vb*

Definitions

USGS maps depict the landscape in a *plan view* format, which means the map shows what the earth would look like if you were looking straight down from an airplane. Contour lines allow the reader to determine or estimate the elevation of a particular point on a map, but you can also measure the distance along slopes between the contour lines (known as the vertical distance between the lines, or the *contour interval*). By measuring contour lines on a map it's possible to construct topographic profiles of land features, an important part of understanding geological formations (recall the original mission of the USGS). For most 1:24,000 scale USGS maps, the distance between successive contour lines is 5 to 20 feet, with 20 feet being the standard interval. A darker brown line is used on elevations divisible by one hundred, making it easier to count contour lines and visualize major changes in slope and elevation. On the peaks of some mountains, the actual elevation in feet is noted in black italic lettering. This is known as a *spot elevation* (see Figure 5-3 below).

You can even tell if a slope is *concave* or *convex* using contour lines. If the

Figure 5-3
Spot elevation as shown for Sugarloaf, California, on a USGS quadrangle.

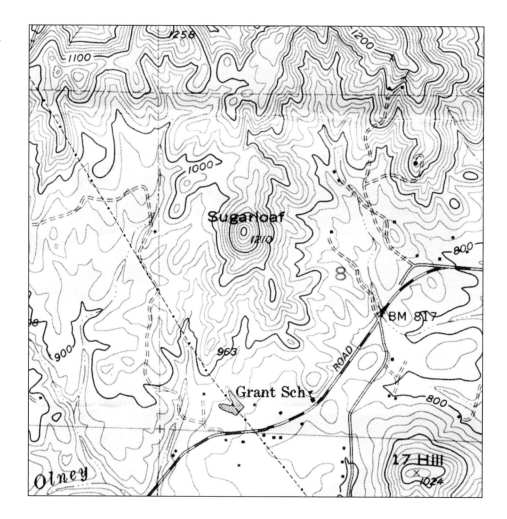

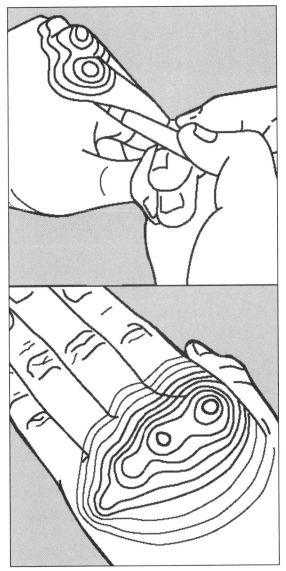

Figure 5-4
To learn how to visualize the land forms that contour lines describe, try drawing a topographic map on the back of your hand. Make a fist and imagine the knuckles represent hill features and the skin between each knuckle forms a swale or shallow valley. Begin drawing small circles on the tops of each knuckle with washable ink. Following the first circle, move down and draw the next circle, trying to keep each line as level as possible. In order to keep the third contour line level you might find your contour spreading across your hand to include those swales and the next knuckle. Continue to draw lines until most of the back of your hand is mapped. Flatten your hand the same way a map flattens out the three-dimensional shapes it represents and observe the way the contour lines look. The "steep" portions of your hand have contour lines that are closer together than the gently sloping areas where the contour lines are spaced farther apart.

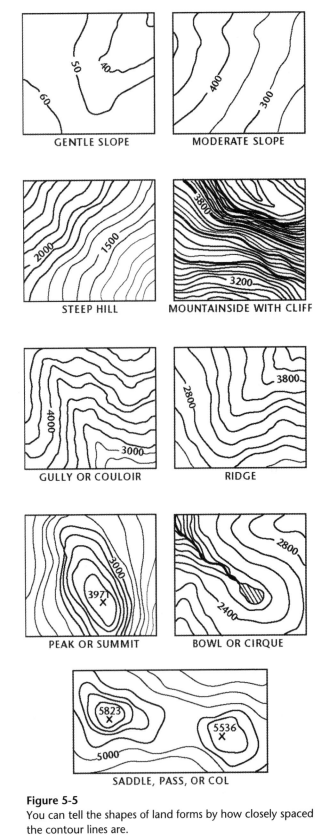

Figure 5-5
You can tell the shapes of land forms by how closely spaced the contour lines are.

103

lines are close together at the top of a slope but widely spaced at the bottom, the slope is concave. If the contour lines are widely spaced near the top and closer together at the bottom, then the slope is convex (see Figure 5-4 on page 103).

One last tip on contour lines involves reading the direction of drainage courses. Topographic maps depict watercourses with a light blue line. Where contour lines cross drainages they meet and form a V. The point of the V *always points uphill*, in the direction opposite of the flow of water (see Figure 5-5 on page 103). The description and direction of drainages can be important when you transfer information found in a property description that references a watercourse as part of the boundary. Chapter six discusses mapping property descriptions.

USGS Maps in Transition

In January 2005, USGS rolled out its newly designed National Atlas Web site complete with several new features for map users. The topographic maps and aerial photographs are also available through <www.nationalatlas.gov.> Pop-up windows supply the dates of the imagery and when it was placed in the National Atlas system. It is easier to search for a particular geographic feature in the Map Maker feature. You type in the name of the feature and a list is returned to you of features with similar place-names. You select the place you want and are taken to the section of the 7.5-minute topographic quadrangle showing that feature. The user can select to display specific information about the map, such as geographic grid information along the side margins in degree, minute and second or decimal degree formats. The default setting is *not* to display this information, so if you want it you must click on a tab labeled "information."

In addition, the National Atlas has Congressional District maps of the 109th Congress, maps depicting federal lands and Indian Reservation boundaries, county boundary maps based on the 2000 census, reference and outline maps of each state that show cities and capitals, state boundaries, interstate highways, selected rivers and waterways, and shaded relief of some areas. The county boundary maps are particularly useful and easy to read—perfect to print and place in your locality file or take with you on that next trip to the library.

Symbols

Close to two hundred different symbols can appear on modern USGS topographic maps. No quadrangle exhibits them all. Some are used exclusively on *provisional maps*, or *p-maps*. P-maps are maps that are "in process" and don't show all the standard information depicted on topographic maps. You can tell a p-map from a regular quadrangle by the color of the lettering in the collar of the map: P-maps have brown lettering rather than the customary black. You will also find hand-lettering of some place-names and features. Roads are shown in black (not the usual red or gray), and the map has no building symbols. P-maps are put together by analysis of air photos and limited fieldwork. P-map editions reduced preparation time and costs by an estimated 25 percent, enabling USGS to meet its goal of finishing the nation's mapping by the 1990 census.

Three classes of symbols are used on topographic maps: relief features, water features, and cultural features. Relief features are printed in brown, water features are depicted in blue, and cultural features related to human activities are usually depicted in black. Some earthwork features such as dams are shown in brown rather than black. Unlike countries such as Canada, who prints its key to map symbols on the back of its maps, the USGS prints its guide to topographic map symbols as a separate publication. You can obtain a free copy of the informational booklet entitled *Topographic Map Symbols* wherever you purchase topographic maps, order it at (888) ASK-USGS, or view an online copy at <http://erg.usgs.gov/isb/pubs/booklets>. An in-depth discussion on the three classes of symbols and the different types within each category is found in *Maps for America* by Morris M. Thompson. This book is out of print but available at many public libraries.

In places with rapid population growth or increased industrial, mining, or agricultural development since the initial quadrangle was completed, a pinkish purple tint is added to portions of the map to show recent changes. The date of these changes is shown and an explanation of the source of the information is also given. For example, on the Redding, California, quadrangle, which depicts the area where I live, the date of the original map is given as 1957 in black and the date of *photorevisions* as 1969.

> Revisions shown in purple compiled in cooperation with California Department of Water Resources from aerial photographs taken 1969. This information is not field checked.

Accessing the same map online through the National Atlas produced a quad with revisions dated 1991. A photo-revised map is not necessarily a map that has been field-checked. Perfected during World War II, aerial photography (known as *photogrammetry*) allows a mapmaker to view vertical aerial photographs with special optical instruments and "see" a small three-dimensional model of terrain and cultural features. Revisions to topographic maps are made based on what the mapmaker or map editor sees on the photographs and his or her experience and training in the interpretation of features. Mistakes are occasionally made. Inconsistencies in the application of the purple tint can be found, too. Prior to the development of the National Atlas Web site, approximately every five to ten years each of the 55,000 topographic quadrangles was compared to new aerial photography and revisions were made in purple—sometimes with crude hand-lettering—in order to maintain a semblance of currency.

Figure 5-6
A helpful map reading tip is to remember that contour lines in hilly regions meet in drainages and form a "V" and that "V" always points uphill or opposite of the direction of flow.

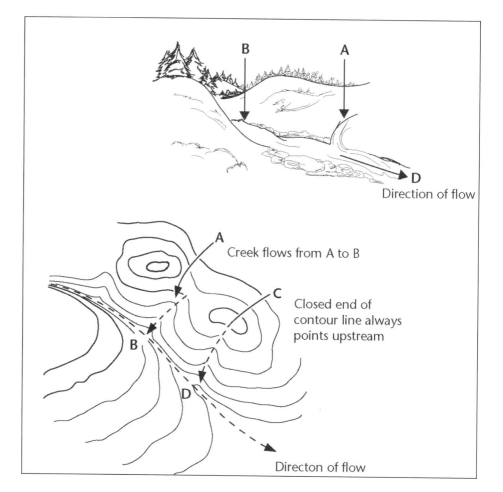

Series and Scale

Although mapping technology has changed greatly since the USGS was founded, the quadrangle system has remained virtually the same since its invention in 1882. USGS publishes several series of maps that are defined by particular geographical dimensions and scale. Most quadrangles are defined by two lines of latitude and two lines of longitude. The standard 1:24,000 scale quadrangle (1 inch = 2,000 feet) that you have been reading about in this chapter is also known as a *7.5-minute quadrangle*. It is defined by 7.5 minutes of latitude between the top and bottom edges and 7.5 minutes of longitude between the right and left margins. The amount of area portrayed on a 7.5-minute quadrangle varies according to latitude—from 64 square miles at a latitude of 30° north (for example, New Orleans, Louisiana) to 49 square miles at a latitude of 49° north (for example, along the border between the United States and Canada). Quadrangles are not perfect geometric rectangles: They are really trapezoid shapes with the bottom edge slightly wider than the top edge of the map as you proceed north in latitude.

So what to do with places like Alaska, where 7.5-minute quads would be extremely thin due to the convergence of longitude lines near the North Pole? USGS used a 15-minute quadrangle (1:63,360 scale, or 1 inch = 1 mile), which is bounded by 15 minutes in latitude and generally bounded by 15 minutes of longitude. The 15-minute quadrangle used to be the standard quadrangle in the United States, but has been replaced by the 7.5-minute size due to its greater detail and ample space for information.

You may occasionally run across another type of 15-minute map published by military agencies (refer to chapter eight) such as the old Defense Mapping Agency or the National Imagery and Mapping Agency (now supplanted by the National Geospatial-Intelligence Agency) that covers some portions of the United States. The scale on these maps is 1:50,000 (1 centimeter = 0.5 kilometer), and they show distances and contour intervals in meters rather than in feet since the military uses meters.

Other USGS series that are available include 30×60-minute quadrangle maps that have a scale of 1:100,000 (1 centimeter = 1 kilometer). The distances and contour intervals (5, 10, 20, or 50) are shown in meters on these maps. The Bureau of Land Management issues maps in this scale and dimension, particularly in the western states where its land holdings are the most extensive.

USGS produces a county map series that covers about 20 percent of the nation's counties on one or more sheets, depending on the size of the county. USGS county maps are similar in content to the 1:24,000 scale maps but are rendered at a scale of either 1:50,000 or 1:100,000. County maps can have contours depicted in either meters or feet. The maps are useful for countywide mapping of resources or population. Several states, like Colorado, are completely mapped in the 1:50,000 scale.

The U.S. Army Map Service originated a 1:250,000 scale (1 inch = approximately 4 miles) series of maps in the 1950s. The entire United States is covered in this series. USGS continues to publish this series, which frequently forms the basis for aeronautical charts and geologic maps. For most of the lower forty-eight states, the series dimensions are one degree of latitude by two degrees of longitude. Aside from geology and navigation uses, these maps are used for regional transportation planning and utility infrastructure. Because the contour interval is quite large (50, 100, 200, or 500 meters or feet), smaller topographic features may not be shown. Genealogists can use these maps when looking at migration patterns. Many of our highways and interstates use the pathways and trails of long ago. These maps portray "big picture" relationships between towns and cities and transportation options for roads, railroads, and rivers.

Many other series are published by USGS, including special maps for states, national parks, and "shaded relief" maps. The shaded relief maps depict landforms with a pictorial effect, featuring halftone shading that makes the map appear to have sunlight and shadows playing across the relief and creating a three-dimensional effect. This technique is an old one but popular with those who are familiar with maps. Not all quadrangles are published in shaded relief format, only locations that have landforms of special interest to the public—ridges that bend and twist back and forth in the Appalachians, most national parks, and even Antarctica.

You may have seen 1:250,000 scale topographic maps created from vinyl. These raised relief maps are three-dimensional with a vertical scale of 1:125,000 (vertical exaggeration = 2:1). These help teach the viewer about regional landforms. Although they look like USGS maps, they aren't produced by the government. A commercial company, Hubbard Scientific (now part of American Educational Products, LLC), compiles them using old topographic Army Map Service maps. You can view their catalog of raised relief maps at <www.shnta.com/Catalog/Raised_Relief_Maps.htm>.

Locations along the coast and on islands have a special series of maps that depict both topographic contours and bathymetric contours (blue contour lines shown underwater known as *isobaths*) that show the shape of the land underwater. The USGS works in conjunction with the National Ocean Service to produce these maps. Genealogists researching locations in the coastal zone might find these maps of interest, as well as those researching lighthouses, wrecks, or any other near-shore cultural features.

USGS topographic maps form the basis of many different types of *thematic maps*, maps that portray a special characteristic of the environment such as geology, soils, or forestry. Recall the quotation at the start of this chapter. USGS is an organization whose purpose is to provide base maps for resource mapping. Genealogists have generally ignored thematic resource maps in their research and opt for the more familiar topographic quadrangle instead. You should consider checking geology and soil maps for several reasons. First, these maps are not updated as frequently as USGS topographic maps. The underlying features and place-names represent landscapes that may be long gone. Geology maps are also good in their detailed representation of not only old highways and main railroad lines, but also spurs, sidings, and abandoned lines. Why? The road cuts made for rail beds and roadbeds provide wonderful views into the local geology of an area. The geologists and soil scientists who mapped resources in the field often used place-names familiar to local inhabitants to help orient the map user. Older geology and soil maps, like old topographic maps, are wonderful repositories of these place-names.

Accuracy

In 1940, the Bureau of the Budget began holding public hearings on the establishment of a national standard of accuracy among mapping agencies and societies for topographic maps funded or produced by the U.S. government. There was concern that some maps published by the government were less accurate than others due to the great number of military and civilian federal agencies producing them. In 1941, the Bureau of the Budget published the first "Standards of Accuracy for a National Map Production Program." This was a momentous move in cartography—some nations, even today, do not have national standards for accuracy for maps their governments produce. The revised version of 1947, the "United States National Map Accuracy Standards," is still in effect today (see Figure 5.7 below).

THIS MAP COMPLIES WITH NATIONAL MAP ACCURACY STANDARDS
FOR SALE BY U. S. GEOLOGICAL SURVEY, DENVER, COLORADO 80225
OR RESTON, VIRGINIA 22092
A FOLDER DESCRIBING TOPOGRAPHIC MAPS AND SYMBOLS IS AVAILABLE ON REQUEST

Federal agencies are not required to subscribe to the standards. However, to use the statement "This map complies with the National Map Accuracy Standards," the map must pass seven tests, including an acceptable rate of error (10 percent or fewer of the points tested) based on the map's scale.

What do the national standards for accuracy mean to a genealogist? For a 7.5-minute quadrangle, 90 percent of the "well-defined" points on a map (like a crossroad that meets at 90°, a corner of a large building, or an intersection of a road and railroad) cannot be greater than $\frac{1}{30}$ of an inch away on the map from their actual location at the given scale of 1:24,000. This means that a point can be as much as 67 feet off and still meet the national standards for accuracy. Not all well-defined points on a map are tested, and 10 percent of the points tested can be substantially off from their correct position. This standard for accuracy takes into account the limits of surveying and mapping equipment and of a human being's hand-eye coordination in drawing the map even with the aid of a computer. The statement "This map may not meet the National Map Accuracy Standards" or dotted or dashed lines with the accompanying phrase "approximately positioned" should be

Notes

taken as serious warnings that the mapped information may not be accurate.

For the most part, large-scale topographic maps are more accurate than those on a smaller scale that are compiled from a variety of sources and must squeeze lots of information into a smaller space. To accomplish this, the mapmaker must *generalize* the information. That is precisely why a 1:250,000 scale map does not show all the information that a 1:24,000 scale map does. In crowded urban settings where a lot of information is crammed together in a relatively small area, some items must be left off so the map remains easy to read. In rural areas, which have greater distances between habitations, symbols and physical features have plenty of room to coexist without too much generalizing. Thompson's *Maps for America* contains a helpful table that lists the features shown on topographic maps for each scale of map produced from 1:24,000 up to 1:1,000,000. By checking this table, you can ascertain that cemeteries are shown on all USGS maps up to 1:250,000 scale, ruins up to 1:100,000 scale, active railroad tracks on all scales up to 1:1,000,000, but abandoned rail lines only up to 1:250,000 scale maps.

USING TOPOGRAPHIC MAPS

As a genealogist, you can use topographic maps to:
- Locate specific cultural features, such as cemeteries, churches, fence lines, ruins, and buildings.
- Search for place-names.
- Study migration trails, canals, roads, and railroads for connections between towns.
- Map property boundary descriptions.
- Measure distances between settlements.
- Navigate in the field. (Depending on the degree of development, this is not recommended unless the map has been recently revised or you have other maps to assist you.)
- Illustrate locations in family histories. (Maps produced by USGS can be reproduced without a copyright violation, but digital versions on CD or online may not be.)
- Envision what your ancestor's physical environment looked like by using historical topographic maps. What did he or she see when looking out the front door?
- Learn about physical obstacles and challenges in the landscape that shaped your ancestor's life. How difficult was it to get to town, to a courthouse, to church, or to go courting? Did he or she have to travel by foot, horseback, wagon, ferry, or a combination?
- List the ways people made a living in the vicinity of where your ancestor

lived. Was there farming, ranching, logging, mining, port facilities, or factories in the area? Do any of these occupations bear on the way your ancestor made a living?

- Imagine the placement of troops on a historic battlefield given the arrangement of local landforms and vegetation.
- Plan research trips.

LOCATING TOPOGRAPHIC MAPS

USGS has participated in the federal depository program for many decades. Regional public libraries and large college libraries may have copies of topographic maps for all fifty states and some territories. Smaller local libraries generally have topographic quads related to the region they serve and sometimes coverage of the entire state. Some libraries keep their old topographic maps, while others cite space constraints or are simply unaware of the value of historical information found on older topographic maps and discard them. **You should also keep in mind that large map libraries will sometimes place copies of their own map collections (not just topographic maps) on microfilm or microfiche.** Always check the library catalog for state and regional topographic map collections that have been filmed.

Microfilm Source

USGS also maintains four regional libraries in Reston, Virginia; Menlo Park, California; Flagstaff, Arizona; and Denver, Colorado. You can access directions and hours of operation of these libraries at <www.usgs.gov/library>.

Every state has an index to topographic sheets that shows all the available maps with their scales and coverage areas. The index is a state map overprinted with a grid to show which quads are available and the name of the quad, and is offered free of charge from USGS. You can consult an index at your local public library at the reference desk or order an index to be mailed to you for free by calling toll-free at (888) ASK-USGS.

You can also access ordering information at the USGS Store online at <http://store.usgs.gov>. Click on "Enter USGS Store," then locate the type of map you want on the left side of the screen. If you want to find the name of a particular 7.5-minute quad, click on that map type. You can locate lists of in-print topographic maps online. None of these ways offers you a graphical display that shows you the relative position of the map, like the free printed paper indexes previously mentioned. You can access the state map lists finding aids at <http://erg.usgs.gov/maplists/selectstatelist.html>. Search by state, series, or latitude and longitude.

You can also purchase USGS maps or obtain information about USGS products and services through its regional Earth Science Information Centers (ESICs) <http://geography.usgs.gov/esic/esic_index.html>. ESICs are located in Anchorage, Alaska; Denver, Colorado; Menlo Park, California;

Reston, Virginia; Rolla, Missouri; and Sioux Falls, South Dakota. USGS maintains a network of commercial retailers of topographic maps and other USGS products. You can locate the nearest USGS business partner by either calling USGS at their toll-free telephone number (888)ASK-USGS or going online and using the clickable map at <http://rockyweb.cr.usgs.gov/acis-bin/choosebylocation.pl?statechoice = none>. Click on a state and you will receive the names of map retailers classified alphabetically by city. Also try inquiring at sporting goods stores that cater to hikers, fishermen, and hunters, or at bookstores, engineering supply stores, and stationery stores. The 7.5-minute quads cost about $6 per sheet.

Historical USGS maps can be located in several ways. The largest and most complete collection of historical USGS maps is in the Library of Congress in Washington, D.C. Unfortunately, their cartographic collection does not circulate on interlibrary loan. The National Archives has ridden to our rescue by microfilming historical topographic maps produced between 1884 and 1979 by USGS. The microfilms are arranged by state, with the quads appearing in alphabetical order on the microfilm. It is important to note that the microfilm is not arranged in state alphabetical order. Topographic map coverage may also spill across state borders, so you may have to look at maps in adjoining states. The Family History Library in Salt Lake City has an almost complete set of 291 reels of microfilm, *Topographic Maps of the United States*, beginning with call number FHL US/CAN 1433631. Each microfilm contains about five hundred maps.

As mentioned previously, mapping the United States has taken more than a century to accomplish. As new quads were added and older ones revised, the names and dimensions sometimes changed. The new indexes do not reflect the names of historical topographic quads. The microfilm collection previously mentioned does not include films of historical quad indexes. In order to find out the names and extent of historical topographic quads, consult Riley M. Moffat's *Map Index to Topographic Quadrangles of the United States, 1882–1940* (Santa Cruz, Calif.: Western Association of Map Libraries, 1986). This book covers maps in the 15-minute, 30-minute, and 60-minute series for all the United States except Alaska. Since they are more recent than the other sizes, locating the names and dimensions of 7.5-minute quads is less difficult.

Topographic Maps Online

Several Web sites display historical topographic maps. It is important to note that no site offers a complete collection of online topographic maps at this time, though. However, more maps are finding their way to the Web every week as libraries digitize their collections to increase access for the public and reduce wear to their map sheets. Several of the best online collections are described below.

Library of Congress Map Collection: 1500–2004
<http://memory.loc.gov/ammem/gmdhtml/gmdhome.html>

This site has more than 7,000 map and atlas images. Topographic maps are a part of the images available, but only a sampling. Maps are being added continually to this collection. You can either download a copy of a map or order a high-quality reproduction at <http://memory.loc.gov/ammem/gmdhtml/gmdorder.html>.

Maptech Historical Maps
<http://historical.maptech.com>

Maptech, Inc., is a private company that hosts historical USGS topographic maps online. Its library of full-color maps covers six New England states plus New York, New Jersey, Pennsylvania, Delaware, Maryland, West Virginia, and Ohio. The maps were originally published between 1885 and the 1950s. Maptech sells a variety of map-related products as well as modern topographic maps on CD (see description below in "Topographic Maps on CD") and encourages viewers to compare older maps available for free on their Web site to the modern versions they sell on CD. The site also offers additional information on historical topographic map series.

University of New Hampshire Library, Government Documents Department, Historic USGS Maps of New England & NY
<http://docs.unh.edu/nhtopos/nhtopos.htm>

This university has posted maps from New England and New York, with links to TopoZone (discussed below in "Topographic Maps on CD"), Terraserver (discussed in chapter ten), and Maptech.

University of California, Berkeley, Historic Topographic Maps of California—San Francisco Bay Area
<http://sunsite.berkeley.edu/histopo>

This site provides historical maps of only the Greater San Francisco Bay Area in 7.5- and 15-minute series. The maps have been published from 1895 to the present. Place-names have been gleaned from each map and cataloged. You can search for any place-name in the Bay Area and come up with a list of historical topographic maps that contain that name.

California State University, Chico, Meriam Library, California Historic Topographic Map Collection
<http://cricket.csuchico.edu/spcfotos/maps/topo_search.html>

This site covers all of California and is easy to use.

David Rumsey Map Collection

<www.davidrumsey.com>

David Rumsey's online collection contains more than 6,400 maps. The collection includes many rare eighteenth- and nineteenth-century maps of North America. You can find early topographic surveys of the western United States, as well as other historical topographic maps of parts of North America.

University of Texas at Austin, Perry-Castañeda Library Map Collection, Historical Maps

<www.lib.utexas.edu/maps/historical/index.html>

Included in this massive worldwide collection of online maps are examples of historical topographic maps.

Topographic Maps on CD

Several dozen companies have taken USGS digital maps and added their own software and value to create a variety of electronic map products. All of today's products are geared for use with GPS receivers (refer to chapter ten for detailed information on these electronic products). As with anything else that has to do with electronics and computers, lists become dated quickly. The CDs below are a place to start looking. All the manufacturers have Web sites with areas where you can examine or download samples to review.

Topo! by National Geographic (formerly produced by Wildflower Productions)

<www.topo.com>

Each CD contains maps of an entire state. The software works seamlessly and is easy to learn. As with all the electronic atlases, you can zoom in and out of maps to control the level of detail depicted. You can also produce shaded relief maps of any area. This product works well with most GPS units.

MapSource by Garmin

<www.garmin.com>

MapSource is an electronic topographic atlas designed to work with this manufacturer's GPS units.

Terrain Navigator and Terrain Navigator Pro by Maptech, Inc.

<www.maptech.com>

These products combine topographic maps with aerial photos at 1-meter resolution. The software combines regional collections of topographic maps with navigation software that permits two- and three-dimensional viewing, customizing and printing, and GPS use.

3-D TopoQuads and Topo USA by DeLorme

<www.delorme.com>

DeLorme is famous for its single-state topographic atlases that became popular a decade ago. The topographic atlases are still being printed, but the company's emphasis has turned to the production of digital state topographic atlases. TopoQuads has the ability to display maps in three-dimensional view. Topo USA covers the entire United States but in less detail than TopoQuads.

Summary Points

★ Topographic maps form the base or framework for mapping by public and private mapmakers, which is why they are referred to as "mother maps."

★ Complete topographic mapping for the entire United States is a relatively recent event, due to the size of the project and the lack of coordinated national effort that plagued the federal government.

★ The USGS National Atlas project will eventually provide continually updated topographic and resource information to the public, but perhaps at the expense of documenting historical changes. The 7.5-minute quads are being updated only in digital formats. That is why commercially produced CDs based on USGS information are more up-to-date than printed USGS maps.

★ Genealogists should take advantage of the wide array of other resource maps that also use topographic base maps and local place names, such as geology and soil maps.

★ Genealogists use topographic maps in a variety of ways to suggest solutions to family history problems. You are limited only by your imagination.

Land Division and County Maps and Atlases

[Section lines shall be] exactly described on a plat; whereon shall be noted by the Surveyor, at their proper distances, all mines, salt springs, saltlicks and mill seats, that shall come to his knowledge; and all watercourses, mountains, and other remarkable and permanent things over or near which such lines shall pass, and also the quality of the lands.

—From "An Ordinance for Ascertaining the Mode of Disposing of Lands in the Western Territory, May 20, 1785" in Lowell O. Stewart's Public Land Surveys: History, Instructions, Methods *(Ames, Iowa: Collegiate Press, 1935).*

I f you fly across the country at 50,000 feet between San Francisco and Washington, D.C., some of the most visible evidences of human habitation are the lines we have inscribed on the surface of the earth. Most often those lines reflect the way we have subdivided the land for the purpose of ownership. Once inscribed on the ground and on maps, the boundaries of land division become part of our inheritance. In some parts of the country those parcels of land have been further modified; in others they remain essentially the same as they were when they were laid out a century or more ago. From an airplane over the Midwest you can see the rectangular pattern of land division that is oriented to compass directions. The roads and boundaries are spaced in an orderly manner, and the landscape appears to be divided in a *systematic* way.

Flying farther east toward Washington, D.C., the pattern becomes haphazard looking, as if parcels of all sizes are tucked up against one another with no discernable order noticeable from our high perch. Instead of relying on the cardinal points of a compass to describe the lines, early surveyors in this area used permanent natural features such as streams and landforms and ephemeral ones like trees or rocks to describe corners and boundaries. When viewed on the ground the lines appear to be straight. For most of the world, land has been described and divided in this *unsystematic* way. This manner of surveying is known as *metes and bounds* or *indiscriminate location*. In places that have had human settlement for hundreds or thousands of years, the pattern of property ownership is often complex, with parcels becoming smaller and spatially disconnected over time, depending on the customs for land disposal through sale or inheritance.

LAND DESCRIPTION SYSTEMS

When the European settlers arrived in America they brought with them a number of different types of land subdivision systems. **Two main types of land partitioning arose: the metes and bounds type in the South and Southwest and the systematic mapping type in the Midwest and New England.**

Notes

In the Southern colonies, where settlements tended to be more dispersed than in the North, people purchased land or acquired it through gifts in large parcels. The earliest settlers grabbed up the lands that were the best no matter what the shape of the parcel. Land that was more marginal in quality—steep slopes, swamps, or rocky soil—occupied odd-shaped parcels tucked in around the larger parcels. As property was exchanged through marriage, inheritance, or sales, parcel shapes became even more complicated and difficult to describe, let alone map. Any genealogist who has tried to map these old property lines can tell you that it is challenging work, although not impossible.

In a metes and bounds survey, a surveyor would walk along the property boundaries and describe landmarks encountered along the way. Little skill was required to describe property boundaries with this method. You would stroll along your property lines with your neighbors and agree on the place-names and landmarks to describe the boundaries. Would that it remained so simple! In time, landowners died, moved away, and stopped the annual custom of walking the property lines with the neighbors. Because these boundaries were often poorly described and based on ephemeral landmarks such as trees, seeps, or rivers, property disputes arose when trees were removed or died, seeps dried up, or rivers changed their courses. Sketch maps created when property was bought and sold sometimes got lost. The introduction of crude survey equipment that could measure distances and compasses that could locate cardinal directions only marginally helped. Most of the land settled was described using the metes and bounds method prior to 1800 in the South.

The harsh winters and thin and stony soils of New England were said to be contributing factors to the development of systematic land partitioning in the Northern colonies. People resided closer together and farmed smaller plots of land than people in the Southern colonies. The land was divided into square parcels known as *towns* or *townships* (see chapter three). The townships were further divided into *lots* or *sections*. The resulting settlement pattern was more compact and systematic in appearance. Everyone shared good and bad land alike under this system.

METES AND BOUNDS SURVEY

A period of steep economic inflation in England during the early part of the sixteenth century encouraged the landed gentry to consider managing their lands more efficiently in order to maximize their crop yield and rent from tenants. One way to actively manage their estates was to draw sketches

FRENCH AND SPANISH LAND PARTITIONING

E. Wade Hone's *Land & Property Research in the United States* (Salt Lake City: Ancestry, 1997) summarizes the different types of property description used in the settlement of our nation and the records that were generated under each system. Early in our nation's development, the federal government established that it would honor valid titles to land granted by foreign governments. This situation works to the genealogist's benefit, as records were created to evaluate these claims and these records have been preserved.

The early French settlements depended heavily on the use of lakes and river transportation to move goods in and out of an area via *bateaux* (long, flat-bottomed boats with sharply pointed bows and sterns). It was important that all property owners have access to the water. Land was surveyed in parallel lines from the waterfront, which created "long lots," also known as "ribbon farms" or "suspender farms" because of their overall long and narrow appearance. The long lots are evident today in certain portions of Canada and the United States that were initially settled by the French. Their long, narrow shape is reminiscent of medieval European *strips*, where renters shared in the good and bad land adjacent to waterways. They were measured in *arpents*, which are equal to about 0.85 acre (0.34 hectare). Plats of early French settlements frequently contained the names of prominent property holders.

Continued on next page

Areas settled under Spanish or Mexican rule in the Southwest and West used methods similar to metes and bounds. Land ownership in the arid and semiarid West focused on water resources—not for travel but for growing crops and watering herds of grazing livestock. Before California became part of the United States, anyone could petition the Mexican governor for land there. Accompanying the petition was a *diseño*, or map. If the governor was of a mind to grant the petition, he forwarded the petition to a local magistrate who would be in charge of verifying its accuracy. The magistrate would summon the neighboring landowners and the petitioner together to establish the boundaries of the parcel. Two horsemen carrying poles would measure the boundaries in *vara* (1 vara = approximately 33 inches). Corners were marked with piles of stones or some other landmark. The magistrate would settle the boundary then and there in the field with all owners present. The original *diseño* would be modified and further refined during this process.

After California became part of the United States, many of these early claims were called into question. The examination of these claims was documented through special surveys by the General Land Office with both the original manuscript *diseños* and the lithographic copies finding their way eventually to the National Archives as part of the General Land Office records. These are found in the National Archives in the "Records of Division 'D' (Private Land Claims Division)" in the *Records of the Bureau of Land Management* (Record Group 49). Maps from private land claim cases in other states (Alabama, Arizona, Arkansas, Colorado, Florida, Illinois, Indiana, Louisiana, Mississippi, Missouri, and New Mexico) can also be found here.

The state of California transcribed and translated the claims petitions documents (known as *expedientes*) and made tracings of the *diseños*. These are in the custody of the Secretary of State in Sacramento, and you can view examples of land grant maps online in the California State Archives in "Spanish and Mexican Land Grant Maps, 1855–1875" <www.ss.ca.gov/archives/level 3_ussg3.html>. A microfilm copy of these records is in the Bancroft Library at the University of California, Berkeley <http://bancroft.berkeley.edu>. Some original manuscript maps and copies of original maps can also be found in the UCLA Library Special Collections at the University of California, Los Angeles <www2.library.ucla.edu/libraries/special.cfm>; the Huntington Library in San Marino, California <www.huntington.org>; and the Bancroft Library at the University of California, Berkeley.

See Also

For more information, see Robert H. Becker's *Designs on the Land: Diseños of California Ranchos and Their Makers* (San Francisco: Book Club of California, 1969).

based on the *butts and bounds* of the tenant's plots. In the language of the day, to "butt" meant to encounter or meet something. So the early surveys and estate maps in England described land according to the corners and where the boundaries met other boundaries. The term *metes and bounds* grew out of this practice.

When English settlers arrived in America they brought with them the familiar concept of metes and bounds to describe their parcels. While the system worked well in the long-settled English landscape, in a heavily forested area with poorly understood colony boundaries that depended on temporary markers like trees or stakes, it proved to be cadastral chaos.

In Virginia, many of the first farms were *headright farms*, awarded to those who paid their own passage across the Atlantic. These first farms were described as more or less 50- and 100-acre squares extending up from a riverbank and capturing a bit of woodland for building materials. Large plantations encompassed 1,000 acres or more. To define the boundaries of their farms and plantations, settlers would measure out a distance square (12 chains and 50 links for a 100-acre farm, 133 chains for a 1,000-acre plantation) and blaze trees, pile stones, scratch boulders, or set stakes at the corners of their parcels. With the inaccurate reckoning, poor measuring, and corners lost over time, it's not hard to see why property boundaries were frequently called into question.

MEASUREMENT CONVERSIONS			
1 mile =	80 chains =	320 poles, rods, or perches =	8,000 links or 5,280 feet
1 chain =		4 poles, rods, or perches =	100 links or 66 feet
1 pole =			25 links or 16.5 feet
1 link =			7.92 inches

Patricia Law Hatcher's *Locating Your Roots: Discover Your Ancestors Using Land Records* (Cincinnati: Betterway Books, 2003) presents a succinct, step-by-step method for mapping metes and bounds property lines. She breaks down the description into *calls* that relate either to a corner location or a line (boundary). An example of a typical deed description is found in the transfer of property between Henry Landis of Rutherford County, North Carolina, who sold land to Adam Mauny of Lincoln County, North Carolina, on 8 December 1789. The property was described in a deed as:

> a parcel of land containing two hundred acres on Cornfield Branch of Indian Creek including his Mill Beginning at a Black Jack on a hill & runs N°35. W. 100 poles to a pine thence S°55.W.100 poles to a Hicory [*sic*] thence S°35.E. 100 poles to a Stake thence to the beginning of the said land was granted unto Thomas Reynolds by patent bearing date fourth day of May Domini 1789 . . .

Hatcher's method breaks out the corners with a "●" and the lines with an "→." Mauny's deed description can be rewritten:

● beginning at a Black Jack on a hill
→ runs N°35.W. 100 poles
● to a pine
→ thence S°55.W. 100 poles
● to a Hicory
→ thence S°35.E. 100 poles
● to a Stake
→ to the beginning of the said land

As you can see, the calls alternate between descriptions of corner locations and lines.

Hatcher also includes a form in her book where you can fill out each call

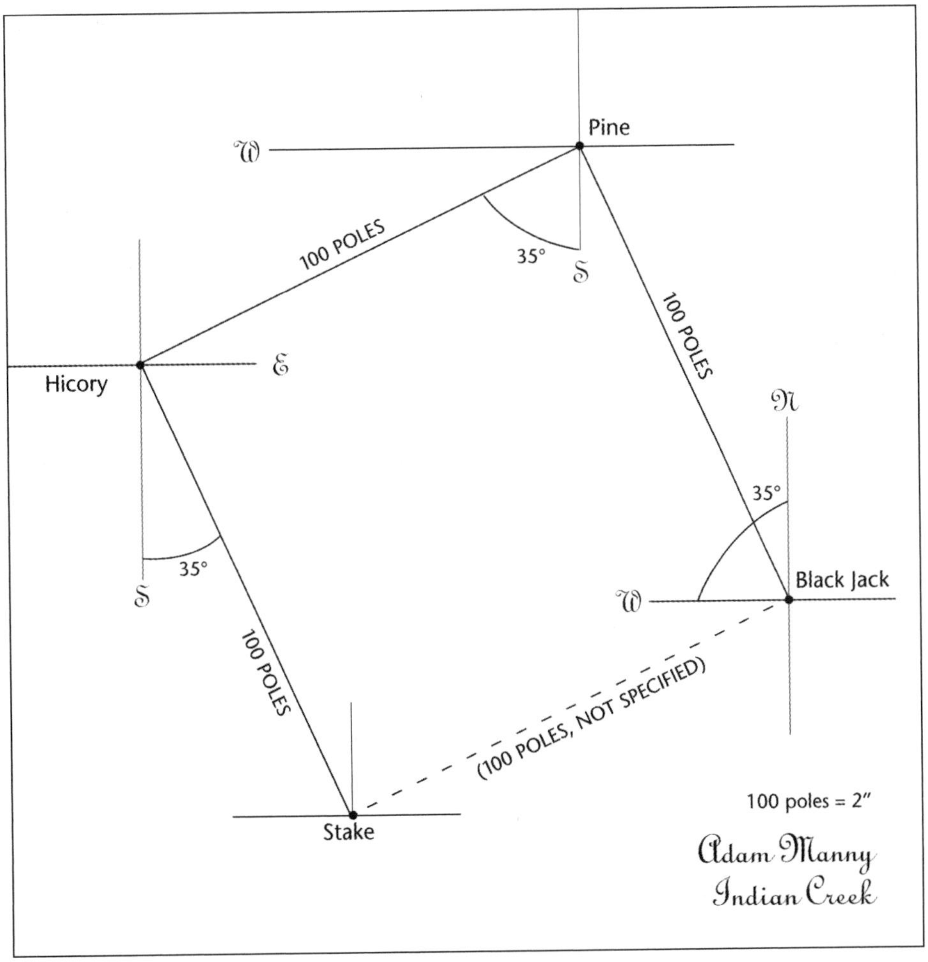

Figure 6-1
Adam Mauny's land deed on Indian Creek drawn from his metes and bounds land description. *Source:* Lincoln County, North Carolina Land Deeds, *Vols. 16-17, 1785–1796, FHL film 0019253.*

line by line to help you organize the information by corner marker, neighbors, direction, and distance.

You can reproduce the shape of the parcel with a protractor and a ruler that can measure in tenths of an inch. All you need to do is decide what you want your scale to be to represent 1 pole of distance on paper. I suggest using graph paper to keep lines straight.

Step By Step

To map the parcel in Figure 6-1 on page 121, I placed a point on the paper to represent the first corner at the Black Jack (an oak) and used a ruler to draw a cross to represent the four compass directions. Recalling that there are 90° in a quarter circle and thus 90° between the west line and the north line, I used the protractor to measure an angle 35° *west* of the north line. In my sketch I elected to make 100 poles equal to 2 inches, so I measured out 2 inches from the Black Jack to the second point (a pine). I drew another cross to represent the four directions and then measured an angle 55° *west* of the south line. I drew a line to represent 100 poles to the third point (the hickory tree). From there I repeated the process until the fourth point (the stake). The fourth line was not specified in this deed other than "to the beginning of the said land." Based on geometry, I could assume that the line was also 100 poles long to close the shape by creating a call with a bearing of N°55W.

Taking the calls found in deeds and platting them is made easier by using the Deed Platter at GenealogyTools.net <www.genealogytools.net/deeds>. Based on the simple method of transcribing outlined by Hatcher, you find the number of lines in the description. Then you select the number of lines for the deed. You fill in the boxes with the direction, degrees, bearing, and distance. You can also annotate your map with additional information—the names of the grantor and grantee, the township, county, location, deed book details, size of parcel, and date. The Web site allows for two different units of distance (such as poles and feet). You can learn a lot about platting by transcribing the calls, playing with the deed platter on this Web site, and then measuring the angles on the resulting printout. If one of the calls is not specified or is a "meander" (a creek or other natural boundary), draw it in with a dotted line by hand like I did in Figure 6-1.

Internet Source

Other commercial programs allow the creation of *connected drafts*—plats of entire "neighborhoods" of land that have been partitioned using metes and bounds. One of the most suitable for genealogical work is Deed-Mapper 3.0 by Steven Broyles <http://users.rcn.com/deeds>.

What if I wanted to map Adam Mauny's land on a USGS 7.5-minute quad? To do that, I need to do a lot more work. The deed description does not give much information about the physical location of this property other than it is near the Cornfield Branch of Indian Creek. The GNIS Web site (chapter two) finds many Indian Creeks in North Carolina (no Cornfield Branches, though). One Indian Creek appears to be promising. It runs through Lincoln County where Adam Mauny was residing when he purchased this property from Henry Landis. A family story indicates that Adam's father Valentine resided somewhere between Cherryville and Crouse, North Carolina. Both of those places are located not too far from Indian Creek. However, to locate Adam, I will need to go back to the Lincoln County land records and read many deeds, starting with the original patent to Thomas Reynolds earlier in 1789, and find out who purchased land around him. Only by collecting all the deeds concerning the adjacent parcels, not just the deed of my ancestor, will I be able to find other physical features that I can tie these parcels to; descriptions of the location of trees and stakes are just not sufficient information to jump to a modern topographic map.

At some point after I have collected adjacent deeds, identified some physical features, and made a few parcel sketches, I will be ready to make that leap to a topographic map. So how do I scale my sketches to fit on a 7.5-minute quad?

I learned to do this from genealogist Mary McCampbell Bell in one of her classes on land platting offered at a National Genealogical Society conference. Recall that a 7.5-minute quad has a scale of 1:24,000 (1 inch on the map equals 24,000 inches on the ground). From the table in this chapter, you learned that:

1 link = 7.92 inches.
25 links = 1 pole, rod, or perch.
7.92 inches (1 link) multiplied by 25 links (1 pole) = 198 inches per pole.
24,000 inches divided by 198 inches = 121.2 poles per inch on a topo quad.

To make measurements easier, Bell recommended that we round off the number of poles per inch to 121. Since my ruler measures in tenths of an inch, I divide 121 by 10 and find that 0.1 inch equals 12.1 poles (rounded to 12). Every 0.1 inch on my topographic map is going to be equal to 12 poles.

When I am ready to map distance in poles, I take the number of poles and divide by 12. This will give me the number of units on the ruler that the line will stretch. Adam Mauny's parcel is 100 poles on each side—giving me a square that is about 0.83 inch per side.

U.S. PUBLIC LAND SURVEY

As early as 1776, the United States Congress of the Confederation was being pressed to form a national land policy for many reasons. A new system needed to be developed that could be easily understood, mapped, and documented: Land had been promised to Revolutionary War soldiers for their service; revenue was needed to pay public debts; newly ceded western lands needed to be inventoried and managed; and the courts were filling up with cases over disputed land claims in states where unsystematic land partitioning was used.

In 1784, Thomas Jefferson and his Congressional Committee on Public Lands proposed a national surveying and mapping program to produce cadastral surveys of the western territory. The land would be subdivided into easily discernable townships of six miles square apiece, each township comprised of sections one mile square, simplifying the inventorying and selling of public land. The quote that begins this chapter comes from the original Land Ordinance of 1785, also known as the Township and Range System or the U.S. Public Land Survey (USPLS), which has been lauded as one of the most important acts of the early government. Unlike other topographic surveys, the main thrust of the USPLS was to set out a uniform system of location so that any parcel, no matter how small, could be easily located and its resources assessed so the government could decide to retain the property or offer it for public sale. The USPLS ultimately created the most extensive region of uniform land surveying in the world.

Two lines form the basis of an original survey tract: a north-south line called the *principal meridian* and an east-west line called the *principal baseline, parallel,* or *geographer's line* (the surveyors were called geographers back then). These lines meet or cross at right angles. In addition, *range lines* were surveyed along meridians at 6-mile intervals north and south of the base line. *Township lines* were surveyed along the parallels at 6-mile intervals east and west of the principal meridian. (See Figure 6-2 on page 125.) The resulting 6×6-mile square parcel was sometimes referred to as a *survey* or *congressional township,* and as mentioned in chapter three, confusingly known as a "township." Each township was divided into thirty-six sections, each section measuring 1 square mile or 640 acres.

Each section is assigned a number from 1 to 36. The sections are numbered *boustrophedonically,* which means that the numbering is in a zigzag fashion much like the Greek meaning of the word—"as oxen plowing a field." The numbers begin with section 1 in the northeast corner and continue westward to section 6, then move south. The numbering then moves eastward from sections 7 through 12, then turns south again and numbers head westward and so on, ending in the southeast corner with section 36. (See Figure 6-3 on page 126.) It is important that you understand this numbering scheme; it will help you locate sections on a topographic map in the event the section numbers in a township are not shown.

Not all sections were available for sale to the public. Section 16 in each township was usually used for education. This section could be sold to raise money to build a school or college (land grant college). Sometimes

For More Info

For more information, see Norman J.W. Thrower's "The Triumph of Geometry over Geography: Cadastral Surveying in the United States," *Mercator's World* 7 (July-August 2002).

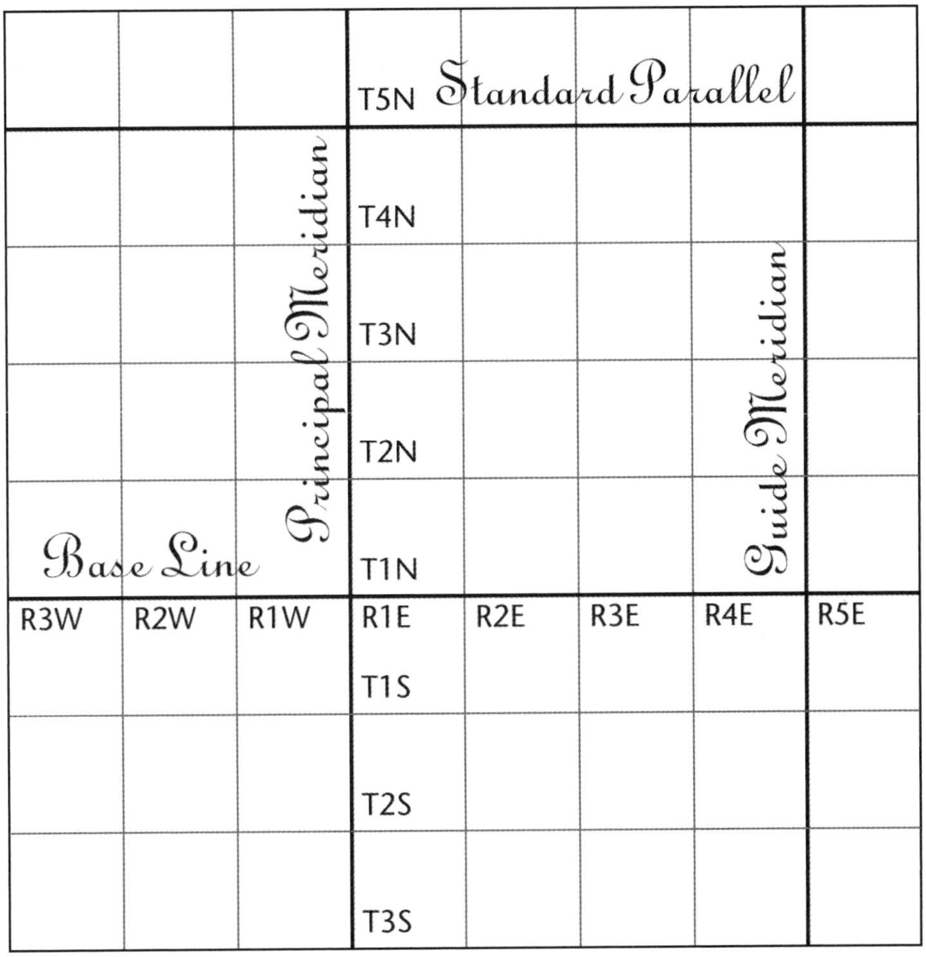

			T5N *Standard Parallel*				
		Principal Meridian	T4N			*Guide Meridian*	
			T3N				
			T2N				
Base Line			T1N				
R3W	R2W	R1W	R1E / T1S	R2E	R3E	R4E	R5E
			T2S				
			T3S				

Figure 6-2
Diagram showing the locations of townships in the United States Public Land Survey (USPLS) which is also known as the rectangular survey system. *Source: Bureau of Land Management*

entire sections were given to companies that created public works, such as railroads or canals, as compensation for their service or to assist in their financing.

The sections were broken down further into smaller units by acreage, such as halves and quarters, or smaller fractional parts known as *aliquot parts* (see Figure 6-4 on page 127). The phrase *forty acres and a mule* originated from the notion that a 40-acre parcel (a quarter of a quarter section) was the minimum amount of land needed to support the average family. An excellent glossary of land-related terms is found in Hatcher's *Locating Your Roots*. An online explanation of the township and range system and legal land terms is found in "Legal Terms in Land Records" <http://users.rcn.com/deeds/legal.htm> at Direct Line Software's Web site.

Field surveyors would determine boundaries by using a magnetic compass (later a solar compass) and measure distances in chains. (The table "Measurement Conversions" on page 120 lists the equivalent measurements.) Section lines and corners were to be plainly marked in the field

Figure 6-3
Sectional diagram of a township showing adjoining sections. *Source: Bureau of Land Management*

36	31	32	33	34	35	36	31
1	6	5	4	3	2	1	6
12	7	8	9	10	11	12	7
13	18	17	16	15	14	13	18
24	19	20	21	22	23	24	19
25	30	29	28	27	26	25	30
36	31	32	33	34	35	36	31
1	6	5	4	3	2	1	6

by blazes on trees or piles of stones, and a description of the immediate vicinity of the corner recorded on the map, including the type of tree and its size, so it could be located again easily. Generally mature, healthy-looking trees were selected for their potential longevity to be a *witness* or *bearing tree* that functioned as a landmark. Today, the Bureau of Land Management (BLM) uses a stainless steel pipe with a bronze cap to mark corners, and points are logged using GPS. Since 1998, several federal agencies have substituted latitude and longitude for the township and range system to describe location. Eventually, describing a land parcel by township and range will be anachronistic.

The details of the USPLS were worked out as they were being applied to a portion of the Old Northwest in eastern Ohio in an area known as the Seven Ranges. The area was known by that name because the Continental Congress required that at least seven ranges of land were to be surveyed before it could be made available for purchase and settlement. In reality, four ranges and no section lines were surveyed before the land office was opened for business in

40 CHAINS 160 RODS 2640 FEET		20 CHAINS		80 RODS	
NW 1/4 160 ACRES		W 1/2 NE 1/4 80 ACRES		E 1/2 NE 1/4 80 ACRES	
1320 FT.	**20 CHAINS**	**660 FT.**	**660 FT.**	**1320 FT.**	
NW 1/4 SW 1/4 40 ACRES	NE 1/4 SW 1/4 40 ACRES	W 1/2 NW 1/4 SE 1/4 20 ACRES	E 1/2 NW 1/4 SE 1/4 20 ACRES	N 1/2 NE 1/4 SE 1/4 20 ACRES	
				S 1/2 NE 1/4 SE 1/4 20 ACRES	
		10 CHAINS	**40 RODS**	**80 RODS**	
SW 1/4 SW 1/4 40 ACRES	SE 1/4 SW 1/4 40 ACRES	N 1/2 NW 1/4 SW 1/4 SE 1/4 5 ACRES	W 1/2 NE 1/4 SW 1/4 SE 1/4 / E 1/2 NE 1/4 SW 1/4 SE 1/4 (330' / 330')	NW 1/4 SE 1/4 SE 1/4 10 ACRES 660 FT.	NE 1/4 SE 1/4 SE 1/4 10 ACRES 660 FT.
		S 1/2 NW 1/4 SW 1/4 SE 1/4 5 ACRES			
		2 1/2 ACS / 2 1/2 ACS	SE 1/4 SW 1/4 SE 1/4	SW 1/4 SE 1/4 SE 1/4	SE 1/4 SE 1/4 SE 1/4
440 YARDS	**80 RODS**	**330' / 5 CHS**	**660 FT.**	**80 RODS**	**40 RODS**

Figure 6-4
Section divided into its ali-quot parts or fractional sections. *Source: Bureau of Land Management*

September 1787. Based on the experience in Ohio, further modification of the system—including the numbering of sections—was made in 1796, and this unified system of surveying public lands has been in use since that time. These public lands are found in thirty states. The twenty "state land states," where the federal government never owned the land, are the thirteen original states plus five that were derived from them (Kentucky, Maine, Tennessee, Vermont, and West Virginia), as well as Texas and Hawaii, which were independent republics prior to becoming part of the United States.

In *Locating Your Roots,* Patricia Law Hatcher astutely notes several geographic anomalies in the split between public land states and state land states:

Portions of public land states with unsystematic surveying: Florida and Indiana.

Portions of state land states with a form of rectangular surveying: Maine, New Hampshire, Vermont, Georgia, Kentucky, New York, Pennsylvania, Tennessee and Texas.

See Also

The curvature of the earth presented early surveyors with a problem: The meridians, like lines of longitude, converge toward the North Pole. The grid could not extend indefinitely without needing correction. The problem was solved with the establishment of *standard parallels* or *correction lines* every fourth township line, and *guide meridians* every fourth range line. You can think of these lines as little correction lines that would limit distortion, which is why mapped grid squares formed by the USPLS are often offset a bit.

It sounds foolproof, but mistakes abound under the USPLS system, not just because of the earth's curvature but also due to surveyor error, corruption, and ineptitude—creating what was colloquially known as "Jack Daniel's Surveys." Up until 1910, most of the land surveying was completed by private surveyors under contract and not government employees. It wasn't until after 1855 (forty-three years after the establishment of the General Land Office in 1812) that a standard method for surveying and recording information was developed. A common practice by surveyors at the time was to put off to the western and northern portions of townships the accumulated survey measurement errors. The result was sometimes an array of peculiar-looking fractional lots that bear little resemblance to the idealized grid. You may need to look in deed descriptions to find two principal meridians in order to clarify a parcel's exact location if the grids on the map don't mesh. Another place to watch for errors is where the USPLS system collides with unsystematic metes and bounds surveys.

Surveyors were required to make maps and field notes that recorded all measurements, locations of water, and comments on the quality of soil and timber (down to identification of species of trees). These field notes and plat maps can provide us with an incredible wealth of information regarding the position of cultural features of the time, including early roads, Indian trails, settlements, and place-names—or not, depending on the abilities of the surveyors. Sometimes the deputy surveyors in the employ of the government were not very talented or truthful, or they held a particular bias. Nevertheless, the field notes and plats are worth searching out and should always be used in conjunction with other sources. Of particular note, place-names were handled differently on USPLS surveys than they were during the topographic mapping described in the previous chapter. Field surveyors were not supposed to name features themselves, but to note the names of all natural landforms and water bodies as *received* from the inhabitants. Thus, many old place-names and field notes contained on these maps might be mentioned in other sources genealogists use but are not found on other map sources. This alone makes these plats and notes worthy of examination.

Three manuscript plats and transcription of the field notes were made from each township survey. One copy of the plat map and original field notes ws retained by the surveyor general (and eventually became the "state copy"). A second copy of the plat and transcribed field notes was sent back to the General Land Office (GLO) in Washington, D.C., and another was retained in the local land office to be annotated with information about specific land transactions. Map librarian Tom Huber has placed a guide to locating GLO survey plats on the Illinois Periodicals Online Web site at Northern Illinois University <www.lib.niu.edu/ipo/il9904232.html>.

A highly readable account of the history of land surveying and its impact on the development of America is Andro Linklater's *Measuring America: How the United States Was Shaped by the Greatest Land Sale in History* (New York: Plume Books, 2003).

Locating GLO Township Plats, Field Notes, and Special Surveys

First, you may want to consult E. Wade Hone's *Land & Property Research in the United States* (Salt Lake City: Ancestry, 1997), which contains a useful appendix—a set of land office boundary maps for each federal land state. This set of maps shows you the boundary line changes that occurred each time a new GLO land office opened or closed. This will give you the name and location of the office and the years it operated. Knowing the name of the local office can help you locate federal copies of plats and field notes within the National Archives and Records Administration (NARA) <www.a rchives.gov> in Washington, D.C, regional branches of NARA, and state-level BLM offices. Public land states have a state BLM office, where original plats and field notes as well as official duplicate copies are often found. Local BLM offices will often have microfiche copies of early General Land Office (GLO) plats and field notes that pertain to their administrative region. The federal copies have been compiled into NARA's *Records of the Bureau of Land Management* (Record Group 49).

Among the BLM records contained in Record Group 49 are the "Records of Division 'E' (Surveying Division)." More than 40,000 township survey plats are included in this category, with some maps showing annotations of land entry numbers and names of *entrymen* (initial grantees). These plats cover Alabama, Indiana, Iowa, Kansas, Missouri, parts of Ohio (Seven Ranges), Wisconsin, the Indian Territory, parts of Oregon, and Washington. The plats and field notes are found in NARA facilities in College Park, Maryland. Some original township plats have been microfilmed, such as *Township Plats of Selected States* (microfilm series T1234). This series is contained on 67 rolls of microfilm and is available through some regional branches of NARA. The plats on the microfilm are arranged by state, principal meridian, range, and township.

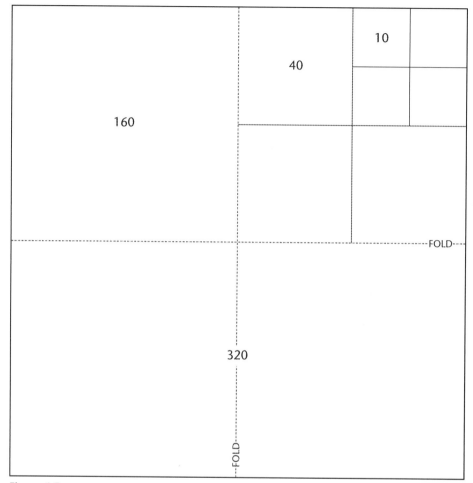

Figure 6-5
An easy way to learn land division is to create your own little "cheat sheet" to take with you to the library or land records office. Select a piece of paper that is square (equal dimensions on all sides of about three or four inches, like a large, square "sticky note") and pretend that it represents a section of land (640 acres). Fold it in half horizontally, then again from left to right. The crease had created a north half and a south half (320 acres each). The upper left one quarter represents the NW ¼, the upper right one quarter is the NE ¼, the lower right one quarter is the SE ¼, and the lower left one quarter is the SW ¼. In the NW ¼ write the number "160" to represent 160 acres (¼ of 640 acres). In the NE quarter draw a cross that divides this quarter equally into four quarters. Each of those four quarters is equal to 40 acres. In the NW ¼ of the NE ¼, write the number "40." Draw a cross in this 40-acre square and you have created four 10-acre parcels.

Some field notes have also been microfilmed, such as *Field Notes from Selected General Land Office Township Surveys* (microfilm series T1240). This series has 280 rolls of microfilm. The states that are covered include Illinois, Indiana, Iowa, Kansas, Missouri, and Ohio. The microfilm is arranged by state and volume number. An index map for each state at the front of the microfilm reel gives you the volume number for a given township and range. The Family History Library has a copy of this series.

List of Cartographic Records of the General Land Office by Laura E. Kelsay (Special List 19, Washington, D.C.: National Archives and Records Service, 1964) is a helpful finding aid for both township plats and many special surveys, including those related to private land claims, town sites, mineral surveys, state boundary surveys, railroad rights-of-way, and American Indian reservations.

Special surveys are particularly useful, because they provide information that might not be on the township plat. The special surveys may have been conducted at a later date than the initial township plat, so they are more up-to-date on settlements, place-names, names of individual landowners associated with numbered sections or fractions of sections, the amount of acreage, and even the entry number of the patent. Special surveys include maps of town sites and Indian lands. Some surveys of Indian land also took place in state land states.

Reading and Mapping USPLS Land Descriptions

Locating a parcel on a map from its legal description is not difficult under the USPLS system. **The trick is to read it backwards, beginning with the principal meridian and working back through the township and range, the section, down to the fractional units of that section.**

Tip

An easy way to learn land division is to take a square piece of paper (equal dimensions of about 3 or 4 inches on all sides, like a large, square self-stick note) and pretend that it represents a section of land (640 acres). Fold it in half from top to bottom. Your crease has created a north half and a south half (320 acres each). In the south half, write the number *320*.

Unfold the paper and fold it in half from left to right. Unfold the paper and you should have four equally divided quarters (160 acres each). The upper left is the NW quarter, the upper right is the NE quarter, the lower right is the SE quarter, and the lower left is the SW quarter. In the NW quarter, write the number *160*.

In the NE quarter, draw a cross that divides that quarter equally into four sections. Each of those sections is equal to 40 acres. In the NW section of this quarter, write the number *40*. In the NE section (the section adjacent to where you wrote *40*,) draw a cross as before. Write *10* in the NW part of this section. These fractional units are known as *aliquot parts*.

An excellent depiction, "Graphical Display of the Federal Township and Range System," is online at Genealogy Resources <www.outfitters.com/genealogy/land/twprangemap.html>.

If you had to write a description from a location on a map, you would start with the smallest fractional unit, then section, township, and range to the principal meridian.

An example for the 10-acre parcel we just created might be:

NW ¼, NE ¼, NE ¼, Sec. 5, T.2N, R.1E, Arkansas 5th Principal Meridian

An expanded description would read:

The northwest quarter of the northeast quarter of the northeast quarter of Section 5 of Township 2 North, Range 1 East, Arkansas Fifth Principal Meridian

Section 5
Township 2 North, Range 1 East
Fifth Principal Meridian

Internet Source

The Bureau of Land Management (BLM) has been placing federal land patents online. These are the initial grants to individuals from the federal government. **You can search the land patent index online at "General Land Office Records" <www.glorecords.blm.gov>.** The directions on the site are pretty straightforward. Make sure to try all possible spelling variations of an individual's name (first and last). Checking a spelling variation enabled me to find two early federal patents issued in 1850 to my great-grandfather, Richard H. Shackelford (Shackleford), in Jefferson County, Florida.

If you find a patent listed in the BLM database, it will give you the legal description, starting with the smallest aliquot parts up through the section, township, range, meridian, state, and county the property was located in from the original patent. In some cases, you can even view and print a copy of the scanned document or order a better, certified copy online.

What if you want to locate this legal patent description on a present-day topographic map? You can do this in several ways, both in the library and online. The 7.5-minute quads discussed in the previous chapter are imprinted in red with section numbers and the USPLS grid in the public land states. Not all the section numbers are printed on every quad. The collar of the quad contains the USPLS grid tick marks and notations for township and range.

You can locate the name of the 7.5-minute topographic quad from the USPLS description by visiting the "Graphical Locator" sponsored by Montana State University <www.esg.montana.edu/gl/trs-data.html>. This Web site converts USPLS descriptions into latitude and longitude information that can help you locate the section on a modern map. Type in the section number, township, and range, select the name of the meridian from a drop-down box, and you will receive information regarding the average elevation of that section and the name of the present state and county the section is located in. You'll also get a list of nearby named places (in order of distance from the section) and a diagram showing the name of the 7.5-minute series quad (bold and in the center), plus the names of all the other adjacent quads. The drawback is the site supports only seventeen western states: Arizona, Arkansas, California, Colorado, Idaho, Kansas, Montana, Nebraska, New Mexico, Nevada, North Dakota, Oklahoma, Oregon, South Dakota, Utah, Washington, and Wyoming.

What if the property you're interested in isn't located in one of these states? You can locate township information in the library by consulting a county map or atlas or by checking Andriot's *Township Atlas of the United States* or the Rand McNally *Commercial Atlas & Marketing Guide*. Both sources show numbered survey townships as well as named civil townships. The Rand McNally atlas does not number each and every section, but it does show meridians and baselines. With a little practice (and a magnifying glass), you can locate a section in its present-day county location. This will give you an idea of where the section is located and what county it appears in on a modern map.

The Bureau of Land Management has an online map "Principal Meridians and Base Lines" <www.ca.blm.gov/pa/cadastral/meridian.html>. It can give you an idea of the general region in which a property is located.

Using TopoZone

Consider my great-grandfather's federal land patents in Jefferson County, Florida. Florida is not in the list of western states supported by the Montana State University's Web site. I printed out the legal description and the scanned copy from the BLM's land patent site. The legal description is:

Aliquot Parts	Sec/ Block	Township Range	Fract.	Meridian Section	State	Counties	Survey Nr.
SWSW	35/	2-N	5-E	No	Tallahassee, FL	Jefferson	[blank]
SESE	35/	2-N	5-E	No	Tallahassee, FL	Jefferson	[blank]

I first checked where the Tallahassee Principal Meridian is located in the Rand McNally atlas and found that it passes directly through the city of Tallahassee. From just the township and range information, I can estimate that the general location will be two tiers north ("2-N") along this meridian and five tiers east ("5-E").

With this information in hand, I could follow several routes. I could go to the USGS store Web site (see chapter five), look up which topographic maps cover Jefferson County, Florida, and order those maps from USGS. The business partner that supports the online maps at the USGS store is Maps a la Carte, Inc., the creator of TopoZone. Since the USGS Web site directs you to TopoZone anyway, I elected to go directly there <www.topoz

one.com> and search for the section I wanted to find. (This site and the USGS Store Web site are best viewed through Microsoft Internet Explorer.) The site allows you to search for a location by its place-name. I found from the Rand McNally atlas that the county seat of Jefferson County is Monticello, so I typed in "Monticello." The city of Monticello is located on the Monticello quad. The name of the quad is linked to the actual quad, and clicking on it takes me to a scanned version of the 7.5-minute Monticello quad.

TopoZone has several features that you can experiment with to help you locate a particular section, and you should try each function until you find the size and scale of a map that you like:

USGS Topo Maps: 1:24K/1:25K; 1:100K; and 1:250K. The program automatically defaults to 1:24K/1:25K, which is the 7.5-minute quad series that shows the greatest amount of detail.

Map Size (small, medium, or large) defaults to small, but I select large because it gives me a view of entire sections on my computer screen.

View Scale the scale matches the series above, except that you also have a choice of a 1:50,000 scale, a 1:100K map, or a 1:24K/1:25K map. The program defaults to 1:50,000. In these scales the township and range lines and section numbers are displayed in red.

Other options allow you to display coordinates in a variety of formats such as UTM or latitude and longitude (in degrees, minutes, seconds, and decimal degrees), and to select the coordinate datum (see chapter ten). I usually select latitude and longitude and leave the datum alone unless I am using a GPS unit.

Warning

Now comes a bit of work. TopoZone maps are seamless, and **because all the maps are knitted together, they don't show the collar information located along the edge of the map.** Scan around until you find either township or range information written in red associated with a line, and then move up or down (north or south) or left or right (east or west) of that point until you find the township you want. Once you find the correct township, search for the proper section. Not all sections are numbered, but if you keep in mind the section numbering diagram in this chapter, you can fill in the missing numbers accordingly. It's important to remember that you can play around with the size of the map.

A version of TopoZone is free to the public. You do not have to register to use the maps. TopoZone Pro is available through a yearly subscription and has many different search options, including links to aerial photographs, street maps, shaded relief maps, elevation displays, extralarge display screens of maps, and USPLS searches that reduce the process to typing in the USPLS description. The program will take you to the center of the section represented by that description. Then you have to map the property boundaries based on the description. This is a time-saver, and if you have lots of properties to locate on topographical maps, a subscription might be worth considering.

You can print out maps on TopoZone, but you can't download them unless you subscribe to TopoZone Pro. A subscription activates both the "topo download" and "photo download" buttons on the upper left corner of the screen. You can print an entire section at the 1:50,000 scale or at 1:24,000, which will take several pages and require some cutting and pasting.

A button located above the download buttons, "Map/Photo Info," gives you the name and date of the quad being displayed. This information tells you how old the quad's base information is and when the most recent revision took place. You should also note that the TopoZone maps are subject to copyright restrictions even though they are based on government maps. You can employ them for personal use but need permission to use them in publications.

Once you print out all the pages you want, cut and tape the section together. I elect to place a piece of tracing paper over the section and draw the property boundaries on it rather than my printout. A method I have used with success is to tape the section to the inside of a letter-size file folder with my tracing paper over it. I also cut out the scale that was printed with the map and tape it to the inside of the folder. I draw the property boundaries on the tracing paper and write the property description or name of the individual on the folder tab. I also place my printouts from the BLM Web site in this folder. All three items are together in one folder—map, description, and document.

COUNTY MAPS AND ATLASES

The middle and later part of the nineteenth century witnessed the development of a new, uniquely North American phenomenon in the map world. *County atlases* or *plat books* (not the same kind of plat book as the federal government produced, but confusingly uses the same name) consist of commercially published cadastral maps of each survey and civil township in a given county. The maps included the property boundaries, the name of the person who owned the land, and the location of various cultural features such as drainages, roads, railroads, mills, schools, factories, cemeteries, and churches. The type of information, scale, and level of detail varied from publisher to publisher, but the atlases were put together in a similar format.

Initially, cadastral mapping was confined to the production of wall maps that would be exhibited in a public building or family home. As the nineteenth century creaked toward the year 1840, when lithography became a popular means of printing maps, county maps became more cheaply avail-

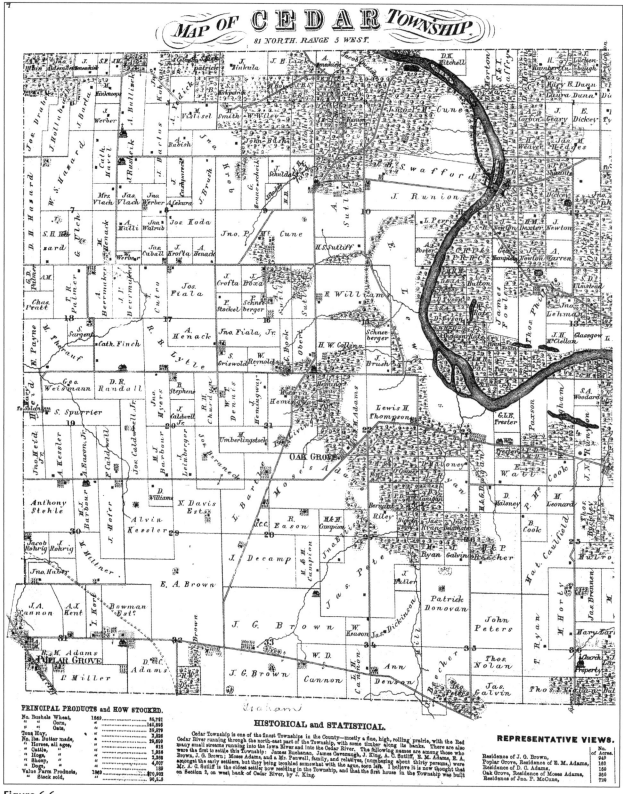

Figure 6-6
County atlas map showing land owners' names in Cedar Township, Johnson County, Iowa. *Source:* Combination Atlas Map of Johnson County, Iowa. *Geneva, Illinois: Thompson & Everts, 1870.*

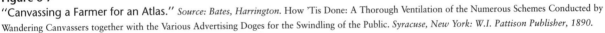
CANVASSING A FARMER FOR AN ATLAS.

Figure 6-7
"Canvassing a Farmer for an Atlas." *Source: Bates, Harrington.* How 'Tis Done: A Thorough Ventilation of the Numerous Schemes Conducted by Wandering Canvassers together with the Various Advertising Doges for the Swindling of the Public. *Syracuse, New York: W.I. Pattison Publisher, 1890.*

able and avenues of greater creativity opened up to publishers. Following the Civil War, the wall maps gave way to books of bound county maps. Although wall maps were quite popular and could be elaborately decorated with pictorial representations of famous landmarks or historical events, they were also subject to greater wear and tear when displayed on a wall, and as a result, fewer of them survived than county atlas books. A book of maps afforded other possibilities for creativity. A publisher could create highly decorated frontispieces—or even market a space on the front page for a portrait of a prominent resident who could afford the price of up to $325 for the privilege.

Most genealogists are aware that printed county history books were created by subscription sales, but county wall maps and county atlases were, too. Just as genealogists are advised to be careful of the information provided in these county histories (also known in the vernacular as "mug books" because of the portraiture that often accompanied the little "potted" biographical statements), the same careful evaluation needs to be made of the information provided on the county maps and atlas pages.

In 1890, during the golden age of the production of these county atlases, Bates Harrington, a nineteenth-century marketing insider, wrote a tell-all book about the sales techniques and dodges practiced on rural county residents—*How 'Tis Done: A Through Ventilation of the Numerous Schemes Conducted by Wandering Canvassers, Together with the Various Advertising Dodges for the Swindling of the Public* (Syracuse, New York: W.I. Pattison Publisher, 1890).

A GRANGER GIVING HIS BIOGRAPHY FOR HIS COUNTY HISTORY
Granger-"What other great things have I done? Well, when I come to Illinois I only had the shillings left. My fellow-citizens, without my asking, have give me the honor to be Road Master four years, and a School Officer two years.

Figure 6-8
"A Granger giving his biography for a county history." *Source: Bates, Harrington.* How 'Tis Done: A Thorough Ventilation of the Numerous Schemes Conducted by Wandering Canvassers together with the Various Advertising Doges for the Swindling of the Public. *Syracuse, New York: W.I. Pattison Publisher, 1890.*

Initially, county atlas subscriptions sold very well in the United States and Canada. Between 1869 and 1877, it is estimated that publishers made $3 million on the sale of county atlases in Illinois alone, and several publishers were reported to have grossed more than a million dollars *a year* between 1870 and 1880. An economic panic in 1873 gradually seeped into the production of atlases and caused orders to slow. Despite this, annual subscription sales continued to be strong until the 1880s, when market saturation in many of the prosperous counties of the Midwest began to catch up. Lastly, the reproduction of lithographic atlases was gradually being replaced by new printing technologies that produced halftone photographs and chromolithographic printing on maps. The county atlases of the 1860s and 1870s were usually colored by hand with the aid of stencils. By the late 1880s, many publishers had converted to chromolithography, which employed machines to do the coloring. Color printing required a type of hard and glossy finished paper typically found in post-1890 atlases.

The companies that were heavily invested in the atlas trade received a little bit of a bounce when President Ulysses S. Grant made a proclamation during the nation's centennial asking Americans to consider documenting local histories in honor of the country's hundredth birthday. As county atlas sales flagged, county history sales began to soar. Text was cheaper to produce than images; county histories bolstered the bottom lines of many county atlas companies. Some of the same boilerplate infor-

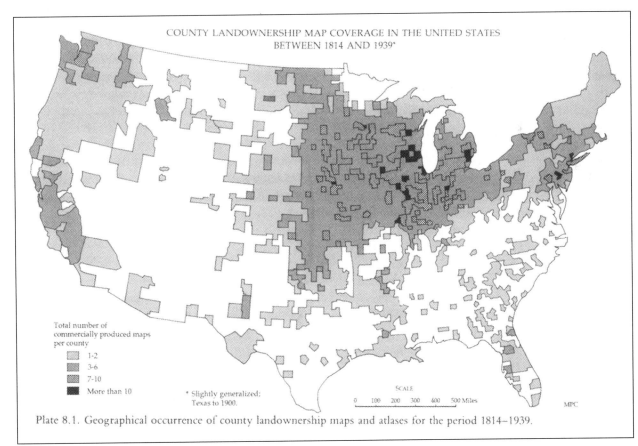

Plate 8.1. Geographical occurrence of county landownership maps and atlases for the period 1814–1939.

Figure 6-9
Map showing the geographical distribution of county landownership maps and atlases published between 1814 and 1939. *Source: Michael P. Conzen. "North American County Maps and Atlases," in David Buisseret (ed). From Sea Charts to Satellite Images. Chicago: University of Chicago Press, 1990, p. 188, Plate 8.1. Used with permission from The University of Chicago Press.*

Reminder

mation that was used for county atlases could be used in county histories. The histories were smaller in format, issued at half the price ($7.50), and contain only one simple county map. Both county atlases and histories published "patrons" or "subscriber lists" in the back of their volumes, but the county history format lent itself to expanding this section to include longer biographical statements and halftone photographs of the subscribers.

To date, more than 5,000 of these county atlases have been discovered. **The largest collection resides at the Library of Congress and can be accessed through** <www.loc.gov>. Another large collection of 2,500-plus county landownership atlases and maps can be found through the online catalog of the Newberry Library in Chicago <www.newberry.org>.

For the most part, county landownership maps and atlases appear most frequently in New England and the Midwest. To a lesser degree, county atlases are found in the western states and in the South. The exceptions were Washington, Oregon, California, and Florida. The map in Figure 6-9 on page 139 gives you a sense of which counties had at least one atlas produced between 1814 and 1939. In some states, such as Wisconsin, Illinois, Michigan, Indiana, and New York, up to ten atlases and maps per county were published during this period.

COUNTY ATLASES

One of the most obvious values county atlases have for genealogical research is the opportunity they afford us to associate a name of a person to a particular place on a map. During the golden age of county landownership maps and atlases, few other geographical resources could do this. County map canvassers sometimes arrived in a county before the surveyors who created topographic maps for the federal government, making the privately sponsored maps the first countywide maps created beyond the initial surveys of the General Land Office.

Using county landownership maps and atlases has certain advantages and disadvantages. An advantage is that, in some portions of the Midwest and New England, you can find several examples of these maps stretching over decades. In this instance, they can provide a sense of landscape change and population expansion. Another advantage is that you can see the association of names in a particular geographic location that is sometimes obscured by the census taker's route. I was searching for the family of William Eaton in Belmont County, Ohio. I had found him in the 1880 federal census living in Morristown with several other Eaton families. When I located him in an 1874 county atlas, I was surprised to see that William Eaton's property adjoined the property belonging to J.R. Eaton. Related? Quite possibly.

Their responses to the 1880 census were separated by several pages, thus obscuring a potential relationship that was made quickly apparent on the map.

It is important to remember that these privately produced county maps and atlases were prepared quickly by people with varied backgrounds and interest in producing an accurate product. One of the first stops for the survey team was the county courthouse and land records office. Boundaries and names were copied from those records. The problem was that everyone living in a county at the time of the survey could not be found among those records. The records focused on landowners, not individuals renting land or squatting on land. The records also didn't record absentee owners who had moved away but left the property still in their name, or people living on land that had been passed down to them through inheritance but had not been recorded in the names of the heirs. If the local land records are ambiguous about property ownership, the county atlas will reflect it, and sometimes magnify it, by capturing "layers" of names, including the earliest land grantees and subsequent purchasers. Just as a page from a medieval manuscript can be a palimpsest filled with partially or incompletely erased information, a county atlas can reflect layers of prior ownership, with names on the maps that do not appear on the census enumeration.

County atlases were especially good at documenting information for parcels greater than 10 acres. The county atlases were also adept at portraying information for states that had landownership patterns described in the township and range system rather than the metes and bounds system. In the metes and bounds states, the atlases tended to show the location of residences and not many land boundaries other than the property lines associated with the initial larger grants of land.

The census was better at documenting people who were not landowners but resided on parcels of farmland as renters. The census was also better at including nonwhite property owners and renters than the county atlases. A brief comparison was made of property owners listed in Henderson County, Kentucky, as depicted on a D.J. Lake atlas in 1880 (*An Illustrated Historical Atlas of Henderson and Union Counties, Kentucky*) to the federal census for Corydon, Kentucky. No African-American residents present on the census could be located on the maps.

County atlases can also provide information that is not readily apparent. Some publishers included information labels on property such as "heirs of S. Powell" or "property for sale." This indicates that not all map canvassers stayed in the county land offices and courthouses, but instead also did a "buggy survey" of the countryside and probably talked to residents to gain additional information. Women's names sometimes appear on the maps or by the occasional notation such as "wid. Tapp" or "Mrs. Minton." Most atlases recorded only the surnames with a first name initial. Sometimes in early atlases only the surnames were recorded, making individual identification quite difficult when more than one person by the same name existed in a given location.

County atlases continue to be published today, but their appearance and content is decidedly different. They are geared toward the real estate market and emphasize parcel numbers, descriptions, and occupancy, rather than the items of cultural and historical interest included in the colorful atlases of the past.

Summary Points

★ Two types of land-portioning systems dominated in North America: metes and bounds, and the USPLS township and range system.

★ The USPLS system is found primarily in the public land states of the Midwest and West.

★ Township plats and surveyors' field notes provide information about the resources and early settlement of an area.

★ County atlases are a type of map unique to North America. Commercially produced county atlases were sometimes the earliest comprehensive maps of a local area beyond the initial township plat.

★ County atlases were produced by subscriptions and should be evaluated as closely as the familiar nineteenth-century county histories (mug books).

Migration Trails Across America

... the new road, it was a 100 miles nearer ... on we went until we came to the first camping place and thair [sic] we found a paper telling how far to the next camping place and then we came to the blue mountains ... when we had crossed the blue Mountains we came to those hard perplexing lakes. Now take the map and look at those lakes which lie between the blue Mountains and the Cascades and you will not see one for every five that theirs [sic] on the ground but you will have some little idea.

—Elizabeth Stewart Warner, in a letter written sometime between 1856 and 1857, in Lillian Schlissel's Women's Diaries of the Westward Journey *(New York: Schocken Books, 1982).*

Overview

- ✦ What kinds of maps show migration information?
- ✦ What kinds of maps did migrants use?
- ✦ Where can I find a map that shows how my ancestor traveled from point A to point B?
- ✦ Are there maps of railroad networks?

FALLING OFF (AND BACK ON) THE MAP

"Where did they go?" is one of the questions that keeps many a genealogist awake at night. To explain the sudden disappearance or appearance of an ancestor, many family historians with tongue in cheek remark that "They must have been abducted by aliens," or "They dropped out of the sky," or, as genealogist Patricia Law Hatcher puts it, "They just showed up." Maps can help us in a variety of ways by suggesting and even explaining the disappearances and reappearances of our ancestors. It is important to know that no one source of migration maps—either in print, online, or a library collection or archive—is going to solve every migration-related question. You have to tailor your use of maps to the problem at hand. This chapter does not retell the history of migration in America; it is an introduction to the wide variety of maps available that can help you understand the movement of people across the landscape of North America.

Tip

Three basic types of maps are helpful in understanding migration. The first category of maps are the small-scale maps that show the routes of trails, canals, railroads, and highways on a national or multistate basis. These are the maps that you typically find in atlases. They are usually the maps that genealogists first encounter when they want to find out how an ancestor traveled between two locations. They suggest the general location of routes but provide little specific detail, such as the counties the trails pass through or near. Unfortunately some family historians begin and end their research with this type of map when actually they should see it as just the beginning—suggestive but not definitive of their ancestors' migration experience.

The second of the three categories are maps that were published as part of government and private surveys of the North American interior. These maps were not specifically targeted to migrants or travelers, but they provided information about internal improvements: roads, canals, and railroads. They were published from the time of the earliest settlements in North America. They tended to be of a larger scale, showing more detail of a particular region than maps in the previous category. Sometimes the maps were of a smaller scale showing regions that were enormous—spanning the entire western half of the United States from the hundredth meridian to the Pacific Ocean.

The last category includes maps specifically targeted to emigrants and travelers. It is the kind of map that Elizabeth Warner refers to in the quote at the beginning of this chapter. During the early to mid-nineteenth century, these maps were commercially published by map publishers, emigrant organizations, and later, the railroads to stimulate interest in migration and settlement in the west. These maps did not always reflect reality, as Elizabeth Warner observed, or were based on a combination of truth, half-truths, and outright falsehoods. They do, however, shed light on the information that was available to migrants at the time of their relocation, such as the location of forts, provisioning stations, depots, isolated farms, and small towns.

UNDERSTANDING MIGRATION STREAMS

It is worthwhile to consider a few things about migration before discussing maps related to the subject.

1. **People choose to leave a place for many reasons:** to preserve their lives through the acquisition of basic necessities such as food or water; to better their lives by obtaining a job, wealth, property, or education; to escape religious and ethnic persecution; to leave involuntarily through conscription, slavery, or by force of arms; to satisfy a need for travel or wanderlust; to reunite with loved ones who went before them; and probably dozens of other reasons beyond these. Sometimes migration is due to only one of these reasons, but more often it is a combination of factors that tip the balance in favor of leaving rather than staying.

2. **Migration is rarely rational.** People migrate even in the face of overwhelming odds, and they don't always go where you might expect. Do you exercise logic in selecting places to shop, reside, or work? Our ancestors didn't, either.

3. **Migration is *bidirectional*—it goes both ways.** People left and people returned. Granted, usually a smaller stream of people returned, but return they did; remember to check records in the last known previous location a decade or two later. My Snow ancestors moved from Oneida County, New York, to Ashtabula County, Ohio, in 1858. They were there in 1860, but by 1870 most of them were not listed in Ohio on the federal census. I checked the 1870 U.S. census in Oneida County, and to my surprise, I found most of them back in their old stomping grounds in New York. They evidently did not like Ohio.

4. **Migration was rarely a nonstop cruise over the landscape between point A and point B.** People halted their journey for all sorts of reasons: bad weather, broken wagon axles, illness, an impending birth, death, running out of money, or even fear of the unknown. The historian Walter Prescott Webb, in *The Great Plains* (Boston: Ginn and Co., 1931; reprinted New York: Grosset & Dunlap, 1957), wrote about a student of his whose family set out from the East to Missouri with the intention of migrating westward from there: "When the women caught sight of the Plains they refused to go farther, and the family turned south and settled in the edge of the timbered country, where the children still reside."

5. **Migration is influenced by both *intervening obstacles* (things that interrupt travel by getting in the way) and *intervening opportunities* (alternative choices that are perceived by the emigrant to be as good as or better than the intended goal).** As a person or group travels, they are continuously bombarded with unforeseen situations, either helpful or harmful. Depending on what those circumstances are, it can cause the migrant to return home, settle where they are, head in a different direction, or otherwise change the original plan.

So, how do you use these five factors to help trace your ancestor? Look at the sources of information your ancestor may have been privy to prior to migration. Scan local newspapers a year or two prior to the ancestor's removal. Were there letters to the editor about how great the farming was in Iowa, or the preponderance of gold in California? Were there ads promoting lands being sold by railroads out west for $10 an acre? What was happening in your ancestor's native area—recession, drought, rumblings of the coming Civil War?

Read published county and town histories and put together a chronological history of events leading up to an ancestor's move. This is *speculative geography*, because unless your ancestor left a diary or letters expressing his or her concerns or state of mind, you cannot be sure of the intentions. However, you can begin to put together a list of potential prods that would have caused an ancestor to consider moving and a list of attractive goal areas that would have drawn an ancestor's attention.

Lastly, make a list of who your ancestor's associates were. People did not move by themselves. They usually traveled in groups. Pay attention to who wrote to the editor of the home newspaper after relocating elsewhere; were those correspondents people your ancestor knew? Look for clues in church lists, land records, local and county histories, military pension records, newspaper articles, notices, obituaries, biographies, probate records, and voter registers that can tell you where people were moving from your ancestor's home area.

Members of a particular ethnic or religious group may be easier to trace by looking at the academic literature. A good place to begin reading about a particular group's geographic movements is the excellent online bibliography "American Ethnic Geography" prepared by Jon T. Kilpinen of Valparaiso University at <www.valpo.edu/geomet/geo/courses/geo200/bibtc.html>. If you locate a particular item of interest in the bibliography, you can request it through interlibrary loan at your local public library.

SMALL-SCALE ROUTE MAPS

Thousands of sources are available that can assist you with understanding the "big picture" of migration in the United States. This section will provide you with a short list of library and online sources that can get you started in your research. These maps were not the maps that the emigrants used to navigate between places, but the ones that came later to describe the history of migration and development of the United States based on routes and means of travel between places.

Previously mentioned in this book is Carol Mehr Schiffman's chapter "Geographic Tools: Maps, Atlases, and Gazetteers" in *Printed Sources*. She describes several major sources for information on early trails and roads, canals and waterways, and railroads. Several sources published after Schiffman's chapter that would be worth consulting include geographer Carrie Eldridge's series of self-published trail atlases (3118 CR 31 Big Branch, Chesapeake, Ohio 45619, <http://home.zoomnet.net/~eldridge1>):

An Atlas of Appalachian Trails to the Ohio River (1998)
An Atlas of Southern Trails to the Mississippi (1999)
An Atlas of Northern Trails Westward from New England (2000)
An Atlas of Trails West of the Mississippi River (2001)

In this series of atlases, Eldridge traces migration routes and describes topographical barriers that influenced trail location and the economic and social factors that influenced migration streams.

The *Atlas of American Migration* by Stephen A. Flanders (New York: Facts on File, 1998) provides an excellent overview of migration streams from the pre-Columbian era to the flight to suburbia from urban centers that took place following World War II. Flanders also addresses forced relocation of American Indians and the trafficking of African slaves and the subsequent relocation of African Americans to northern urban areas following the Civil War.

William Dollarhide's article "Locating Colonial Wagon Roads on a Modern Map" (*HeritageQuest* 20 [February 2004]: 30-37) explores using modern road atlases to discover the routes of colonial wagon trails. The premise is that modern highways were often built on top of or near the earlier trail traces and wagon roads because engineers noticed that earlier residents often traveled the route of least resistance, which often was the most efficient place to build a modern road. The article was derived from an earlier book he published, *Map Guide to American Migration Routes, 1735–1815* (Bountiful, Utah: HeritageQuest, 1997). In this article he suggests tracing the modern routes across county lines shown in the road atlases and then observing how the configuration of the county boundaries has changed over time. This can lead to ancestral records located in parent counties. His classic reference with William Thorndale, *Map Guide to the U.S. Federal Censuses, 1790–1920*, could be one way to research county boundary changes within the time frame of the decennial censuses. However, many of the eastern trails used by early emigrants predate the 1790 census by decades.

Another way to research county boundary changes with respect to trails in the eastern and midwestern states would be to consult the eleventh edition of *The Handybook for Genealogists*. The last section contains contemporary county outline maps of eastern and midwestern states with trail routes marked on them. With the *Handybook* and *Map Guide to the U.S. Federal Censuses* laid side by side, place a sheet of tracing paper over the map closest in age to the 1920 census and trace the trail of interest. Be sure to also trace the state boundaries; they function as a registration mark so you can match state lines and trails with earlier maps in census guides. In this manner you can move backward in time, census by census, and observe county boundary changes.

You can perform the same exercise in a more high-tech way using AniMap 2.5 Plus software <www.goldbug.com>. Using the *Handybook* as a reference guide, you can trace the route of a historical trail on a modern county boundary map by using the "markers" tool available in the program. You can place up to fifty reference point markers on a map in thirteen different designs and color-code them according to trail name. Once the markers are placed, they will remain as you click on the dates of earlier maps and move backward through time. The county boundaries will shift with respect to your marked trail. Notes will appear on each map, letting you know the names of parent counties and the status of newly formed ones. I performed this exercise researching the Russellville-Shawneetown Trail that passes through Webster County, Kentucky, where my ancestors settled. Figures 7-1A, B, and C on page 149 show a map with markers delimiting a trail with the AniMap program. The maps suggested that I should consider looking at courthouse records in Henderson, Christian, and Lincoln counties since the modern Webster County was at one time associated with these larger parent counties. Depending on the state, AniMap has maps that date back to the earliest formation of counties in America during the seventeenth century. It also has an overlay that shows the location of rail lines and the names of the major railroads associated with those routes circa 1970.

Many Web sites pertain to migration routes. One of the most comprehensive is Cyndi Howells's "Cyndi's List: Migration Routes, Roads & Trails" <www.cyndislist.com/migration.htm>. Some of the sites cataloged on Cyndi's List link to emigrant lists of those who traveled various routes.

Michael K. Smith placed his genealogy class syllabus online at "Historical American Migration & Settlement Patterns: A Selected Bibliography" <http://book-smith.tripod.com/migration-top.html>. The bibliography covers many of the classic works consulted by historians studying migration across the United States.

INTERNAL IMPROVEMENT MAPS

Chapter eight details the role the military played in early topographic mapping of the United States following the Revolutionary War. The government had interest in both military defense and civilian commerce. With the General Survey Act of 1824, the War Department became an active participant in the development of roads, canals, and to a certain extent, railroads through the mapping and surveying of routes. Although maps that depicted the growing network of roads, canals, and railroads were not specifically developed for emigrant use, they were consulted by

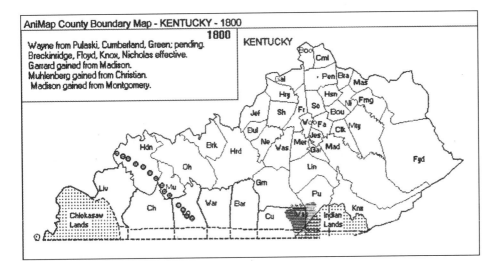

AniMap County Boundary Map - KENTUCKY - 1800

1800

Wayne from Pulaski, Cumberland, Green: pending.
Breckinridge, Floyd, Knox, Nicholas effective.
Garrard gained from Madison.
Muhlenberg gained from Christian.
Madison gained from Montgomery.

AniMap County Boundary Map - KENTUCKY - 1825

182

Edmonson from Grayson, Hart, Warren.
Laurel from Whitley, Clay, Knox, Rockcastle; pending.
Russell from Cumberland, Adair, Wayne; pending.
Allen gained from Barren, Monroe.
Trigg gained from Caldwell.
McCracken organized.

AniMap County Boundary Map - KENTUCKY - 1939

1939

Cumberland gained from Metcalfe.

Figure 7-1A, B, C

Three maps showing county boundary changes along the Russellville-Shawneetown Trail during the years 1800, 1825, and 1939. Understanding the configuration of early county boundaries with reference to trails, rivers, roads, canals, and railroads will help you identify local record sources. These maps were created using AniMap 2.5 Plus County Boundary Map software and are reproduced with permission from Art Lassagne, The Gold Bug.

some emigrants. The depiction of early paths and trails on these historical government maps can be valuable to genealogists. The topographic surveyors noted all conditions, including preexisting paths and trails used by American Indians and settlers.

These maps were created both by commercial publishers and, increasingly after 1824, by the federal government. Between 1824 and 1838, Congress repeatedly approved funding for roads and canals in eastern and midwestern states. Many of these transportation improvements were built by the War Department, the Quartermaster Department, and the Corps of Topographical Engineers. The preproject survey maps, the maps showing the finished roads and canals, plus many other maps related to the internal transportation network in many western states are described in Patrick D. McLaughlin's *Transportation in Nineteenth-Century America: A Survey of Cartographic Records in the National Archives of the United States* (Reference Information Paper No. 65, Washington, D.C.: National Archives and Records Service, 1973).

The maps resulting from these topographic surveys did not pass unnoticed by commercial publishers who published guidebooks for emigrants and travelers. They were often copied and used as base maps for maps created to satisfy the prospective migrant. Sometimes the commercial mapmakers identified their government source and sometimes they did not. Throughout the nineteenth century, as survey accuracy improved, commercial mapmakers were quick to mention their government sources as well as the names of well-known explorers such as Lewis and Clark, Zebulon Pike, and Stephen H. Long to increase the value of their maps in the consumer market. The next section will describe the emigrant publications created by these private mapmakers.

Warning

Locating these maps can be a bit of a challenge because so many places exist to look for them. You may want to begin with map collections in large public libraries or college libraries. Historical societies, especially those dedicated to documenting roads, canals, and railroads, are another source. State and federal agency archives should not be overlooked either. At the federal level, the collections at NARA, the Library of Congress, and the USGS libraries contain thousands of examples of internal improvement maps. The American Memory Web site at the Library of Congress <http://memory.loc.gov> and NARA's Archival Research Catalog <www.archives.gov/research_room/arc/index.html> are two places to look for route maps related to historical transportation projects.

NARA has placed *Special List 29: List of Selected Maps of States and Territories* online, which includes maps delineating many early trails, roads, canals, and railroads. You can read the entire list at <www.archives.gov/publications/finding_aids/special_list_29/index.html>. You click on a state and the list of maps appears, complete with annotations about each map. A link enables you to order copies of any of these maps from NARA.

Two important regional lists of American maps are of interest to those seeking route maps. The *Checklist of Printed Maps of the Middle West to 1900* (Robert W. Karrow Jr., general editor; 14 vols., Boston: G.K. Hall, 1981) lists almost 26,000 maps by state and region in thirteen volumes, with the fourteenth volume a cumulative index to the set. Carl Wheat's monumental *Mapping the Transmississippi West, 1540–1861* (5 vols., San Francisco: Institute of Historical Cartography, 1957) not only describes but reproduces the featured maps. His bibliography includes material through 1884, which includes the railroad building era. A separately published index by Charles Seavey makes Wheat's work more accessible: *Mapping the Transmississippi West, 1540–1861: An Index to the Cartobibliography* (Winnetka, Ill.: Speculum Orbis Press, 1992).

Several published directories to map collections are available. Two of the best sources are a bit dated: David K. Carrington and Richard W. Stephenson's *Map Collections in the United States and Canada: A Directory*, 4th ed. (New York: Special Libraries Association, 1985) and Christopher J.J. Thiry, ed., *Guide to U.S. Map Resources*, 3rd ed. (Lanham, Maryland: Scarecrow Press, Inc., 2005). Sometime in 2005 a new published survey of map collections in the United States will be published by the American Library Association's Map and Geography Round Table (MAGERT) <http://magert.whoi.edu>.

The Web sites of the Perry-Castañeda Library Map Collection at the University of Texas at Austin <www.lib.utexas.edu/maps> and the John R. Borchert Map Library of the University of Minnesota <http://map.lib.umn.edu> maintain extensive links to worldwide online map collections.

EMIGRANT AND TRAVELER MAPS

Emigrants across the United States were not entirely ignorant of the rivers, trails, roads, canals, and railroads they used to traverse the country. By the 1830s, commercial publishers had discerned growing public interest in travel books with foldout maps, as well as maps published singly, catered to the traveler and emigrant. These maps are quite rare today because they were printed on cheap paper and handled frequently. Such books had titles such as A.T. Goodrich's *The North American Tourist* (1839), Lansford Hastings's *The Emigrants' Guide to Oregon and California* (1845), and J.H. Colton's *Colton's Map of the United States, the Canadas & Showing the Rail Roads, Canals, & Stage Roads* (1850). These commercially published books and maps were compendiums of earlier surveys by adventurers, government contractors, traders, and commercial concerns such as the Hudson's Bay Company, as well as maps and published diary accounts of early travelers. Some publishers like John Melish based his maps on his own observations as well as the work of others and created numerous editions of his maps. Others were based on a combination of truths and half-truths and driven by greed; for example, Hastings had property interests in California, and his book was long on promotion and short on actual advice. The tragedy of the Donner Party in 1846 largely discredited Hastings's work but not before many copies were sold at $3 apiece.

Figure 7-2
Samuel Augustus Mitchell was one of several commercial map publishers who capitalized on the growing market of tourists and migrants who were eager to purchase maps and guidebooks about newly acquired American territories in the West. Mitchell's publication was one of his most popular "pocket maps"—a map that could be folded and easily stored during travel. Although containing misstatements of fact, this edition was reprinted in 1849, 1851, and 1852 to satisfy gold seekers. The map accompanying this guidebook can be viewed at <www.davidrumsey.com>.
Source: Private collection.

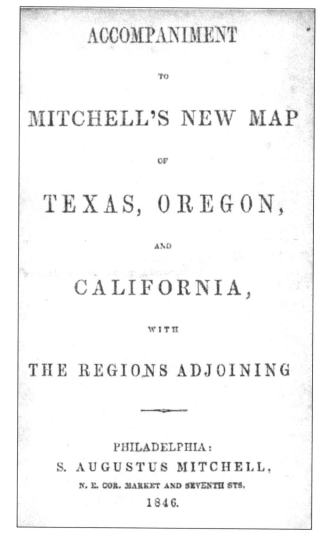

ACCOMPANIMENT

TO

MITCHELL'S NEW MAP

OF

TEXAS, OREGON,

AND

CALIFORNIA,

WITH

THE REGIONS ADJOINING

PHILADELPHIA:
S. AUGUSTUS MITCHELL,
N. E. COR. MARKET AND SEVENTH STS.
1846.

Guides for specific ethnic and religious groups were available, as well as guides for women. *The Latter-day Saints' Emigrants' Guide: being a table of distances, showing all the springs, creeks, rivers, hills, mountains, camping places, and all other notable places from Council Bluffs, to the valley of the*

Great Salt Lake by William Clayton (St. Louis: Republican Steam Power Press—Chambers & Knapp, 1848) was used by Mormons and non-Mormons alike. It was considered by some to be one of the more accurate emigrant guides available in 1848.

As railroads moved west, they devoted more time and money to promoting their services and advertising the land that they owned for settlement. Every major rail line had its own stable of writers, sketch artists, and, later, photographers who helped create promotional brochures and guidebooks to stimulate travel. **The Newberry Library in Chicago <www.newberry.org> has a large collection of guidebooks and maps published by Rand McNally in the late nineteenth and early twentieth centuries for many railroad clients.**

Printed Source

Locating Traveler and Emigrant Maps

Numerous trail guides and maps have survived, and they are also a popular item for reprinting. The bicentennial of the Lewis and Clark expedition from 2003 to 2006 has increased public interest in tracing explorer and pioneer trails. Several major bibliographies can help you locate traveler and emigrant guides and maps. Previously mentioned were the two finding aids for maps: Wheat's cartobibliography *Mapping the Transmississippi West, 1540–1861* and Karrow's *Checklist of Printed Maps of the Middle West to 1900*. In addition:

Townley, John M. *The Trail West: A Bibliography-Index to Western American Trails, 1841–1869.* Reno, Nevada: Jamison Station Press, 1988. This bibliography is particularly valuable because it indexes material by trail segment and chronologically.

Wagner, Henry R., and Charles L. Camp. *The Plains and the Rockies: A Critical Bibliography of Exploration, Adventure, and Travel in the American West, 1800–1865*, edited by Robert H. Becker. 4th ed. San Francisco: J Howell-Books, 1982. Although not specifically a bibliography of map sources, the materials reviewed contain maps, and the bibliographies of the references are also helpful in locating maps the authors used in their research.

A related genre of maps are those found in travel guides, such as the ones published by Baedeker, Nagel, or Frommer's. These are scattered throughout library collections. The maps of small towns and neighborhoods can be quite detailed, down to the number of floors in individual buildings. The older guides preserve historical place-names of streets and neighborhoods. When searching in library catalogs you can search by the name of the place, by name of the publisher, or by the phrase *travel guide* or *emigrant guide*.

Maps that were part of emigrant and travel guides are found in many public and private collections. The Utah Academic Library Consortium has sponsored a digital archive based on material from the special collections of several Utah universities—Brigham Young University, the University of Utah, and Utah State University. "Trails of Hope: Overland Diaries and Letters, 1846–1869" contains not only textual material but also forty-three maps from Mormon and non-Mormon emigrant guides <http://overlandtrai ls.lib.byu.edu/guides.html>.

The "David Rumsey Map Collection" Web site <www.davidrumsey.c om> also has examples of emigrant guides. Several of the maps that appear on Rumsey's site were reproduced in Paul E. Cohen's *Mapping the West: America's Westward Movement 1524–1890* (New York: Rizzoli International Publications, 2002).

RAILROAD MAPS

Railroad maps depicting historical and present-day rail systems can be just as revealing as highway road maps. They suggest connections between locations and, therefore, new places to look for ancestors and their records. Rand McNally & Company began in 1856 as a small print shop in Chicago that specialized in the printing of railway tickets and schedules; by 1872, they were publishing maps. In 1876 they published their first *Rand McNally & Company's New Railroad and County Map of the United States and Canada*, which was later renamed their *Business Atlas*. It contained pages that could be published singly and embellished according to the needs of individual railroad or other business clients. This successful product ultimately evolved into their *Commercial Atlas & Marketing Guide*.

Earlier editions of the *Commercial Atlas* and *Business Atlas* are valuable sources of geographic information related to railroads—names of railroads and the segments of track they operated on. Earlier editions listed distances between cities (shipping points) by railroad segment. Today, the modern atlases list distances by highway segment. Older atlases also include maps of other nations, but, with the exception of Canada, they contain fewer transportation details than maps of America. A 1904 edition of *Rand McNally's Enlarged Business Atlas* suggested how my great-great-grandfather eloped with my great-great-grandmother. He spirited her away from her small hometown in Ohio and married her in Conneautville, Pennsylvania (via the Lake Shore & Michigan Southern and the Bessemer & Lake Erie railroads). He delivered her back home before her family realized what had happened.

Rand McNally was not the only map publisher that catered to the railroads, shippers, and passengers. Maps from an 1895 atlas and an

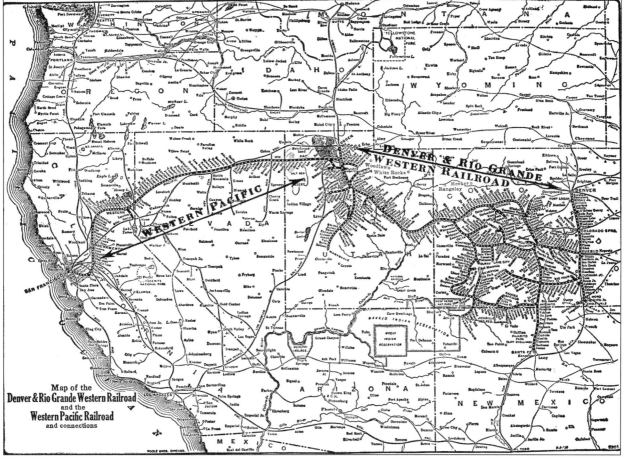

Figure 7-3
This map designed for tourists appeared in a souvenir booklet that names all the stops along the route between Denver and Salt Lake City and Salt Lake City and the San Francisco region. Such maps are valuable not only to the genealogist as mementos of a journey taken by a family member, but also as the source of historic place-names. The traveler who owned this route book wrote the date and times of each station stop encountered along the way from San Francisco to Denver. *Source: The Inter-State Company.* Rocky Mountain Views: On the Rio Grande "Scenic Lines of the World," *Denver: Smith-Brooks Printing Company, 1917. Private collection.*

1891 edition of *Grain Dealers and Shippers Gazetteer* have been placed online at the Mardos Memorial Library's Web site <www.memoriallibrary.com>.

The Library of Congress has one of the largest collections of railroad maps in the world. A Library of Congress publication, *Railroad Maps of North America: The First Hundred Years,* by Andrew M. Modelski (Washington, D.C.: Library of Congress, 1984), traces the history of the first one hundred years of railroad mapping and reproduces a selected set of examples that give you a feel for what types of maps were created for local, regional, and transcontinental railroad routes. The same author wrote a selective annotated bibliography of the library's American railroad maps between 1828 and 1900, which is available on microfiche at the Family History Library: *Railroad Maps of the United States: A Selective Annotated Bibliography of Original 19th-Century Maps in the Geography and Map Division of the Library of Congress* (Washington, D.C.: Library of Congress, 1975). A revised version of the introduction to this bibliography, "History of Railroads and Maps," gives a short history of railroad maps and is available online at the Library of Congress's American Memory site <http://memory.loc.gov/ammem/gmdhtml/rrhtml/rrintr o.html>. All of the maps discussed in this bibliography have been digitized and placed online at "Railroad Maps: 1828–1900" <http://lcweb2.loc .gov/ammem/gmdhtml/rrhtml>.

Research Tip

NARA has custody of many different types of maps related to federal involvement in railroads, both in the United States and abroad. NARA's collection includes maps related to specific railroad land grants from the federal government and plans of "land grant" towns created by the railroads. These were towns created by the railroads between 6 and 10 miles apart, particularly in the Midwest, to serve farmers and ship their products to market. Most of the railroad land grant maps are contained within "Records of Division 'F' (Railroads, Rights-of-Way, and Reclamation Division)" of the *Records of the Bureau of Land Management* (Record Group 49). The *Valuation Records of the Interstate Commerce Commission* (Record Group 134) includes track maps, plans of stations and rail yards, and right-of-way maps that show the names of adjacent property owners and the value of their land. Contained within this record group are field notes concerning land acquisition. There are also maps related to railroads that operated during the Civil War (Record Group 94, *Records of the Adjutant General's Office 1861–1895*) and World War I (Record Group 120, *American Expeditionary Forces*). The Central Intelligence Agency also produced maps (1971–1986) of foreign rail networks. These maps are available in the *Records of the Central Intelligence Agency* (Record Group 263) at NARA.

An introduction to the breadth of railroad records and related maps can be found online in a series of three articles by David A. Pfeiffer, entitled "Riding the Rails Up Paper Mountain: Researching Railroad Records in the National Archives," published in the Spring 1997 issue of NARA's magazine *Prologue* <www.archives.gov/publications/prologue/ spring_1997_railroad_records_1.html>.

The Routledge Historical Atlas of the American Railroads (New York: Routledge, 1999) by John F. Stover summarizes regional railroads. The maps do not detail rail routes through counties but show where they link or did not link up for decades due to regional differences in gauge size.

Two online locations to begin searching for information on railroad maps and atlases, histories of various railroad lines, and links to railroad museums and archives are "Cyndi's List of Genealogy Sites on the Internet: Railroads" <www.cyndislist.com/railroad.htm> and RailServe's "Directory of Railroad, Railway & Model Train Links" <http://railserve.com>.

Summary Points

★ Genealogists find three broad categories of maps valuable for research: small-scale maps showing migration routes; internal improvement maps that depict the location of roads, canals, and railroads; and maps designed for the use of emigrants and travelers.

★ Transcontinental migration was rarely nonstop, point-to-point. Maps show locations where people stopped, as well as topographic barriers to migration.

★ Maps can assist family historians in identifying and speculating about routes between locations. Points along those routes represent places where an ancestor may have stopped and created records. Emigrant guides often contained at least one map that identified locations to obtain provisions, find safety, and purchase land.

★ Government-sponsored internal improvement maps were used by commercial map publishers as references to compile their own maps for emigrants and travelers.

★ To enhance your chance of success in locating someone who has migrated, you need to identify the time period they moved, what contributed to their decision, and what information was available on different places that might have beckoned them.

Military Maps

Every day I feel more and more in need of an atlas, as the knowledge of geography in its minute details is essential to a true military education.

—quote attributed to Union General William Tecumseh Sherman

Overview

⊕ How has war influenced the way we draw maps?

⊕ What types of maps produced by military agencies are helpful to genealogical research?

⊕ Where can I find military maps; aren't they all top secret?

[We] knew no more about the topography of the country than they did about Central Africa. Here was a limited district, the whole of it within a day's march of the city of Richmond . . . and yet we were profoundly ignorant of the country, [we] were without maps, sketches, or proper guides, and nearly as helpless as if we had been suddenly transferred to the banks of the Lualaba (Congo River).

—*Confederate General Richard Taylor, quoted in Christopher Nelson's* Mapping the Civil War: Featuring Rare Maps from the Library of Congress *(Golden, Colo.: Fulcrum Publishing, Inc., 1992)*

I nterest in maps is always highest during times of war, so it comes as no surprise that some of the greatest achievements in the history of mapmaking are a result of war. Resource inventories and political boundary surveys are created by military agencies in preparation for war, battles are documented, the aftermath is depicted, the care and settlement of war refugees is tracked, and communities directly damaged by conflict are surveyed and their renewal documented. Maps are also used during times of war as propaganda tools. Our evening news broadcasts and Internet news are lush with maps to illustrate current events in the Middle East and elsewhere around the globe. Geographic knowledge is synonymous with power and authority.

Many military organizations have been involved with mapping activities in the United States. Several date back to the Revolutionary War, but as their missions have been modified over time their names have changed to reflect new emphases, which leaves the diligent researcher with a variety of both historical and present-day organizations to scour for maps and aerial photographs. Some organizations have kept their information out of the public eye, while others have declassified their materials and deposited them with public institutions. The first challenge is to identify the type of map needed and then search the appropriate collections. Luckily, we live in an era that has a plethora of geographic information available to the public that has been collected and mapped by military organizations, in spite of (or perhaps because of) international turmoil and homeland security concerns. This chapter briefly outlines the contributions to mapping made by various military organizations, identifies types of maps and geographic information collected by military organizations, and lists online and print resources associated with particular wars, conflicts, and interventions involving the United States. As you study the life of an ancestor who served in the military, maps help illuminate their experience by providing insight into the location and configuration of training locations and forts, battles, troop movements, transport by ship, and journeys home.

TYPES OF MILITARY MAPS

Many types of maps are either created by military organizations or related to military subjects that are of interest to the family historian. Only one's time, money, imagination, and occasionally national security are barriers to locating these fascinating maps.

As mentioned in chapter five, it was not uncommon for the earliest topographic and resource maps to be produced by military engineers on behalf of a national government. To locate nineteenth-century and early twentieth-century topographic maps, particularly those from foreign countries, you will have to become familiar with the names of the various military organizations that were charged with mapping in that nation. The references listed in chapter five are a good place to start. A quick reference that is helpful for learning about all mapping, including military mapping, is R.B. Parry and C.R. Perkins's *World Mapping Today*, 2d ed. (München: K.G. Saur, 2002). This reference is encyclopedic in composition and will give you the history of mapping for any modern nation, including addresses of govern-

TIME LINE OF MILITARY MAPPING IN THE UNITED STATES

1777   Lacking detailed maps during the American Revolution, George Washington appeals to the Continental Congress for assistance to form a unit of geographers and surveyors to make maps. He is granted permission, and he forms the Military Cartographic Headquarters at Ringwood, New Jersey, for the purpose of collecting geographic intelligence and creating maps to assist in the war effort.

1803   President Thomas Jefferson, who is also a surveyor and mapmaker, sends Army officers Captains Meriwether Lewis and William Clark into the newly acquired Louisiana Territory.

1807   President Jefferson orders a survey of the eastern coast of North America for the purpose of creating accurate maps to assist in navigation. He creates the Survey of the Coast, the forerunner to today's U.S. Coast and Geodetic Survey.

1814   William Clark's map is published, adding significantly to topographic and cultural knowledge as well as military reconnaissance.

1818   The United States begins centralizing the Army's topographical engineers into the Office of the Chief of Engineers (Record Group 77).

1830   The U.S. Navy Depot of Charts and Instruments is created to reduce American reliance on British and commercial navigation chart publishers.

1831   The Topographical Bureau is established in the War Department.

1832   The complete mapping of the nation's waterways and coastlines begins in earnest, and the first charts are published and circulated in America.

1836   The first war in which maps are extensively created and used by American military personnel is the Seminole Indian campaign between 1836 and 1842.

1838   The U.S. Army Corps of Topographical Engineers is founded for the purpose of conducting reconnaissance surveys of newly acquired territories.

1841   New Army regulations require that topographical engineers accompany all armies into the field.

1843   "Map of the Hydrographic Basin of the Upper Mississippi River, from Astronomical and Barometrical Observations, Surveys and Information" is published and raises the bar of mapping standards and accuracy in the United States.

1844	New York Harbor is completely mapped, and charts are issued to navigators.
1846	The Bureau of Topographical Engineers not only is engaged in mapping ahead of military operations but, for the first time following a battle, creates "order-of-battle" maps that detail troop movements before, during, and after an engagement.
1847	Every commanding officer of a post is required to form reconnaissance parties and survey the area around their posts and create sketches and descriptions, duplicates of which are to be forwarded to general headquarters.
1853	The passage of the Army Appropriations Act directs Secretary of War Jefferson Davis to survey possible routes to the Pacific through the War Department's Office of Exploration and Survey (whose records were eventually transferred to the Department of the Interior, Record Group 48).
1853–1856	Five east-west running routes that roughly follow lines of latitude are surveyed by parties under the supervision of the Topographical Corps of the Army.
1861	The official documentation of the routes is published in the twelve-volume *Reports of Explorations and Surveys, to Ascertain the Most Practicable and Economical Route for a Railroad from the Mississippi River to the Pacific Ocean . . . 1853–1856.*
1863	The responsibilities of the U.S. Army Corps of Topographical Engineers are divided between the Corps of Engineers, the Treasury Department's U.S. Coast Survey, and the U.S. Navy Hydrographic Office.
1871	The federal government provides funding for a nationwide coastal survey, and the Coast and Geodetic Survey (C&GS) is created from the prior Coast Survey.
1907	The Aeronautical Division of the Army Signal Corps is created in anticipation of the potential use of aerial photography in military mapping.
1941	The War Department requests to share mapping data with the Tennessee Valley Authority Forest Service, USGS, and the Coast and Geodetic Survey, which ultimately produced more accurate maps.
1942	The Army Map Service is created and prints 500 million maps by the end of WWII.

Continued on next page

1948   The Library of Congress's Geography and Map Division acquires one of the best collections of Confederate maps, which includes the diaries, correspondence, and private papers of Jedediah Hotchkiss, topographical engineer of the Confederate Army.

1972   The Defense Mapping Agency (DMA) is formed through the consolidation of the Army Topographic Command (the agency that took the place of the Army Map Service in 1968), the U.S. Air Force Aeronautical Chart and Information Center, parts of the Naval Oceanographic Office, and the Mapping Office of the Defense Intelligence Agency (DIA).

1993   Severe flooding in St. Louis destroys the DMA Map Library, which is located within the DMA compound, which in turn is located on a flood plain. Estimates of the number of maps lost during the flood are as high as 175,000.

1996   The DMA becomes part of the National Imagery and Mapping Agency (NIMA), whose primary duties include supplying geospatial information to the military.

2003   NIMA becomes the National Geospatial Intelligence Agency, expands its mission to include surveillance, and, as a result, limits access to some of its maps and imagery.

Sources: Campbell, Albert H. "The Lost War Maps of the Confederates." *Century Magazine* XXXV (January 1888): 479-481; Ehrenberg, Ralph E. "Taking the Measure of the Land." *Prologue* 9 (Fall 1977): 128-150; Modelski, Andrew M. *Railroad Maps of North America: The First Hundred Years*. Washington, D.C.: Library of Congress, 1984; Sorkin, Michael D., and Robert L. Koenig. "Map Agency Losses Put at $11 Million." *St. Louis Post-Dispatch*. October 1, 1993.

ment and commercial map publishers. *World Mapping Today* also lists any restrictions on the availability of maps, particularly those developed by military organizations. For example, it is illegal to export topographic maps produced by the Greek government.

Most of these maps are printed, but manuscript maps and sketches can be found in libraries and archives. The Confederate Engineers' Collection in the Jeremy Francis Gilmer Collection at the Virginia Historical Society is a good example of hand-drawn topographic maps that were created by field operations in advance of front lines. This particular collection has been microfilmed by the Library of Congress. Several of these maps are also available online and in color (roads red, drainages blue, vegetation green). They are important to genealogists because they show the names of residents and the loca-

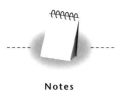

Notes

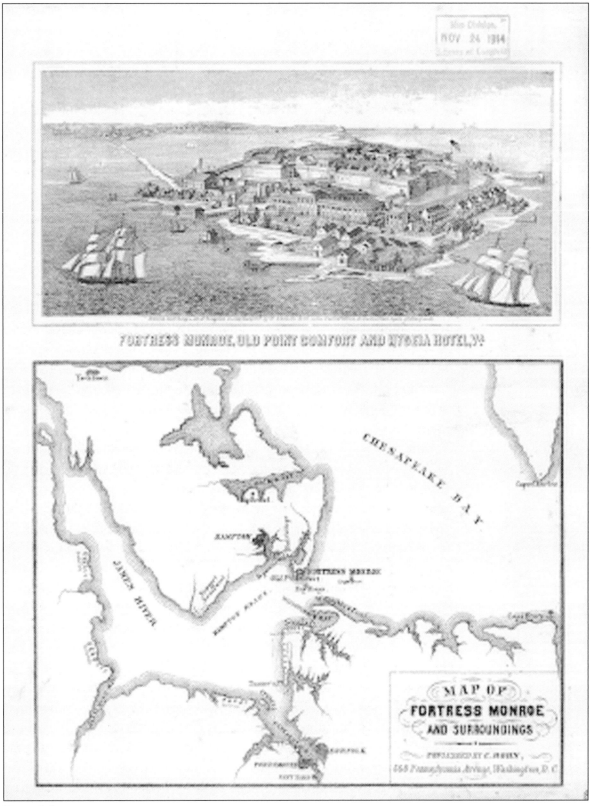

Figure 8-1
Panoramic map of Fortress Monroe on the James River in 1861. *Source: Library of Congress American Memory Web site.*

tion of their homes. Since there were relatively few county atlases of Southern states, these maps are precious to anyone researching Southern ancestry. Other features are shown in black ink, such as topographic hachures, trails, property owners' names, factories, mills, railroad lines, churches, and many other cultural features, including the occasional still.

Military mapmakers also created maps to guide battle decisions and illustrate official reports of field commanders to their superiors. Locating these maps takes a little bit of extra work, but the dividends could be enormous—particularly if the battle was a minor one located in an isolated region of the world. Each branch of military service maintains its own archival repository, and many Department of Defense files have made their way to the National Archives.

Along with maps that illustrated battles, other maps documented the layout of forts, battlements, trenches, military outposts, and training grounds. These plans were published separately, found as part of bound reports or regimental histories, and even appear as "bird's-eye" panoramas produced by commercial map companies. During the late nineteenth century, improvements in printing technology and competition among commercial printers drove the cost down and enabled more people to afford maps and prints to decorate their homes. Military-themed bird's-eye maps were very popular with the public due to the interest in the Civil War (see Figure 8-1 on page 163).

Military schools such as the U.S. Military Academy at West Point and the U.S. Naval Academy at Annapolis trained students to create maps in the field. The vicinity around many of the nation's forts and military training centers have been mapped for decades by students as part of their training. Those maps as well as the maps their teachers created for post-operation classroom examples could be of interest to the genealogist because of the level of detail. Reference librarians at military training institutions or military historical archives may help you locate maps drawn by students or faculty cataloged by the area they represent.

In the United States the National Oceanic and Atmospheric Administration distributes contemporary military navigational charts through Ocean-Grafix <www.oceangrafix.com>. Historical navigational charts can be particularly valuable for topographic and cultural information related to islands and coastal regions. Navigational charts sometimes show much more than just a coastline, as they used points far inland to aid the accuracy of their survey. Historical navigational charts may depict older, locally recognized place-names. College map libraries and large public libraries that function as repositories for federal maps are two sources for historical navigational charts.

Historical aeronautical charts developed by the military can be found at

NARA among the records of the Army Air Corps and Army Air Forces (*Records of the Army Air Forces*, Record Group 18). The National Archives has an incomplete set of maps issued by the Aeronautical Chart Service during World War II (1939–1947); though incomplete, the collection has more than 5,200 charts. The U.S. Air Force succeeded the Army Air Force in 1947. Its map collection is found at NARA under "Aeronautical Chart and Information Center" records (*Records of United States Air Force Commands, Activities and Organizations*, Record Group 342).

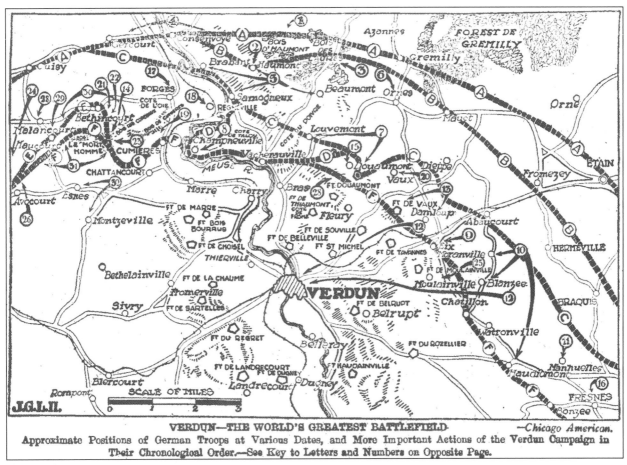

Figure 8-2
This map proclaims "Verdun—the world's greatest battlefield." History books that reprise battles are often excellent sources of maps and geographical descriptions of conditions during a war. You need to pay attention to copyright restrictions if you plan to publish a map on the Web or in a printed family history. *Source: Russell, Thomas H.,* America's War for Humanity A Pictorial History of the World War for Liberty. *New York: L.H. Walter, 1919.*

Maps appearing in military history books are another good source of geographic information. Following the Civil War and for every war since that time, both governmental and commercial publishers rushed books to market following major conflicts in attempts to capitalize on their relevancy. An important point to remember is that battles sometimes had more than one name, depending on which side's cartographer was wielding the pen. For example, the Civil War has several major battles that were called one name by the Union side and referred to by another name on the Confederate side, like Antietam or Sharpsburg, and Bull Run or Manassas.

Order-of-battle maps are maps that reproduce the positions of troops and enemy forces on a given day or defined period of time. They are useful in documenting the progress of a battle, movement of forces, lines of communication, placement of headquarters, artillery locations, frontlines, jump-off lines, positions of relief, billeting areas, and lines of resistance. Often they accompanied official reports from the field to headquarters. They are found both within governmental documents and as loose maps within governmental record groups. World War I order-of-battle maps are described in NARA's *Cartographic Records of the American Expeditionary Forces* (Record Group 120), which not only contains maps from U.S. army sources, but also Belgian, French, and British army maps. The Library of Congress' American Memory Web site <http://memory.loc.gov> has nearly a year's worth of daily troop positions for the Battle of the Bulge operation during World War II. Other interesting map sources include the "Records of U.S. Army Commands in the Philippines (1870–1941)" found in NARA's *Records of United States Army Overseas Operations and Commands* (Record Group 395), which contains blueprint copies of maps from the Office of the Chief Engineer depicting American order-of-battle operations against insurgents.

By the end of World War II, the Army Map Service was producing more than 5,000,000 maps *per month* for use in the war abroad and at home. Postwar survey maps exist within many different government record groups. For example, maps related to postwar port and navigation are contained in the Office of the Hydrographic Survey or with the Army Map Service. To find postwar conditions maps, you will have to search by military organization (such as the Army Map Service) or by region or country. Reconstruction of war-torn areas (such as Germany and Japan) was supervised by the U.S. military, and you would have to search the records of those branches of the military involved.

Internet Source

Interest in locating the graves of ancestors who served in the military or were killed in battle has increased with the online publication of several databases, such as the National Park Service's site "Civil War Soldiers and Sailors System" <www.civilwar.nps .gov/cwss>. Maps of national military cemeteries are slowly finding their way onto the Internet also. The Arlington National Military Cemetery is not administered by the Veterans Administration but through the Military District of Washington. You can view the "Arlington National Cemetery Interactive Map" at <www.arlingtoncemetery.org/interactive_map/index.html>.

The Army's "Records of the Graves Registration Service" are found within NARA's *Records of the Office of the Quartermaster General* (Record Group 92). These records also contain a large collection of maps related to national cemeteries in the United States and its territories and possessions between 1903 and 1917. It also has ground plans of American cemeteries established during World War I in France, England, and Belgium.

The American Battle Monuments Commission was created after World War I to commemorate the service of all American military personnel who fought throughout the world. This agency is charged with establishing and maintaining permanent cemeteries, monuments, and memorials where their remains have been buried. The agency's Web site <www.abmc.gov> has several searchable databases for military casualties from World War I, World War II, and the Korean War. Each soldier listing generally includes name, service number, rank, unit, date of entry into the service, medals, date of death, and occasionally the name of the cemetery and sometimes the exact burial location. The databases are also searchable by state and by cemetery. Unfortunately, cemetery names are not linked to maps or individual gravesites, but with the name of the cemetery or exact location of a grave, procuring a map, if it exists, is made easier by contacting the cemetery. NARA has also compiled the agency's records in the *Records of the American Battle Monuments Commission* (Record Group 117).

Genealogist George G. Morgan's "Military Cemeteries: Honor and Glory on the Internet" (*HeritageQuest* 20 [June 2004]: 52-59 <www.heritaqueststmagazine.com/pdf/morgan_june.pdf>) lists detailed information about the American Battle Monument Commission as well as foreign military services, and includes addresses of online databases that help in locating their military casualties.

The Veterans Administration Web site has links to aid in finding military graves on its "Burial & Memorial Benefits" page <www.cem.va.gov/nmc.htm>. Although this database is not specifically designed to locate Confederate graves, some Confederate graves and cemeteries are being added as they appear in cemeteries with other war dead.

For maps of historic battleground memorials and monuments, check the National Park Service's Web site <www.nps.gov> or NARA's *Records of the National Park Service* (Record Group 79). You can find maps of national military parks such as Gettysburg and Shiloh. The National Park Service has also published maps of Civil War operations at Tullahoma, Chickamauga, and Chattanooga. The Perry-Castañeda Library Map Collection site at the University of Texas at Austin also lists links to maps of specific historic battlefields that are now preserved as parks and monuments, in "Historical Map Web Sites" <www.lib.utexas.edu/maps/map_sites/hist_sites.html>. The Tennessee Valley Authority (TVA) has also published historical maps of several post–Civil War southern communities. These are available at its

"TVA Map & Photo Records" Web page <https://maps.tva.com>.

Aerial photographs of battle zones can be found from as early as World War I. Most of the photographs were oblique (taken at an angle) rather than from overhead because of perilous ground fire from enemy positions. Aerial photography became much more sophisticated and useful during subsequent wars. For historical aerial photographs, the best collections are found among the records of the Library of Congress and the National Archives. Historical satellite imagery has only recently become available through the USGS in the last decade through the declassification of these records by President Bill Clinton. These images are scattered throughout university map collections and military institutions—such as the U.S. Naval Postgraduate School's Dudley Knox Library <www.nps.edu/Library> in Monterey, California—that functioned as federal depositories for satellite imagery created by the National Imagery and Mapping Agency (NIMA) and the Defense Mapping Agency (DMA). Satellite imagery of modern conflicts in Afghanistan and Iraq remain for the most part classified and unavailable to the public by decree of the U.S. Department of Defense.

MILITARY MAP INTERNET SITES

Listed below are some of the best Web sites for locating military maps.

American Civil War Research Site for Maps and Timeline

<www.americancivilwar.com/civil.html>

The site is organized by state and by periods during the war. I was surprised to find that it contains maps of even minor battles; for example, the Battle of Natural Bridge, in which my grandfather participated, that took place in northern Florida on 6 March 1865.

American Military History, by Roger Lee

<www.historyguy.com/american_military_history.html>

This site is more history-oriented than geography-oriented but has great links to all wars, including the most recent military interventions and conflicts. Some of the linked resources have maps related to particular wars and battles.

Combined Arms Research Library, Maps and Graphics, Command & General Staff College

<http://cgsc.leavenworth.army.mil/carl/gateway/maps.asp>

This military Web site has a list of links to various online map collections. The Digital Library collection of World War II documents contains some maps within the reports, surveys, and publications related to this conflict.

Digital History

<www.digitalhistory.uh.edu/maps/maps.cfm>

This gigantic Web site has links to chronologically arranged historical maps such as "Revolutionary Era," "Early National Period," "Nineteenth Century," and "Civil War." Maps are also indexed by topic; for example, "French and Indian War," "War of 1812," "Plains Indian Wars," and "National Parks and Battlefields."

Perry-Castañeda Library Map Collection

<www.lib.utexas.edu/maps>

See specifically "Maps of United States National Parks and Monuments" and "Historical Maps of the United States." This is an excellent Web site to begin research on any type of map, including maps related to battlefields.

Library of Congress, American Memory Collection

<http://memory.loc.gov/ammem>

Several map collections have obvious connections to military history—the American Revolution Collection and the recently expanded Civil War Collection. They have placed an illustrated introduction to the history of mapping the Civil War at <http://lcweb.loc.gov/ammem/collections/civil_war_maps/cwmpm.html> The Panoramic Maps Collection contains battlefield views produced by nineteenth-century commercial map publishers. The Civil War touched many families, so it was popular for people to want to purchase views of famous battles that their relatives had participated in during the conflict. Many of these battlefield views were advertised in newspapers along with advertisements of the familiar bird's-eye-view maps of towns and cities.

Another collection, "Map Collections: 1500–2004," contains maps within the public domain and available for downloading. The "Military Battles and Campaigns" section covers many military operations throughout the world. For example, if you were interested in a particular region and time period such as Germany during the last days of World War II, you can find several hundred maps detailing troop positions.

Dudley Knox Library Map Collection, U.S. Naval Postgraduate School, Monterey, California

<http://library.nps.navy.mil/home/mapcollection.htm>

This wonderful Web site has many links for military and nonmilitary maps. The military maps links include listings of military cemeteries, military bases, peacekeeping missions, and wars from ancient times through the modern era.

NEWSPAPER MAPS AND WAR

After leaving school, how did our ancestors learn about other places? Before movies and television were invented, newspapers were *the* major source of geographic information. Later, newsreel footage accompanied movies or was included in television news broadcasts. Today we are literally awash in maps from many journalistic sources, including the Internet and 24-7 satellite news channels. The next time you watch a news broadcast on television, count how many maps are shown and notice how many different ways they are used, for everything from simple location to predicting what tomorrow's weather will be.

As a genealogist you might occasionally delve into newspapers to locate vital record information or announcements related to your ancestor. Have you ever considered looking at the maps displayed in newspapers? These maps have value to us because they illustrated the news stories our ancestors read. They suggest places that our ancestors might have wanted to move to (or away from).

As you have seen, maps are a powerful means to communicate a lot of information about a place in a succinct manner. For this reason alone, you would have thought that from the very beginning newspapers would have employed maps, but that was not the case. Maps were expensive graphics to produce. Initially newspaper maps were created by carving them into wood blocks and setting the blocks into the frames along with the rest of the movable type. During the mid-eighteenth century, newspapers and monthly periodicals employed maps especially in the coverage of events related to wars and specific battles. It did not take long for publishers to notice that war stories illustrated by maps sold newspapers and magazines.

Today, maps are used in newspapers in several ways: to provide explanation in a new story; to act as a "fact graphic," such as showing the location of an accident or fire; to add interest to a story by showing changes over time; to anticipate a forthcoming event, such as a traffic closure for a parade; and to add "flavor" to a news article by using eye-catching colors on the map or by printing maps in unusual shapes (as in *USA Today*.) Travel articles frequently employ maps to attract readers' eyes. A darker side to the use of maps in journalism is their use for propaganda purposes. As you have read in chapter four, maps can be manipulated to highlight a particular feature or de-emphasize other aspects of a situation. Mark Monmonier's book *Maps with the News: The Development of American Journalistic Cartography* (Chicago: University of Chicago Press, 1989) is an excellent introduction to the uses and abuses of maps as they appear in newspapers and on television.

Maps in news stories came into their own during the American Civil War. People hungry for information from the front lines where their loved ones were serving clamored for maps illustrating particular battles. News editors responded by hiring wood-block artists to work in teams, each taking small portions of maps to engrave. These small sections were joined together into larger blocks, thus reducing the production time of these maps. The news was urgent and maps sold newspapers. *Civil War Newspaper Maps: A Cartobibliography of the Northern Daily Press* by David Bosse (Westport, Conn.: Greenwood Press, 1993) is an excellent aid to locating Civil War maps that appeared in northern U.S. newspapers.

Following the Civil War, photographic engraving replaced woodblocks as the means to create maps in newspapers. Another technical innovation that further encouraged the use of maps in newspapers was the invention of "stereotyping boxes," which used precut mats as templates to create map plates cast from molten lead. These mats could be easily shipped by mail or delivered.

The year 1935 was the turning point for the use of maps in newspapers. In that year the Associated Press (AP) rolled out its subscription wire photo network. Dedicated phone lines transmitted what we call "faxes," which took seven to eight minutes per image to send. News editors finally had a reliable source of graphic imagery that included both maps and photographs to use to illustrate national news stories. Other companies such as ACME Newspictures and United Press followed suit by offering the same services as AP by subscription. Eventually the equipment became faster and more sophisticated. Today, maps are beamed via satellite in an instant to hundreds of thousands of subscribers all over the world.

The most recent advance in newspaper cartography came with the advent of the desktop computer and the development of graphic software that enabled even small newspapers to create their own maps for a fraction of the previous cost of designing maps for local stories. Maps covering neighborhood stories were another way to sell local newspapers by communicating to readers that "we care about your issues, too," not just about the big news stories such as wars.

You locate maps in historical newspapers the same way you would locate any other story or photograph. National and state microfilming projects of historical newspapers are ongoing. The Library of Congress American Memory Collection has a selection of Civil War-era maps from newspapers. They make excellent illustrations for family histories describing an ancestor's participation in a particular battle or as background to events that occurred in a region where an ancestor may have resided.

Through its Serial and Government Publications Division, the Library of Congress (LOC) maintains one of the most extensive collections of newspapers in the world. It has more than 9,000 U.S. titles and 25,000-plus non-U.S. titles in its collec-

Continued on next page

tion. You can learn more about its collection in the Newspaper and Current Periodical Reading Room <www.loc.gov/rr/news/ncp.html>.

The Library of Congress is one of the cosponsors of the U.S. Newspaper Program, which is funded by the National Endowment for the Humanities (NEH). The NEH and LOC sponsor this program for the purpose of locating, cataloging, and preserving U.S. newspapers on microfilm. The programs they have funded are listed by state and national repository programs at their Web site <www.neh.gov/projects/usnp.html>.

An excellent overview by James L. Hansen, his chapter "Research in Newspapers" on how to locate newspapers, is found in Loretto Dennis Szucs and Sandra Hargreaves Luebking's *The Source: A Guidebook of American Genealogy* (Salt Lake City: Ancestry Publishing, 1997). He lists the major bibliographies of historical newspapers, including religious, ethnic, and military newspapers (the latter is listed under the heading "Specialty Newspapers"). He also lists a short bibliography of state newspaper resources.

Increasingly newspaper publishers are placing their newspaper content on the Web. Some of these newspapers offer their daily newspapers for free online. Archived copies of past editions are sometimes free but more often are seen as part of the revenue stream of newspapers and require a small fee in order to access articles from older issues. Some larger newspapers store the articles and original graphics such as maps together, while smaller newspapers might not to save space.

Korean War Project
<www.koreanwar.org/html/maps.html>

This Web site is privately sponsored and contains detailed maps published by the Army Map Service (1:250,000 or 1 inch = 4 miles). This map series is excellent for locating small villages and fine landscape detail.

National Defense University Library Map Resources
<www.ndu.edu/library/maps.html>

This megasite contains links to military organizations and maps related to specific conflicts, peacekeeping, government mapping sites, and satellite imagery.

Office of Coast Survey, Historical Map and Chart Collection
<http://chartmaker.ncd.noaa.gov/csdl/ctp/abstract.htm>

This branch of the government is not directly related to defense, but during times of war supplies information and shares resources with military organizations. The collection contains maps from the late 1700s to the present day and includes many Civil War battle maps and resource survey maps related to ports and navigable waters that were involved in wars. Historical maps and charts are not available for purchase, but the scanned maps are highly detailed and worth pursuing.

West Point Atlas of Major Conflicts

<www.military.com/Resources/
HistorySubmittedFileView?file = History_Maps.htm>

This site is organized by century and contains hundreds of maps from the earliest colonial wars up to the intervention in Somalia (1994). At one time West Point was the leading American institution that taught military cartography, so its map collection reflects maps published by others as well as maps produced by students as part of their training and maps produced by faculty for "lessons learned from battle" classroom instruction.

U.S. Army Corps of Engineers, "Where We Are"

<www.usace.army.mil/where.html>

The official mapping branch of the U.S. Army provides many types of maps and geospatial information to the public, including maps of major U.S. waterways and ports through the Public Affairs Office of any corps district or division listed on this Web site. Other government maps may be available for purchase through either the USGS National Geospatial Data Clearinghouse at <http://geography.usgs.gov>, or for historical military maps or foreign maps through the National Geospatial-Intelligence Agency (NGA)<www.nga.mil>

U.S. Geological Survey

<www.usgs.gov>

The USGS distributes declassified intelligence satellite photographs. More than 880,000 high-resolution photographs taken between 1959 and 1972 by CORONA satellites were declassified by President Bill Clinton's 1995 executive order. The collection is held at the USGS EROS Data Center near Sioux Falls, South Dakota. Copies of spy satellite imagery are available for sale to the public and are described in a USGS fact sheet <http://erg.usgs.gov/isb/pubs/factsheets/fs09096.html>.

LIBRARY AND ARCHIVE SOURCES

Family History Library

35 North West Temple Street
Salt Lake City, Utah 84150-3400

(801) 240-2584
(800) 346-6044
<www.familysearch.org>

The Family History Library Catalog (FHLC) can be searched through the Web site of the Church of Jesus Christ of Latter-day Saints <www.family search.org>. Their collection contains original maps, reproductions of maps, and maps on microfilm or microfiche. They also have several finding aid books for other cartographic collections and subjects, such as the National Archives and the Library of Congress. You can search the FHL catalog by place, surname, keyword, title, film/fiche number, author, subject, or call number. Some of the results you obtain will not be map materials but other histories and rosters, which may contain useful maps.

The Army Map Service produced millions of maps during World War II. Try searching the FHL catalog by keyword using the phrase "Army Map Service."

Library of Congress, Geography and Map Division

101 Independence Avenue SE
Madison Building, Room LM B01
Washington, D.C. 20540-4650
(202) 707-6277
fax (202) 707-8531
maps@loc.gov
<www.loc.gov/rr/geogmap>

The Library of Congress has the largest map collection in the United States, with maps for almost any military conflict both at home and abroad. It has an active microfilming project that includes collections related to military subjects. It may be possible to receive microfilms of maps through interlibrary loan to your public library. Larger public libraries and university libraries may own some of the microfilm collections related to the Revolutionary War or Civil War.

U.S. Army Military History Institute

The Army Heritage and Education Center
950 Soldier's Drive
Carlisle, PA 17013-5021
(717) 245-3971
usamhi@carlisle.army.mil
<http://carlisle-www.army.mil/usamhi>

This library has posted a detailed twenty-two-page finding aid that describes the many collections that make up this repository. Of particular interest is the collection of information on modern and historic forts and military installations in their manuscript collections. The map collection contains more than 12,000 maps, filed in chronological order from the Civil War to the present. The collection's strength is WWI and WWII maps, but the curators are actively building a collection of maps of the Korean War and Vietnam War. All maps must be used at onsite as none circulate via interlibrary loan.

Navy Department Library

Naval Historical Center
805 Kidder Breese SE
Washington Navy Yard
Washington, D.C. 20374-5060
(202) 433-4132
fax (202) 433-9553
<www.history.navy.mil/library>

This library's large collection of maps includes charts of wrecks, admiralty charts, charts of naval engagements, and many other types of maps related to naval operations. At this time, 99 percent of its maps are uncataloged. Slowly its cartographic collection is being processed, and as the entries are cataloged they are being placed on its Web site (address given above). If you're interested in a particular naval battle, a call to the reference librarian is necessary. A preliminary inventory to NARA's *Naval Records Collection of the Office of Naval Records and Library* (Record Group 45) is a place to start, but it is not the complete listing for this category of records.

U.S. Army Center of Military History

Collins Hall
103 Third Avenue
Fort Lesley J. McNair, D.C. 20319-5058
(202) 685-2714
cmhanswers@hqda.army.mil
<www.army.mil/cmh-pg>

The collection shines best in its World War II and Vietnam War-era holdings. Reference assistance is limited, so it is advised that you call for an appointment prior to your visit.

National Archives and Records Administration (NARA)
Cartographic and Architectural Branch
8601 Adelphi Road
College Park, MD 20740-6001
(301) 713-7030
fax (301) 713-7488
carto@arch2.nara.gov
<www.archives.gov>

No single reference source exists for information on federal cartographic collections housed in the National Archives because it grows daily, but the *Guide to Cartographic Records in the National Archives*, published in 1971 by NARA, gives an overview of the federal agencies and their record groups that have military maps. It is a fine compendium but not a complete listing of all maps created or collected by the federal government, as many maps are published as part of reports and may not be listed as part of the cartographic collection. The *Guide to the National Archives of the United States* published in 1987 by NARA adds additional record groups with military-related cartographic collections. This publication's brief descriptions of cartographic records include record group number, date of materials, and number of items or number of linear feet, depending on the size of the collection. It has a helpful listing of record group numbers and agencies in its Appendix C. The most recent printed guide to the entirety of NARA's collection is the *Guide to Federal Records in the National Archives of the United States*, compiled by Robert B. Matchette, et al. (Washington, D.C.: NARA, 1995).

For the most up-to-date listing of cartographic holdings, check the online version of *General Information Leaflet No. 26: Cartographic and Architectural Records* at <www.archives.gov/publications/general_information_leaflets/26.html>. *The Archives: A Guide to the National Archives Field Branches*, by Loretto Dennis Szucs and Sandra Hargreaves Luebking (Salt Lake City: Ancestry, 1988), is also helpful, but it is not geared specifically to locating military cartographic records.

Map Sources for Specific Wars
Colonial Wars, 1607–1763

Esposito, Vincent J., ed. *West Point Atlas of American Wars*. 2 vol. New York: Praeger, 1959; reprint, New York: Henry Holt, 1995. This source contains detailed topographical maps from battles during the Colonial era through the Korean War.

Fite, Emerson David, and Archibald Freeman. *A Book of Old Maps, Delineating American History from the Earliest Days Down to the*

Close of the Revolutionary War. Cambridge: Harvard University Press, 1926. Microfilmed by Genealogical Society of Utah, 1966. FHL US/ CAN film 0430099.

Historical Atlas of Canada. Volume I: From the Beginning to 1800. Toronto: University of Toronto Press, 1987.

Indian Wars, 1775–1890

Goetzmann, William H. *Army Exploration in the American West, 1803– 1863*. New Haven, Conn.: Yale University Press, 1959.

Morris, John W., Charles R. Goins, and Edwin C. McReynolds. *Historical Atlas of Oklahoma*. 3d ed. Norman: University of Oklahoma Press, 1986.

National Archives. *Memoir of Reconnaissances With Maps During the Florida Campaign, April 1854–February 1858*. Microfilm series M1090. Includes maps.

Prucha, Francis Paul. *Atlas of American Indian Affairs*. Lincoln: University of Nebraska Press, 1990.

Revolutionary War, 1775–1783

Barnes, Ian. *The Historical Atlas of the American Revolution*. New York: Routledge, 2000.

Cappon, Lester J., ed. *Atlas of Early American History*. Princeton, N.J.: Princeton University Press (for the Newberry Library and the Institute of Early American History and Culture), 1976.

Clark, David Sanders. *Index to Maps of the American Revolution in Books and Periodicals: Illustrating the Revolutionary War and Other Events of the Period 1763–1789*. Westport, Conn.: Greenwood Press, 1974.

Ferrell, Robert H., and Richard Natkiel. *Atlas of American History*. New York: Facts on File, 1987.

Greenwood, W. Bart, comp. *The American Revolution, 1775–1783: An Atlas of Eighteenth Century Maps and Charts*. Washington, D.C.: Naval History Division, 1972.

Guthorn, Peter J. *British Maps of the American Revolution*. Monmouth Beach, N.J.: Philip Freneau Press, 1972.

War of 1812, 1812–1815

Cartographic Archives Division. "Unpublished Guide to Maps of the War of 1812, In-house Finding Aid." Washington, D.C.: National Archives, no date.

Crawford, Michael J., et al. *The Naval War of 1812: A Documentary History, Vol III, 1814–1815*. Washington, D.C.: Naval Historical Center, 2002.

Dudley, William S., ed. *The Naval War of 1812: A Documentary History, Vol. II, 1813*. Washington, D.C.: Naval Historical Center, 1992.

Heidler, David S., and Jeanne T. Heidler, eds. *Encyclopedia of the War of 1812*. Santa Barbara, Calif.: ABC-CLIO, 1997.

Mexican War, 1846–1848

Bauer, K. Jack. *The Mexican War, 1846–1848*. Lincoln: University of Nebraska Press, 1993.

Traas, Adrian G. *From the Golden Gate to Mexico City: The U.S. Army Topographical Engineers in the Mexican War, 1846–1848*. Washington, D.C.: Center of Military History, 1993.

Civil War, 1861–1865

Abell, Sam, and Brian Pohanka. *The Civil War: An Aerial Portrait*. Charlottesville, Va.: Thomasson-Grant, 1990.

Bosse, David, comp. *Civil War Newspaper Maps: A Cartobibliography of the Northern Daily Press*. Westport, Connecticut: Greenwood Press, 1993.

Hotchkiss, Jedediah. *Make Me a Map of the Valley: The Civil War Journal of Stonewall Jackson's Topographer*, edited by Archie P. McDonald. Dallas: Southern Methodist University Press, 1973.

Kennedy, Frances H., ed. *The Civil War Battlefield Guide*. 2d ed. Boston: Houghton Mifflin, 1998.

LeGear, Clara Egli, comp. *The Hotchkiss Map Collection: A List of Manuscript Maps, Many of the Civil War Period, Prepared by Major Jed. Hotchkiss, and Other Manuscript and Annotated Maps in His Possession*. Washington, D.C., 1951; reprint, Falls Church, Va.: Sterling Press, 1977.

McElfresh, Earl B. *Maps and Mapmakers of the Civil War*. New York: Harry N. Abrams, 1999.

National Archives. *A Guide to Civil War Maps in the National Archives*. Washington, D.C.: National Archives, 1986.

Nelson, Christopher. *Mapping the Civil War: Featuring Rare Maps from the Library of Congress*. Golden, Colo.: Fulcrum Publishing, 1992.

O'Reilly, Noel S., David C. Bosse, and Robert W. Karrow Jr. *Civil War Maps: A Graphic Index to the Atlas to Accompany the Official Records of the Union and Confederate Armies*. Chicago: Newberry Library, 1987.

Phillips, David. *Maps of the Civil War: The Roads They Took*. New York: MetroBooks, 1998; reprint, New York: Barnes & Noble Publishing Inc., 2005.

Sharpe, Michael. *Historical Maps of Civil War Battlefields*. San Diego, Calif.: Thunder Bay Press, 2000.

Stephenson, Richard W., comp. *Civil War Maps: An Annotated List of Maps and Atlases in Map Collections of the Library of Congress.* Washington, D.C.: Library of Congress, 1961.

——. *Civil War Maps: An Annotated List of Maps and Atlases in the Library of Congress.* Washington, D.C.: The Library of Congress, 1989.

Symonds, Craig L. *A Battlefield Atlas of the Civil War.* 3d ed. Baltimore: Nautical and Aviation Publishing Company of America, 1993.

U.S. War Department. *Atlas to Accompany the Official Records of the Union and Confederate Armies.* Washington, D.C.: Government Printing Office, 1891–1895; reprint, New York: Barnes & Noble Publishing Inc., 2003.

Spanish-American War, 1898, & Philippine Insurrection, 1898–1903

Armstrong, Le Roy. *Pictorial Atlas Illustrating the Spanish-American War: Comprising a History of the Great Conflict of the United States with Spain.* Washington, D.C.: R.A. Dinsmore, 1898.

Lawson, Don. *The United States in the Spanish-American War.* New York: Abelard-Schuman, 1976.

Marrin, Albert. *The Spanish-American War.* New York: Atheneum, 1991.

Rand McNally & Company. *History of the Spanish-American War, with Handy Atlas Maps.* Chicago: Rand McNally & Company, 1898.

Shewey, A.C. *Shewey's Spanish American War Atlas.* Chicago: A.C. Shewey, 1898.

World War I, 1914–1918

Clark, Thomas D., ed. *World War I, 1914–1918, European Theater.* Indianapolis: George F. Cram Company, 1956.

Forty, Simon. *Historical Maps of World War I.* London: PRC, 2002.

Gilbert, Martin. *Atlas of World War I.* 2d ed. New York: Oxford University Press, 1994.

Livesey, Anthony. *The Historical Atlas of World War I.* New York: Henry Holt, 1994.

Lord, Clifford Lee, and Elizabeth H. Lord. *Historical Atlas of the United States.* Rev. ed. New York: Henry Holt, 1953.

U.S. Military Academy. Dept. of Military Art and Engineering. *A Short Military History of World War I, with Atlas.* West Point: U.S. Military Academy, 1950.

World War II, 1939–1945

Gilmore, Donald L., ed. *U.S. Army Atlas of the European Theater in World War II.* New York: Barnes & Noble Books, 2004.

Goodenough, Simon. *War Maps: World War II, from September 1939 to August 1945, Air, Sea, and Land, Battle by Battle*. New York: St. Martin's Press, 1982.

Keegan, John, ed. *The Rand McNally Encyclopedia of World War II*. Chicago: Rand McNally, 1977.

Messenger, Charles. *The D-Day Atlas: Anatomy of the Normandy Campaign*. New York: Thames & Hudson, 2004.

Natkiel, Richard. *Atlas of World War II*. New York: Military Press, 1985.

Pimlott, John. *The Historical Atlas of World War II*. New York: Henry Holt, 1995.

Pitt, Barrie. *The Month-by-Month Atlas of World War II*. New York: Summit Books, 1989.

Swift, Michael. *Historical Maps of World War II, Europe*. London: PRC, 2000.

U.S. Military Academy. Dept. of Military Art and Engineering. *A Military History of World War II*. West Point: U.S. Military Academy, 1953.

Cold War, 1945–1991

Carnes, Mark C., and John A. Garraty. "America and the World After WWII." In *Mapping America's Past: A Historical Atlas*. New York: Henry Holt, 1996.

Swift, John. *The Palgrave Concise Historical Atlas of the Cold War*. New York: Palgrave Macmillan, 2003.

Korean War, 1950–1953

Atlas of the Arab-Israeli Wars, the Chinese Civil War, and the Korean War. Wayne, N.J.: Avery Publishing Group, 1986.

Grant, Reg. *The Korean War*. Milwaukee, Wisc.: World Almanac Library, 2004.

Kirk, John G., et al. *Atlas of American Wars*. New York: Arch Cape Press, 1986.

Indochina or Vietnam War, 1956–1975

Grant, Reg. *The Vietnam War*. Milwaukee, Wisc.: World Almanac Library, 2005.

Summers Jr., Harry G. *Historical Atlas of the Vietnam War*. Boston: Houghton Mifflin, 1995.

Strategies for Locating Map Resources

1. Check several of the previously mentioned megasites that are gateways to military and civilian information related to military history and geography.

2. Search the Library of Congress catalog at <http://catalog.loc.gov>. With the largest collection of maps in the United States, the Library of Congress is bound to have something of interest for any military conflict. Also, you should contact special military libraries and archives directly.

3. Check the Government Printing Office Web site <http://bookstore.gpo.gov> for their most recent catalog. Items, because of customer interest, are added with great frequency on modern wars and conflicts. The site has a section on atlases and maps for sale to the public. The online sales catalog is searchable by subject, such as "Korean Conflict" or "Marine Corps." Searching by subject can help you find military histories that may contain maps as exhibits.

4. Visit the cartographic section of the United Nations Map Library <www.un.org/depts/dhl/maplib/maplib.htm>. The map collection at the United Nations in New York contains more than 80,000 maps and 3,000 other geographical references.

OBTAINING MILITARY MAPS

Several vendors for military maps have been mentioned in this chapter. The National Geospatial-Intelligence Agency (NGA) Web site would be a place to start, although they make their maps and imagery available through the USGS map store, which can be accessed online or via telephone or fax. The U.S. Government Printing Office has a section on military atlases, maps, and foreign country briefing books for sale to the public.

For foreign military maps, you should consult Parry and Perkins's *World Mapping Today* for a brief recitation on the names of the government military organizations involved with national mapping campaigns abroad. Purchasing or exporting these maps overseas may be restricted.

Two commercial vendors that offer military maps and international topographic maps in their selection are:

Map Link, Inc.
30 South La Patera Lane, Unit #5
Santa Barbara, California 93117
(805) 692-6777; fax (805) 692-6787
(800) 962-1394; fax (800) 627-7768
USGS Topo Dept. fax: (800) 627-1839
E-mail: custserv@maplink.com
<www.maplink.com>

Map Link is the world's largest commercial distributor of maps.

Omni Resources
1004 South Mebane Street
P.O. Box 2096
Burlington, North Carolina 27216-2096
(336) 227-8300
fax (336) 227-3748
E-mail: custserv@omnimap.com
<www.omnimap.com>

Summary Points

★ Historically, collecting geographic information and creating maps has been advanced more often than not by the requirements of the military.

★ Military organizations create a variety of geographic products useful to genealogists—maps, atlases, and gazetteers.

★ Incorporating battle maps into family histories not only provides insight into an ancestor's geographical movements but also a heightened awareness about an experience in his or her life and how it connects to national and international events.

★ A wealth of military maps is available from the time of the Civil War. For security reasons, maps related to recent events may be more restricted for public use than those related to prior wars, although maps since World War II are continually being declassified and made available to the public.

CHAPTER 9

Fire Insurance and Other Urban Maps

You can always tell a Midwestern couple in Europe because they will be standing in the middle of a busy intersection looking at a wind-blown map and arguing over which way is west. European cities, with their wandering streets and undisciplined alleys, drive Midwesterners practically insane.

—Bill Bryson, The Lost Continent: Travels in Small-Town America *(New York: Harper & Row, 1989).*

Overview

⊕ *What types of maps are available for towns and cities?*

⊕ *What are panoramic or bird's-eye-view maps?*

⊕ *How are fire insurance maps useful in genealogical research?*

⊕ *Where do I locate historical maps of towns and cities?*

A mericans like orderly cities, and our maps reflect that underlying desire to create perfect grids. This chapter focuses on several examples of large-scale city mapping. In previous chapters, cities have been addressed as related to transportation networks and landownership. Many kinds of maps about towns and cities are available, but unfortunately you won't find the majority of them in college library or public library map collections.

These maps reside in the files and archives of local municipalities and courts. When blueprinting became an affordable technology, these maps and plans were reproduced "on demand" in response to a request. Most of these maps were created with a specific purpose in mind related to the administration, planning, or engineering of cities or neighborhoods in progress. Just because these maps can be challenging to locate, you should not

---

BLUEPRINTING

Blueprinting was invented in 1837 when it was discovered that light created a reverse image on paper that had been coated with silver chloride. The resulting print was white lines on blue paper. Blueprinting was one of the first means for a mapmaker, architect, or engineer to publish maps and drawings on demand. The process went out of fashion in the 1950s when it was replaced by other related processes such as Ozalid and blueline. Blueprinting, Ozalid, and blueline offered mapmakers easy and affordable reproduction, though the prints tended not to be very durable.

---

be dissuaded from looking for them. Urban maps created at the neighborhood level can provide the genealogist and local historian with insight into the lives of ordinary people and the neighborhoods where they lived. Historical utility maps showing the location of water connections, sewer lines, electrical and gas lines, telegraph and telephone lines, and public and private alarm systems are often found in the archives of larger cities. Cities generated school district maps to assist with the placement of students and administer tax and bond money associated with school development. Road right-of-way maps with the names of adjacent property owners are another genre of urban maps often overlooked by the genealogist.

PANORAMIC AND BIRD'S-EYE MAPS

During the nineteenth century, a popular type of map that excited our ancestors' imaginations was the panoramic or "bird's-eye" map. This cartographic form was common prior to photography to promote communities to settlers and emigrants, as well as show off a town's accomplishments or illustrate a story about an event such as the California gold rush. The roots of this type of map are old, dating back to the late Middle Ages and early Renaissance when printers slipped in a panoramic view of a town or city or a slightly elevated, oblique view of European cities to illustrate their books and atlases.

The popularity of these maps reemerged in the early nineteenth century in North America when printers in New York, Philadelphia, Chicago, and, later, San Francisco began churning out prints depicting either panoramic views or slightly elevated views of American and Canadian towns and cities. Between 1825 and 1900, several thousand communities were sketched by artists or freelancers. **By midcentury, a higher view, dubbed** *bird's-eye views* **as the oblique perspective appeared to be from a higher vantage point than earlier**

\di'fin\ *vb*

Definitions

Figure 9-1
Bird's eye view of Sacramento, California, circa 1890. *Source: Warren, F.K. (ed.)* California Illustrated Including a Trip Through Yellowstone Park. *Boston: De Wolfe, Fiske & Company, 1892.*

renditions, began to routinely appear. (See Figure 9-1 above.) At the same time, commercial publishing was moving away from engraving metal plates toward the chemical process of lithography. The result was maps and prints that showed intricate details that could be tinted by hand or, later, by machine. These maps could also be reproduced quickly and sold affordably—for as little as $0.75 for a black-and-white copy or as much as $5 for hand-tinted versions.

The value of these maps to genealogists and local historians is manifold, as they not only show what some of these communities looked like but what our ancestors wanted them to look like—prosperous, clean, progressive, orderly, and peaceful. Some communities were sketched more than once during the nineteenth century, and you can compare physical sprawl as well as economic development, transportation networks, and recreation opportunities from map to map. The post–Civil War maps tended to be more accurate than earlier maps. They depict towns and cities in such detail that individual buildings can be spotted as well as railroad and street patterns and the physical terrain.

Many maps were designed to be hung or displayed in the home or business. The border often was composed of detailed renderings of individual homes and businesses. As with county atlases, you could pay to have your home or business either depicted in extra detail on the map or appear as one of the sketched buildings in the border. Railroads were also quick to pick up on the renewed interest in these town and city prints, and they commissioned artists to draw their railroad towns.

No complete list exists of the thousands of printed maps that fit into the category of panoramic and bird's-eye maps. A number of publishers were involved in this market. Some images had small print runs based on subscription sales, while other maps were made to promote a specific business and given away as a premium to customers.

The largest collection of these maps is found in the Library of Congress. The Library of Congress American Memory site has several hundred examples of these fascinating maps available at "Panoramic Maps 1847–1929" <http://memory.loc.gov/ammem/pmhtml/panhome.html>. A dozen or so prolific artists traveled from city to city sketching, but rarely taking more than a week or two to complete each map. Most of the views were created of midwestern, northeastern, western, and southwestern towns and cities—particularly those on the frontier. Gold rush mining towns appear as frequent subjects that were reproduced by printers in London and sold throughout Europe. There is no question that these maps stimulated migration, investment, and development along the American frontier.

Like its relative, the subscription county atlas, the bird's-eye map should be compared to other maps and later photographs of the city to detect the level of accuracy. For the most part, many were more accurate than you might suppose because subscribers would have scrutinized their homes and buildings as well as those belonging to their neighbors and friends for any inaccuracies. Sketch artists also wanted to be as accurate as possible to capture future commissions.

For additional information, see:

Hébert, John R., comp. *Panoramic Maps of Cities in the United States and Canada: A Checklist of Maps in the Collection of the Library of Congress, Geography and Map Division.* 2d ed. Revised by Patrick E. Demsey. Washington, D.C.: Library of Congress, 1984. A checklist of the 1,726 maps in the Library of Congress collection. The introduction to this work is posted online at the American Memory Web site <http://memory.loc.gov/ammem/pmhtml/panintro.html>.

Reps, John William. *Views and Viewmakers of Urban America: Lithographs of Towns and Cities in the United States and Canada: Notes on the Artists and Publishers, and a Union Catalog of Their Work, 1825–1925.* Columbia: University of Missouri Press, 1984.

Watson, Douglas S. *California in the Fifties: Fifty Views of Cities and Mining Towns in California and the West, originally drawn on stone by Kuchel & Dresel and other early San Francisco lithographers.* San Francisco: J. Howell, 1936.

Historic Urban Plans reproduced facsimiles of panoramic and bird's-eye-view maps of cities throughout the world. They can be reached at P.O. Box 276, Ithaca, New York 14851, <www.historicurbanplans.com>. An online vendor of panoramic maps is the U.S. Historical Archive <www.ushistoricalarchive.com>.

FIRE INSURANCE MAPS

In *Fire Insurance Maps: Their History and Applications*, map historian Diane Oswald (College Station, Tex.: Lacewing Press, 1997) calls fire insurance maps "the footprints of America's industrial revolution." That's not a bad description of them. Fire insurance maps were developed during the eighteenth century in Great Britain, the seat of the European industrial revolution, as a reference tool for insurance underwriters. As the insurance industry grew and began to insure buildings farther away from their headquarters, it became less convenient to dispatch someone to check individual buildings and assess potential risks prior to deciding whether to issue a policy. **Entrepreneurial engineers and map publishers in Europe and later North America created detailed plans that showed physical characteristics of individual buildings, such as the type of material used in construction and its shape and size.** As time progressed, the maps became more detailed and included a basic street plan with the names of the streets and the locations of alleys, cisterns, fire-fighting equipment, and alarms. The type of land use (residential, commercial, industrial, etc.) was also noted, as well as the type of businesses and any other information that could help assess the potential risk of fire or explosion.

Important

Researchers from many different fields find these maps useful, including historians, architects, environmental research companies involved in hazardous waste remediation, geographers, and especially genealogists. Although not many people's names appear on fire insurance maps, when combined with other resources such as deeds, city directories, and federal census records, they become a powerful reference source useful in reconstructing urban landscapes in the nineteenth and early twentieth centuries.

After the American Revolution, British insurance companies began writing policies on American properties. In 1790, the first fire insurance map was published of Charleston, South Carolina, by the Phoenix Assurance Company, Ltd. of London. Later, as simmering hostilities between the U.S. and Great Britain grew into the War of 1812, American businesses lost their fire insurance from British companies almost overnight. Following the end of the war, American insurance companies that had struggled prior to 1812 found a ready market almost free of competition from British insurance companies. The American insurance business grew quickly and became centered in cities such as New York, Philadelphia, and Hartford, Connecticut. As the century progressed, industrial growth with the prospect of potential jobs attracted people to cities. More population squeezed together into less space meant greater incidence of fires, particularly in those cities that were built primarily of wood structures. Periodic devastating fires increased local insurance company losses and pushed their reserves to low levels. In 1835 a major fire in New York City caused more than $20 million in losses and nearly wiped out the American insurance industry. State and local laws were enacted that changed insurance business practices, and the industry began to reorganize. Rather than wait for bankruptcy, local insurance companies began to merge and create larger, regional companies that had greater reserves. For these regional companies it was not practical to visit each and every property on which a request for insurance coverage had been made. The stage was set for the American fire insurance mapping industry to be born.

In 1852, the first set of American-made fire insurance maps specifically designed for use by insurance underwriters was published by William Perris and George T. Hope; it consisted of three wards in New York City. While these maps were being compiled, Hope and Perris convened a committee of New York fire insurance officials to find out what information their prospective clients needed and how to portray it in a cost-efficient manner and format. This committee developed the standardized colors, symbols, format, and scale (1 inch = 50 feet) of fire insurance maps that we are familiar with today. Their system provided a basis for consistency, reliability, and accuracy not yet seen in the large-scale mapping of American cities.

The success of Perris and Hope did not go unnoticed, and in 1857 Ernest Hexamer and William Locher established their own firm in Philadelphia to make maps at the same scale (1 inch = 50 feet). Other small firms sprang up in major American cities, only to fall by the wayside during the Civil War when civilian mapping was severely restricted by the war.

The Sanborn Map Company

Following the Civil War, in 1867, D.A. Sanborn, a surveyor from Massachusetts, established the D.A. Sanborn National Insurance Diagram Bureau in New York City. It eventually grew into the Sanborn Map Company through its reliable product, good business practices, and strategic mergers with competing fire insurance map firms such as Perris and Browne in 1889, Rascher Map Company in 1891, the Whipple Agency in 1902, and Hexamer and Sons in 1915. Eventually Sanborn held a monopoly in the American fire insurance mapping market. By 1902, Sanborn's company catalog listed maps and atlases for nearly 5,000 towns and cities. By 1912, that number grew to 7,500. In 1924, that number nearly doubled with 11,000 communities included on its list.

Sanborn's entrance into the fire insurance mapping market was fortuitous because it coincided with the development of railroads, which, in turn, stimulated industrial and commercial development—more cities. Immigration from abroad also pushed the spread of cities outward and upward, further necessitating insurance maps to be drawn. This is why Diane Oswald's observation quoted earlier in this chapter seems particularly apropos. Eventually, the Sanborn Map Company would publish maps for more than 13,000 U.S. towns and cities at the scale of 1 inch equals 50 feet on sheets the size of 21 inches by 25 inches. The maps of large cities were bound into books, which later evolved into loose-leaf volumes whose pages could be easily updated and replaced.

The Sanborn Map Company's success was due in part to the company's devotion to uniformity, accuracy, and format. Like the county atlas business described in chapter six, fire insurance map companies depended on the research of people in the field. These employees, who were known as "striders," "trotters," or "pacers," pored over maps in courthouses, real estate offices, and municipal engineering offices to locate base maps—the source maps on which most maps for a city are based. In places with no base maps (for example, fast-growing western mining towns) they were expected to measure their territory with a tape line and plot their own notes on map sheets that were gridded with 1-inch squares. Each sheet translated to about four to eight blocks of mapped structures. Striders had to make note of close to one hundred characteristics in order to adequately describe a structure, adjacent land uses, and the location of fire prevention resources, as well as potential obstacles that would hinder firefighting or situations that would increase the possibility of a fire or explosion, such as certain types of industries.

The maps were incredibly detailed, (see Figure 9-2 on page 190) showing everything from the location of mansions, factories, worker housing (sometimes identified by ethnicity of residents), outhouses, and brothels

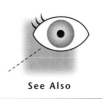

See Also

For more information, see Vlad Shkurkin's "Fire Insurance Maps as Primary Historic Records," <www.utah ice.com/sanborn/firemaps .htm>.

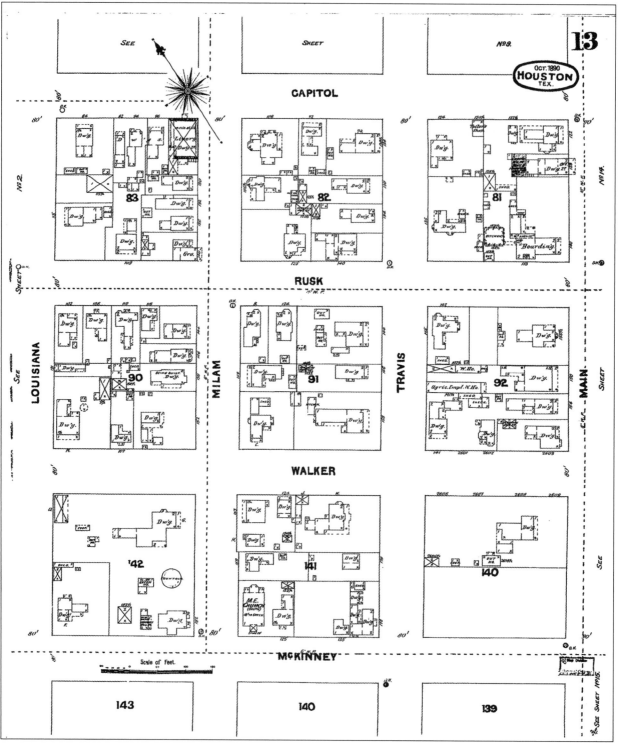

Figure 9-2
This Sanborn fire insurance map depicting a Houston, Texas, neighborhood in 1896 shows residential and commercial land uses.
Used with permission from EDR™ Environmental Data Resources, Inc., Milford, Connecticut.

(sometimes noted primly as "female boarding establishments"). The striders focused their attention on the parts of a town or city that were the most densely packed with businesses and population. This usually meant the central business district and a few blocks around it. The degree to which a community was mapped was a judgment call based on the experience of the strider and the requirements of insurance company clients. It is not uncommon to see on a fire insurance map a boundary line with the phrase *no exposure beyond*, which meant that the area had few structures or that they were sufficiently spaced apart that a fire would do limited damage.

How often a town was mapped by Sanborn and other mapping companies is a matter of debate. If a lot of development occurred in a particular area, then remapping would take place at shorter intervals in order to maintain a particular level of accuracy. Their clients depended on these maps to help them evaluate whether to write a policy, so it was important that they reflected what was currently on the ground. Generally, it is believed that the striders would make revisions about every five to six years. Sanborn maps produced after World War I had a "correction record" form stamped on them below the map key, where subscribers could track the revision number, date of the revisions, and who applied them to the map.

The peak decade for production of maps in the fire insurance market appears to be the 1930s. The slowing economy of the late thirties began to sap the market for these maps. The Sanborn Map Company provided an expensive service to its subscribers. As insurance applications dropped off, so did interest in subscribing to fire insurance maps. In response, the Sanborn Map Company devised a method to reduce costs for customers by offering cash discounts to subscribers and "paste-overs": The company would send its subscribers updates printed on small pieces of paper to paste over their maps in the appropriate locations and mark the revisions on the correction record block on the map. Eventually, the company also tried to reduce costs by changing the scale on their maps to 1 inch equals 100 feet or 1 inch equals 200 feet.

World War II and the decade that followed essentially spelled the end of the fire insurance mapping industry. During the war, mandatory restrictions were placed on civilian mapping. The slow postwar economy also affected map sales. The development that began in the 1950s to accommodate the postwar baby boom did not occur in central business districts or industrial areas, but in the suburbs where densities were lower and the need for mapping fire insurance risks was much less. Today, the Sanborn Map Company services a few insurance clients but mostly focuses attention on satisfying the mapping needs of engineers and architects. They revise existing map and atlas products for thirty to fifty cities per year.

Notes

Locating Fire Insurance Maps

By far, the world's largest collection of Sanborn fire insurance maps resides at the Library of Congress. Their fire insurance collection is composed of 50,000 maps and atlases that represent 700,000 individual map sheets. The collection was built in three ways: from direct deposit of maps during the copyright registration process, the transfer of a substantial number of maps from the Census Bureau in 1967, and contributions by individuals or institutions. The donated material from the Census Bureau was particularly valuable because that agency was a subscriber to the Sanborn maps and thus received those little printed, paste-over revisions as well as new sheets and entire books. The copyright deposit materials received by the Library of Congress did not reflect subsequent additions or deletions, only the original map.

Published in 1981, *Fire Insurance Maps in the Library of Congress: Plans of North American Cities and Towns Produced by the Sanborn Map Company: A Checklist* (Washington, D.C.: Library of Congress) lists these maps by state or province, city, and date for the entire collection. In 1996, Environmental Data Resources, Inc. (EDR) purchased the library of historical maps (and rights) from the Sanborn Map Company. At present, you can make copies of pre-1923 Sanborn maps held by the Library of Congress without obtaining permission from EDR. The Library of Congress has a policy that maps published after that date require permission from EDR before they can be reproduced. At present, pre-1923 Sanborn maps are not part of the online American Memory collection of maps at the Library of Congress Web site.

During the 1980s, Chadwyck-Healy, which today is part of ProQuest Information and Learning, microfilmed the Library of Congress's collection of Sanborn maps on 1,099 rolls of microfilm. That microfilm has since been digitized by ProQuest, and access is sold on a subscription basis to libraries and institutions. The collection includes maps produced between 1867 and 1970. The quality of the online images varies greatly, as some microfilmed sheets produced digitized images that are clearer than others. Libraries that subscribe to the collection report heavy use by many different researchers, including genealogists.

The maps are accessed by first selecting the state, then the city, and lastly the date of the map. Some cities have one date to choose from, while others have a half-dozen or more. Unlike the printed paper copies of the Sanborn maps, the online maps are displayed in black and white. You can zoom in and out and print or download entire sheets or sections of map sheets for personal use only. Maps that have been digitized by ProQuest have a new copyright date, and permission must be sought from both ProQuest and EDR in order to use their digitized versions in publications. Permission to use maps that have not been digitized (paper format) and that were published after 1923 must be obtained from EDR.

Environmental Data Resources, Inc.
440 Wheelers Farms Road
Milford, CT 06460
(800) 352-0050
<www.edrnet.com>

ProQuest Information & Learning
300 North Zeeb Road
P.O. Box 1346
Ann Arbor, MI 48106-1346
(800) 521-0600
<www.proquest.com>

An important tip for using the ProQuest digitized collection is to look for the index to the map or a street index on the first sheet of the map. The index will tell you which sheet (or sheets) a particular street is located on, reducing your search time for a particular address. Sanborn maps recorded street names and addresses, so it is important to have a specific address in mind. A city directory published close to the time the Sanborn map was published will assist you in this endeavor. Remember that the names of owners were generally not recorded unless the name was part of a specific business or business block, and even then the maps usually recorded only generic designations, such as *dry goods store* or *opera house*.

Using Sanborn maps is a bit voyeuristic. The maps record intimate details of individual buildings, properties, and neighborhoods. After looking at a street your ancestor resided on, you can see the places nearby where he or she shopped, attended school or church, and worked. A city directory can give you the names of those neighbors and help fill in additional information about your ancestor's life. There really is no other source like them in American mapping history other than the county atlases for rural places. Besides reconstructing urban neighborhoods, one of the other values of fire insurance maps is assistance in identifying buildings in photographs or dating photographs.

Sources for Sanborn Fire Insurance Maps
Appendix A lists large map collections in the United States, some of which have fire insurance collections; these have been noted with an asterisk. For a more complete and continually updated list of institutions that own fire insurance maps (not just Sanborn), check the "Union List of Sanborn & Other Fire Insur-

Printed Source

ance Maps" at the University of California at Berkeley map library Web site <www.lib.berkeley.edu/EART/sanbul_about.html>. This is derived from an earlier publication: R. Phillip Hoehn, William S. Peterson-Hunt, and Evelyn L. Woodruff's *Union List of Sanborn Fire Insurance Maps Held by Institutions in the United States and Canada*, 2 vols. (Santa Cruz, Calif.: Western Association of Map Libraries, 1976–1977).

MAPS IN MUNICIPAL OFFICES, ARCHIVES, AND COURTS

The majority of historical maps related to cities are tucked away in files, boxes, basements, and storage units. These are the maps that were created to serve a specific purpose related to the administration, planning, and engineering of towns and cities. Unless donated with the personal papers of someone who worked for a city, they usually do not make their way into map collections. Some might be given to historical societies and museums, particularly if they are related to an important public work or issue, but sadly, most are seen as space wasters and eventually are tossed. Some larger cities maintain their own archives, in which case it is easier to locate old maps. For the most part, old city maps are scattered among several local agencies, including courts, and it takes a bit of patience and luck to locate them. They can be worth the time and effort; people's names do show up on these maps, particularly maps related to rights-of-way, easements, and street-widening projects.

Several important considerations:

- Learn the structure of the city, county, or court. As mentioned in chapter three, no two administrative units are structured in the same way. Find out how the planning department relates to the public works department: Are they separate entities? Are they the same department? Were they always separate? When did they split? The answers to these questions and others will help you decide where historical maps are filed. Sometimes departments retained the old records while spawning off a new department, as sometimes you will locate your ancestors' records in the parent county of the county in which they resided.

- Be considerate and sincere in your quest. The first local record custodian you ask may not be sure where to find the old map you are seeking. Be prepared to ask several different people the same question. You may be surprised how answers vary. You may also be surprised how often the location of old maps is part of the "corporate memory" of an agency—the oral history, if you will—that may or may not be imparted prior to someone leaving or retiring. You may find yourself asking the question at the tax assessor's office, the recorder's office, the public works department, and the historical society. Be patient.

- If you are looking for a specific property, make sure that you have both the street address and the parcel or tax assessor's number associated with that location. Street addresses changed in some cities as they grew. The street address on the census record or city directory may not be the most reliable guide, but an assessor's number combined with a property description will help keep you on track.

- Always be on the lookout for maps created for a special purpose, such as ethnic mapping or settlement patterns.

- Carry Mylar film or tissue paper for tracing or a digital camera in the event an old map cannot be photocopied because it is faded or too fragile. As described in chapter four, always note important information such as scale and symbols used on the map. You think you won't forget what they mean, but you will!

Summary Points

★ The variety of historical urban maps is dazzling, but most of the maps never find their way into map collections. Generally, they must be accessed through local municipal archives and courts.

★ Panoramic and bird's-eye-view maps provide important geographic information about cities in the early to mid-nineteenth century prior to most fire insurance mapping. Many of our ancestors purchased these maps and hung them on their walls as a form of art that was both decorative and useful.

★ The fire insurance map is the only widespread, large-scale urban mapping of North American cities in the late nineteenth and early twentieth centuries. If your ancestors dwelt in cities, this is a type of map you really should consult.

CHAPTER 10

Using Global Positioning Systems

GPS has become a global utility. It benefits users around the world in many different applications, including air, road, marine, and rail navigation, telecommunications, emergency response, oil exploration, mining, and many more [applications].

—*President William Clinton,* Statement Regarding the United States' Decision to Stop Degrading Global Positioning System Accuracy, *1 May 2000*

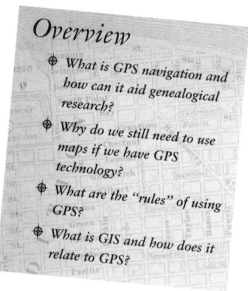

Overview

- What is GPS navigation and how can it aid genealogical research?
- Why do we still need to use maps if we have GPS technology?
- What are the "rules" of using GPS?
- What is GIS and how does it relate to GPS?

WHAT IS GPS NAVIGATION?

Whether you think it is a navigator's dream, an answered prayer to someone lost or in need of assistance, or the latest shiny new gadget available to consumers, Global Positioning System (GPS) navigation is here to stay for as long as the federal government allows the public to have access to it. The heart of the system is twenty-four satellites that began on a U.S. Department of Defense (DOD) drawing board as Navigation Satellite Timing and Ranging (NAVSTAR) in the early 1970s. DOD planners dreamed of a reliable system that would replace the old radio navigation system for air and sea travel.

Military users of NAVSTAR are able to locate any place on the earth within 3.28 feet (1 meter) accuracy. Civilian users can expect to be able to

HOW DOES A GPS OBTAIN DESTINATION INFORMATION?

There are several ways a GPS gets destination or *waypoint* information. The first way is to set a point after you have waited five minutes and acquired satellite position and give it a short name or assign it an icon that you will remember. The second way is obtaining location coordinates from a source such as a map and manually entering the location of the point (and give it a unique name or icon) into the memory of your unit. My GPS' memory can hold several hundred of these destinations in its memory. The third way you can obtain a waypoint is for someone to give you the coordinates and entering the information manually, or receiving the coordinates electronically via a signal between similarly equipped units. The fourth way is to download point coordinates from a Web site such as the Geocaching Web site <www.geocaching.com>.

locate something only within 10 to 30 feet (3 to 10 meters), but still have the advantages of a system that operates twenty-four hours a day, anywhere with a clear view of the sky, even in bad weather. The satellites orbit the earth twice a day at an altitude of about 11,000 miles. They continuously beam time-coded radio signals back to five ground stations on earth. These signals contain information about each satellite's position, altitude, and speed and are used by the ground stations to confirm each satellite's location from a fixed position on the earth. At any given time, eight to twelve satellites are available to your GPS receiver. The GPS calculates time and distance from the satellites in order to acquire a position and sense movement.

The GPS units come in many forms, from handheld versions the size of a cell phone to units mounted in cars, boats, semi trucks, and even farming equipment. GPS units are found integrated into cameras, cell phones, telescopes, two-way radios, personal digital assistants (PDAs), and a host of other consumer items. The most useful ones are the single-purpose units.

Around 1995, the public began using GPS units with a typical manufacturer's advertised accuracy of about 328 feet (100 meters). When many publicly available receivers routinely delivered an average accuracy closer to 82 feet (25 meters), the DOD became concerned about national defense and introduced a random error known as *selective availability* (SA) to radio signals received by the public. Until the year 2000 two types of signals were generated by the satellites: one for the military, which was highly accurate, and one for the public, which was less precise (accurate to about 100 meters). The quote at the beginning of this chapter was drawn from a statement made by President Clinton when the federal government eliminated SA for civilian use with the proviso that it could be reinstated at any time. Since that time, the DOD has figured out a means to degrade civilian GPS signals regionally—currently in the case of Iraq—rather than affecting the entire GPS system. In a short time the world has become dependent on GPS signals for civilian navigation in the air and on the seas, as well as emergency services on the ground. The disruption of the GPS system would be a disaster.

Warning

Accuracy can be affected by many conditions. For a GPS receiver to be fully functional, it must have a clear view of the sky. At times, the signal can appear to "bounce around," especially if you are standing under trees or walking near tall buildings, in a canyon, near a sheer rock wall, or around areas that have many reflective surfaces with metallic content or even snow. This is called *multipath error*. Although GPS receivers can work in the pouring rain (most are water resistant if not waterproof), shifts in the earth's ionosphere can affect their operation as a result of solar storms. The thicker the earth's ionosphere, the slower the radio signals travel through it. Atmospheric interference is sometimes referred to as *dithering*, which can cause errors of several meters.

Other types of error that can affect GPS units include the satellites breaking down or even wobbling a bit in their orbits. This situation can introduce error into their signals. A GPS unit receives a time correction every nanosecond and continuously updates its location with reference to the orbiting satellites. The smaller the difference in time between the satellite's atomic clock and your personal unit, the more accurate your location information will be. GPS units used for mapping by surveyors or the military rely on larger, more expensive equipment with external antennas and other paraphernalia that virtually eliminate that time gap.

For a GPS unit to work optimally, it should receive many satellite signals from a variety of positions spread across four quadrants of the sky. The twenty-four satellites constantly move through space, thus their positions relative to your position on earth also constantly change. Sometimes you might receive information from five satellites; other times you might have close to ten. This number changes continuously as satellites move in and out of range. Some GPS units display a satellite map showing where the satellites are located at that moment above your head. (See Figure 10-1 on page 199.) Your position is located at the center of the map. The inner circle on the map represents 45° above the horizon. The outer circle represents the horizon. The system works best when you receive information from at least four satellites spaced within that inner circle and at least one satellite within the outer ring. On a mountain or out in the ocean with a clear view of the horizon, theoretically you could receive information from as many as twelve or thirteen satellites. Three satellites sending you information is the minimum number required to operate your GPS, and five is best to achieve a consistent level of accuracy.

The GPS receiver calculates the distance from its position in your hand, car, or boat continuously. The system is designed to be most accurate when you occupy a location for three to five minutes. The compass of your GPS operates only when you are moving at least 1.5 miles per hour. Your navigation arrow locks on the last direction of movement, not the direction you are facing. The two rules of using a GPS for navigation to a selected destination are follow the arrow and close the distance to that point until it reaches zero, or very close to it.

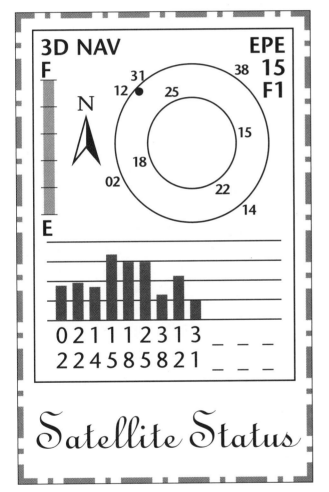

Figure 10-1
Sample map showing satellite positions and relative reception strength from a GPS unit. The inner circle represents 45° above the horizon, the outer circle represents the horizon. In this example, nine satellites are being tracked.

GPS AND GENEALOGICAL RESEARCH

You are probably thinking that this is all very interesting, but what is the payoff for genealogical research? With a GPS unit you can locate any point on the earth's surface within 30 feet or less (about 10 meters). Using a

Tip

GPS unit properly, you can expect to locate your ancestors' graves, house foundations, fields, libraries, courthouses, or any other cultural or physical feature with far greater precision than reading and estimating latitude and longitude off a topographic map. **With a handheld unit and a mapping program, you can walk and record property boundaries, fence lines, old roads, and any other linear feature you can imagine.** You can also estimate the acreage of land parcels using a GPS. Any point, line, or geometric figure can be located on the ground and on a map, no matter the age of the point for which you are searching. The location grid used by GPS satellites and receivers is based on either the familiar geographical location system of latitude and longitude or the military-based Universal Transverse Mercator (UTM) system, both of which have been used to chart land for many years and will be around for a long time to come. Grave sites can become lost, buildings knocked down, and house foundations removed, but the coordinates of where they were located can be permanently noted and useful for future generations.

Genealogist and technology guru Beau Sharbrough says in his article

Figure 10-2
Sample screen showing navigational bearing. Remember to keep moving when using a GPS unit for navigation—otherwise you may obtain an erroneous location. Many GPS units allow you to adjust the compass so the arrow can represent direction of movement or behave as a traditional compass.

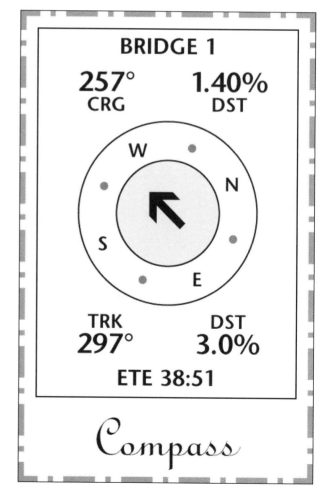

"Rootworks: Travel, Part 1—GPS" (*Ancestry Daily News*, 23 August 2001) <www.ancestry.com/library/view/news/articles/4462.asp> that one of the less obvious benefits of using GPS is saving time; a GPS can help you plan a trip and prevent you from getting lost in unfamiliar surroundings. Rather than waste time looking for a grave site, the library, the hotel, or the gas station, you can program in coordinates of a goal or use a saved *waypoint*, a position that you marked with your GPS during a previous visit. For urban explorations, you can use waypoints with trip planning software such as Microsoft's Streets & Trips, Rand McNally's TripMaker Deluxe, or De-Lorme's AAA Map 'n' Go. For rural expeditions you can use Maptech's Terrain Navigator Pro or National Geographic's Topo!, which are electronic versions of USGS 7.5-minute quads. Many electronic atlases are available on the market; you need to check them out either in the store or on the Web to see which one is compatible with your GPS unit and your personal computer.

Where do you find coordinates, especially if you haven't been to a location and set a waypoint yourself? Increasingly, city's chamber of commerce Web sites or other sites promoting local attractions list geographic coordinates. You can use the Geographic Names Information System (GNIS) to obtain latitude and longitude for any place-named on a USGS quad (refer to chapter two). You can also measure latitude and longitude or UTM grid coordinates yourself from a USGS topographic map with a sharp pencil and a centimeter ruler. The publication "An Introduction to Using a Garmin GPS with Paper Maps for Land Navigation," available online for free from Garmin International <www.garmin.com/manuals/UsingaGarminGPSwith PaperLandMaps_Manual.pdf>, has a handy mapping tool you can copy onto overhead projector film to use in reading and converting latitude/longitude and UTM coordinates from maps. See chapter five for how to locate latitude and longitude and UTM grid ticks in the collar of a topographic map. You can convert your measurements with great ease for use with your GPS to whatever datum format you need at JeEep.com <http://jeeep.com/details/coord>. Your measurements may not be absolutely precise, but you will have enough information to input the coordinates needed to get you close to your intended goal.

The USGenWeb Project hosts a Web site, "G.P.S. Satellite Mapping" <www.rootsweb.com/~scoconee/gps_lxl.html>, that provides information and links to using GPS in genealogical research, specifically the mapping of cemeteries.

You can generate a quick map showing a location you have marked with your GPS unit by using MapQuest. You can input your position in MapQuest in latitude and longitude <www.mapquest.com/maps/latlong.adp> using either degrees, minutes, seconds (00° 00″ 00.0′) or decimal values

(00.0000). In North America, you always need to remember to place a minus sign (-) in front of the longitude coordinate to indicate our position *west* of Greenwich, England.

An obvious use of GPS in genealogical research is the US GeoGen Project, a national network of county Web pages that lists locations of interest with their geographical coordinates <http://geogen.org>. Project organizer Bob Maley is looking for volunteers to contribute geographical coordinates and links to personal Web pages that contain information about locations. The database listing these coordinates is free to all and is searchable by type of feature (cemetery, ghost town, monument, mine, homestead, or historical post office), waypoint, state, county, or latitude and longitude.

MAPPING CEMETERIES WITH GPS

Using a GPS to locate a grave site or cemetery is one of the best means for preserving its location for future generations. No matter what happens to the individual markers or even the entire cemetery, the location can be traced using its geographic coordinates. Some genealogical database programs, such as The Master Genealogist by Wholly Genes Software, include geographic coordinates as part of the description of places where historical events occurred.

Notes

You can use a GPS in several ways to assist you in mapping a cemetery. First, you can stand in the middle of a cemetery and create a waypoint that represents the general location of the cemetery. You can also use GPS to mark individual grave locations within a cemetery, keeping in mind that precise locations from publicly available GPS units can be difficult to reliably achieve and depend on satellite reception. Your GPS can double as a tape measure to measure distances across the cemetery or between stones, which will help you describe the cemetery on sketch maps you draw or create using a mapping program. An example of marking individual grave sites and creating an online database is James A. Shepherd II and Barbara Barrett Kitterman Shepherd's "Kitterman Cemetery" <http://soli.inav.net/~shepherd/kitt/kit_cem/cem1.html>. The cemetery is located in Wapello County, Iowa.

The GPS can be used as a compass to locate the cardinal directions and orientation of headstones, but only as you are walking. Unless your GPS is equipped with a magnetic compass option, don't try to take a compass reading while standing still.

Step By Step

Another way to use a GPS is to mark the corners of the cemetery (as best you can find them). You can use your GPS as a tape measure and measure the distance along a boundary by setting a waypoint on one corner and walking to the next and noting the distance reading from the waypoint. On a sheet of graph paper you can draw each side of the cemetery and then calculate the area of the enclosed shape or use the GPS to calculate the area for you. A trick to using a GPS to estimate an area in acres is to walk along each boundary without stopping until you come to within 20 or 30 feet from your starting point. There, stop and ask the GPS to calculate area. By not closing the boundaries of the cemetery, the acreage will be approximate. The GPS will not calculate the acreage if it detects that you have crossed your track, which is why you stop about 30 feet away from your starting point. An online example of how GPS helped document a missing section of an old cemetery by comparing the modern area configuration to a 1944 German air force aerial photograph is described at Thomas F. Weiss's "Jewish Cemetery in Rozhnyatov" <www.shtetlinks.jewishgen.org/Rozhnyatov/RozhCemetery.html>.

Robert L. Brown has posted an elaborate map of cemetery locations at "Cemeteries on USGS Maps: Laurel County, Kentucky" <www.cem-maps.com/usgskylaurel.htm>. The map displays the geographic coordinates for each cemetery as you move your computer's cursor over the mapped cemetery location. Each cemetery has been located using a GPS. The map has GPS coordinates, links to GNIS, links to USGS maps via TerraServer, and links to the U.S. Census Bureau TIGER map showing each cemetery location. Each cemetery entry is annotated to indicate whether it is shown in GNIS, and its USGS quad is identified.

See these additional sources for more information:

Birth, Elvin E. "Technology Improves County Cemetery Survey." *Genealogical Computing* 18 (Winter 1999). <www.ancestry.com/library/view/gencomp/2186.asp>.

Johnson, Steve Paul. "Using a GPS Device." *The Cemetery Column* (8 January 2001). <www.interment.net/column/records/gps>.

"Use of GPS in Locating a Cemetery or Gravesites." *Saving Graves.* <www.savinggraves.org/education/print/gps.htm>.

DO WE STILL NEED MAPS?

A GPS receiver should never be used as a replacement for a map, but rather in conjunction with a map, traditional compass (to double-check direction and in case the GPS breaks or runs out of batteries), and common sense. You still need a map to orient yourself, observe detailed information about terrain and cultural features, and obtain important information such as geographic grid location (latitude and longitude or UTM). Your GPS might give you a bearing to follow and can display a map on its screen if you have downloaded map information from a CD or off the Web. However, depending on the map software, the tiny maps displayed on some handheld models have so little detail that you might have difficulty locating yourself in the landscape and not be able to tell what obstacles lie between you and your intended goal. A GPS tells you the straight-line path ("as the crow flies") between positions or waypoints. You may need to alter your GPS-recommended course to avoid obstacles or dangerous conditions, and you'll need a map to do it.

Never assume that the GPS is going to do all the work for you and tell you exactly where to go, and don't presume that you're ready for a jaunt into unfamiliar territory just because you're armed with a GPS and a cell phone. Your GPS unit may not work and you might not have cell phone reception even close to a town because of lack of antenna coverage or interference with terrain. You place yourself and your theoretical rescuers in potential danger when you aren't properly prepared with a map, compass, extra batteries, clothing appropriate for the environment, and common sense.

ON THE ROAD WITH GPS

A fun way to use your GPS is to connect it to a laptop computer and head out on the road. The small screen on a GPS unit can be difficult to see. When you attach it to a laptop, your navigator can enjoy a larger, more detailed map view. It can actually be quite mesmerizing to watch your position move along the map depicted on the laptop's screen.

Many possible combinations of GPS, laptop, and map software are available, so remarks in this section will be general.

Important

Minimally, what you will need is:

- A laptop with plenty of disk space to accommodate map software. (Read the software requirements before you purchase, because you will load the CD contents into the laptop, unless you don't mind switching disks during the trip.)
- Electronic map software that either depicts streets for urban driving or topographic maps for driving through the countryside. (For example, I use Topo! by National Geographic.)
- A GPS unit with the ability to export information to the laptop computer.
- An adapter that will draw power from the cigarette lighter socket in the car and send data from the GPS unit to the laptop computer. Typically, these adapters have Y-shaped wires. The bottom of the Y plugs into the car, leaving one wire each for the GPS and the serial port on the laptop. My Garmin eTrex Legend uses a Pfranc eCombo cable. If your laptop has a USB port but no serial port, you can purchase a port converter or a special USB-to-serial port cable—search for manufacturers online.

It takes three to five minutes to acquire satellite reception with the GPS propped up on the dashboard of the car. The GPS unit should stay on the dashboard or be held by your navigator near the window to maintain contact with the satellites as you travel. You can use Velcro to attach the GPS to the dashboard.

All manner of GPS units are available, plus corresponding software and laptop configurations. Trip planning software can help you locate specific addresses, direct your turns by audible voice commands, estimate trip time and expenses by legs, and many other features. You can find any number of articles online that compare the features of map software. As in anything else having to do with electronics, price is dictated by the amount of features: The more bells and whistles, the greater the cost. I enjoy using Topo! because it saves the track I drove and allows me to annotate maps with text. I can print topographic maps in color for the entire trip or any segment of it in either two-dimensional or three-dimensional view.

For other setups with a GPS and laptop, you might want to consult the articles by Sharbrough, Kerstens, or Eastman mentioned elsewhere in this chapter.

ADVICE FOR USING GPS

- Never turn on the GPS receiver and immediately mark a waypoint; wait three to five minutes until you have reception from four or five satellites. This is one of the most common errors people make when using GPS units. Wait those extra few moments next to that tombstone or parked vehicle before marking its location and heading off to your next target!

- Weird but true: A GPS unit *is not* a compass unless you are moving at least 1.5 miles per hour. It can tell you direction *only* if you are moving. Always take a compass to check where north is. Many types of good compasses priced at about $20 are available at your local sporting goods store. Look for one that can be adjusted to accommodate magnetic declination. Do not rely on a compass that comes on a keychain or as a cereal box prize. They are not made to be accurate. In an emergency, your wristwatch can double as a compass to estimate the location of north. Be sure it is set to the correct time zone, then hold the watch horizontally and point the hour hand at the sun. South will be located halfway between the hour hand and twelve o' clock. North will be directly opposite that. Your genealogy comrades will be duly impressed by your display of geographic panache.

- Always pack extra batteries. This is a mistake you need to make only once to ruin a research trip.

- Make sure your GPS is advertised as waterproof. If not, carry several resealable sandwich bags to encase your GPS unit and keep it dry if rain is predicted.
- When venturing out into unfamiliar territory on foot or by car on lonely back roads, take a buddy with you. Let people know where you are going. If you plan to park your car and then hike, leave a note somewhere in the car as to where you are going. Even a cemetery in an urban area in broad daylight can be unsafe. Use common sense and be aware of your surroundings and not so fixed on your GPS's screen that you step into a gopher hole at a cemetery, trip over a tree root, or fall off a curb (said sheepishly by one who has done all three).
- Do not trust elevation information unless your GPS is equipped with an altimeter to measure it. Receivers without an altimeter may be off by as much as 200 feet. Those with an altimeter may be able to measure elevation within 5 feet.
- Bad information in means bad information out. Be careful of the format of the coordinate points you put into your GPS. Always input information in the proper datum and the proper position format. The most common is WGS 84 (World Geodetic System of 1984), which is programmed into most GPS units at the factory (dd mm.mmm or 00, 00.000). At one time there was no internationally recognized prime meridian. In the absence of a single geographic coordinate system, nations began mapping their countries based on their own *datum*, or fixed starting point from which they commenced their mapping. Historical latitude and longitude coordinates in different datums may look similar to those in use today, but they won't be same. That difference can get you into trouble if you are not aware of which datum is being used. Topographic maps use either NAD-

For More Info

NAD-27 AND NAD-83

These stand for *North American Datum of 1927* and *North American Datum of 1983*. A datum is a mathematical model that represents the three-dimensional earth's sphere on a two-dimensional map. A datum can be used to describe one portion of the earth or the entire earth as in WGS-84 (internationally recognized World Geodetic Survey of 1984). Over the centuries many different datums were used to create maps. The number preceding the words "North American Datum" reflects the year a particular model was selected to be used to construct maps depicting North America. Most USGS maps rely on the NAD-27 or NAD-83.

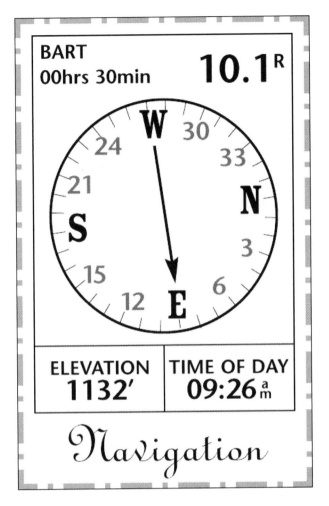

BART
00hrs 30min   10.1ᴿ

ELEVATION
1132′

TIME OF DAY
09:26 ᵃₘ

Navigation

Figure 10-3
Datum information from a USGS topographic quadrangle is found in the lower left hand corner of the map. A very common error committed by new users of GPS devices is to use a datum source that is different than the one used to compile the map they are using. Most GPS receivers come pre-programmed with WGS-84 which is different than the datum used on USGS topographic maps. Be sure to consult your GPS owner's manual and find out how to check your datum source before heading out on a trip.
Source: USGS

27 (North American Datum of 1927) or NAD-83 (North American Datum of 1983), depending on the government agency or commercial mapmaker who published the map. On a USGS topo quad, you will find the datum information in the lower left-hand corner of the map. (See Figure 10-3 above.) Consult the instructions that came with your GPS to check the datum that is being used to display coordinates. Make sure that you check it periodically, especially if you have loaned your GPS to someone else who may have intentionally or unintentionally reset the datum. If the datum in the GPS does not match the map datum, location coordinates could be off by hundreds of yards if not a mile or two.

- Clear the track log before you set out to ensure you have enough memory to record all your route points and retrace your steps.
- Program at least one or two waypoints that you are familiar with (like the location of your home) so that when you turn your GPS on you can check and make sure that it is working properly.

- If you want to practice using a GPS, try *geocaching*. Geocaching is a game in which people hide objects in a given location, log the GPS coordinates online, and let others attempt to find the location of the hidden "treasure," or cache. Sometimes the coordinates take you to a box of trinkets that you can exchange with trinkets you bring along or to a particularly scenic or historic location. Some geocaches are located in and around cemeteries, but their placement is guided by strict game rules involving public access and no possible harm to tombstones and premises. You can find out more about geocaching online at Geocaching.com <www.geocaching.com> or by consulting Mike Dyer's *The Essential Guide to Geocaching: Tracking Treasure with Your GPS* (Golden, Colo.: Fulcrum Publishing, 2004).

SOURCES OF INFORMATION

Since GPS became popular, a number of books and Web sites regarding the subject have appeared on the market. Below is a selected list to get you started learning how to use your unit to its maximum potential or to finding guidance on purchasing one. As with all consumer electronics, any recommendations published in books or posted on the Web become outdated quickly due to continual improvements in technology. Your local community college or recreation department may also offer a course in using a GPS.

Books

Featherstone, Steve. *Outdoor Guide to Using Your GPS*. Chanhassen, Minn.: Creative Publishing International, 2004. This book has practical exercises to help you become more adept at using a GPS.

Ferguson, Michael. *GPS Land Navigation*. Boise, Idaho: Glassford Publishing, 1997. This book is becoming dated, but the procedures outlined hold even for contemporary GPS units.

Online

Bartlett, Don. "A Practical Guide to GPS-UTM." <www.dbartlett.com>. Geared to hikers, hunters, and fisherman, but has practical information about using GPS.

Dana, Peter H. "Global Positioning System Overview." *The Geographer's Craft Project*. <http://colorado.edu/geography/gcraft/notes/gps/gps_f .html>.

Eastman, Dick. "Using a GPS for Genealogy." *Eastman's Online Genealogy Newsletter* (10 April 2002). <www.ancestry.com/library/view/colu mns/eastman/5528.asp>.

Garmin International. *An Introduction to Using a Garmin GPS with Paper Maps for Land Navigation.* Olathe, Kan.: Garmin International, 2003. <www.garmin.com/manuals/UsingaGarminGPSwithPaperLand Maps_
Manual.pdf>.

——. *GPS Guide for Beginners.* Olanthe, Kan.: Garmin International, 2000. <www.garmin.com/manuals/GPSGuideforBeginners_Manual .pdf>. Both Garmin manuals are excellent references even if you do not own a Garmin GPS.

Kerstens, Elizabeth Kelley. "Lost? Get a GPS." *Genealogical Computing Extra* (6 July 2000). <www.ancestry.com/library/view/gencomp/ 1871.asp>.

Mehaffey, Joe, Jack Yeazel, and Dale DePriest. "GPS Information Website." <http://gpsinformation.net>. This is a great place to start your GPS research because it has reviews of hardware and software as well as tutorials.

Trimble Navigation. "All About GPS." <www.trimble.com/gps/index .html>.

Summary Points

★ A GPS is not a compass. It is a navigational tool to be used with a map, a traditional compass, and a bit of common sense.

★ Consider using a GPS in conjunction with a map (paper or digital version) to locate places relevant to your family. Record the geographic coordinates for posterity in your genealogical database as part of the place description or even in the notes section.

★ Reread the GPS "rules" in this chapter.

★ Make sure your datums match—those on the map and those you input into the GPS, as well as those shared between GPS users or found on Web sites. Specify in your genealogy notes which datum you used.

Major Map Collections in the United States

Note: Asterisk denotes major fire insurance map collections.

Alabama

Alabama Department of History and Archives, Montgomery
Auburn University, Auburn
Birmingham Public Library, Birmingham*
Samford University, Birmingham
University of Alabama, Tuscaloosa*

Alaska

Alaska State Historical Library, Juneau*
University of Alaska, Fairbanks

Arizona

Arizona Historical Society, Tucson*
Arizona State Archives, Phoenix*
Arizona State University, Tempe*
University of Arizona, Tucson*

Arkansas

Arkansas State Archives, Little Rock*
University of Arkansas, Fayetteville*

California

California Historical Society, San Francisco*
California Institute of Technology, Pasadena
California State Library, Sacramento*
California State University, Chico*
California State University East Bay, Hayward*
California State University, Fresno
California State University, Northridge*
California State University, Sacramento*
Claremont Colleges, Claremont*
Humboldt State University, Arcata
The Huntington Library, San Marino*
Los Angeles Public Library*
Naval Post Graduate School, Monterey
Oakland Public Library*

Pomona Public Library*
San Diego Public Library*
San Francisco Public Library*
Sonoma State University, Sonoma
Stanford University, Palo Alto*
Whittier College, Whittier
University of California, Berkeley*
University of California, Davis*
University of California, Los Angeles*
University of California, Riverside
University of California, Santa Barbara*
University of California, Santa Cruz*
University of California, San Diego*

Colorado

Colorado School of Mines, Golden
Denver Public Library, Denver*
State Historical Society, Denver*
University of Colorado, Boulder*

Connecticut

Bridgeport Public Library, Bridgeport*
Connecticut State Library, Hartford*
New London County Historical Society, New London*
University of Connecticut, Storrs*
Yale University, New Haven*

Delaware

Delaware Public Archives, Dover
Historical Society of Delaware, Wilmington*
University of Delaware, Newark

District of Columbia

District of Columbia Public Library
Library of Congress*
National Archives
National Geographic Society

Florida

Florida State University, Tallahassee*
Miami-Dade Public Library, Miami*
Miami University, Coral Gables

State Library of Florida, Tallahassee*
University of Florida, Gainesville*
University of West Florida, Pensacola

Georgia

The Georgia Archives, Morrow
Georgia Historical Society, Savannah*
Georgia Institute of Technology, Atlanta*
University of Georgia, Athens*

Hawaii

Bishop Museum, Honolulu*
Brigham Young University, Laie
Hawaii State Archives, Honolulu*
Lyman Museum, Hilo*
University of Hawaii, Hilo
University of Hawaii, Honolulu*

Idaho

Boise State University, Boise
Idaho State Historical Library, Boise
Idaho State University, Pocatello
University of Idaho, Moscow*

Illinois

Chicago Historical Society*
Illinois State University, Bloomington*
The Newberry Library, Chicago*
Northwestern University, Evanston*
Southern Illinois University, Carbondale*
University of Chicago, Chicago
University of Illinois, Urbana*

Indiana

Allen County Public Library, Fort Wayne*
Ball State University, Muncie
Indiana State Library, Indianapolis*
Indiana University, Bloomington*
Purdue University, Lafayette

Iowa

Burlington Public Library*
Iowa State University, Ames

State Historical Society of Iowa, Iowa City*
University of Iowa, Iowa City*

Kansas
Kansas State Historical Society, Topeka*
University of Kansas, Lawrence*
Wichita State University, Wichita

Kentucky
Kentucky Historical Society, Frankfort
Kentucky Libraries and Archives, Frankfort
University of Kentucky, Lexington*

Louisiana
Louisiana State University, Baton Rouge*
New Orleans Public Library*
State Library of Louisiana, Baton Rouge*
Tulane University, New Orleans
Williams Research Center of the Historic New Orleans Collection

Maine
Bangor Public Library, Bangor*
Colby College, Waterville
Maine Historical Society, Portland*
Maine State Archives, Augusta
University of Maine, Orono*
University of Southern Maine, Portland

Maryland
Enoch Pratt Free Library, Baltimore*
Johns Hopkins University, Baltimore
Maryland State Archives, Annapolis
National Archives, Cartographic and Architectural Branch, College Park
University of Maryland, College Park*

Massachusetts
American Antiquarian Society, Worcester*
The Bostonian Society, Boston*
Clark University, Worcester*
Harvard University, Cambridge*
Massachusetts Archives at Columbia Point, Boston
Massachusetts Historical Society, Boston

Massachusetts Institute of Technology, Cambridge*
New England Historic Genealogical Society, Boston
State Library of Massachusetts, Boston*
Tufts University, Medford
University of Massachusetts, Amherst

Michigan

Detroit Public Library, Detroit*
Eastern Michigan University, Ypsilanti
Library of Michigan, Lansing
Michigan State University, East Lansing
Michigan State Archives, Lansing*
University of Michigan, Ann Arbor
Western Michigan University, Kalamazoo*

Minnesota

Minneapolis Public Library, Minneapolis*
Minnesota Historical Society, St. Paul*
Saint John's University, Collegeville*
University of Minnesota, Minneapolis*

Mississippi

Mississippi Department of Archives and History, Jackson
Mississippi State University, State College*

Missouri

Mercantile Library, St. Louis
Missouri State Archives, Jefferson City
Missouri Historical SocietyLibrary and Research Center, St. Louis*
St. Louis Public Library, St. Louis*
State Historical Society of Missouri, Columbia
University of Missouri, Columbia*

Montana

Montana Historical Society, Helena*
Montana State Library, Helena
Montana State University, Billings

Nebraska

Nebraska State Historical Society, Lincoln*
University of Nebraska, Lincoln*

Nevada
Nevada Historical Society, Reno*
Nevada State Library and Archives, Carson City
University of Nevada, Reno*

New Hampshire
Dartmouth College, Hanover*
Keene State College, Keene
New Hampshire Division of Records Management and Archives,
    Concord
New Hampshire Historical Society, Concord*
New Hampshire State Library, Concord*

New Jersey
New Jersey Historical Society, Newark*
New Jersey State Archives, Trenton
New Jersey State Library, Trenton
Rutgers University, New Brunswick*

New Mexico
Albuquerque Museum, Albuquerque*
New Mexico Institute of Mining and Technology, Socorro
New Mexico State Library, Santa Fe
New Mexico State Records Center and Archives, Santa Fe
University of New Mexico, Albuquerque*

New York
Brooklyn Historical Society, Brooklyn*
Brooklyn Public Library*
Buffalo and Erie County Public Library*
Columbia University, New York
Cornell University, Ithaca*
Hamilton College Library, Clinton*
Farmingdale State University, Farmingdale*
New York Historical Society, New York*
New York Public Library, New York*
State University of New York at Binghamton
State University of New York at Stony Brook
Syracuse University, Syracuse*
United Nations Library, New York
U.S. Military Academy, West Point

North Carolina
Appalachia State University, Boone
Duke University, Durham
North Carolina State Archives, Raleigh*
University of North Carolina, Chapel Hill*

North Dakota
Minot State College, Minot
North Dakota State Library, Bismarck
North Dakota State University, Fargo
State Archives and Historical Research Library, Bismarck
University of North Dakota, Grand Forks

Ohio
Bowling Green State University, Bowling Green
Kent State University, Kent*
Ohio Historical Society, Columbus*
Ohio State University, Columbus*
Toledo-Lucas County Public Library, Toledo*
Western Reserve Historical Society, Cleveland*

Oklahoma
Oklahoma Historical Society, Oklahoma City
Oklahoma State University, Stillwater
University of Oklahoma, Norman*

Oregon
Oregon Historical Society, Portland*
Oregon State Library, Salem*
Oregon State University, Corvallis*
Portland State University, Portland*
Southern Oregon University, Ashland
University of Oregon, Eugene

Pennsylvania
Bryn Mawr College, Bryn Mawr*
Carnegie Library, Pittsburgh
Free Library of Philadelphia*
Historical Society of Pennsylvania, Philadelphia*
Kutztown University, Kutztown
Pennsylvania State Archives, Harrisburg
Pennsylvania State University, University Park*

State Library of Pennsylvania, Harrisburg
Temple University, Philadelphia
University of Pennsylvania, Philadelphia
University of Pittsburgh, Pittsburgh

Rhode Island

Brown University, Providence*
Newport Historical Society, Newport*
Princeton University, Princeton
Rhode Island Historical Society, Providence*

South Carolina

The Citadel, Charleston
South Carolina Department of Archives and History, Columbia
University of South Carolina, Columbia*

South Dakota

South Dakota State Historical Society, Pierre
University of South Dakota, Vermillion

Tennessee

Chattanooga Public Library, Chattanooga*
East Tennessee History Center, Knoxville
Tennessee State Library and Archives, Nashville*
University of Tennessee, Knoxville*
Vanderbilt University, Nashville

Texas

Dallas Public Library, Dallas*
El Paso Public Library, El Paso*
Southern Methodist University, Dallas
Texas A&M University, College Station*
Texas State Library, Austin
University of Texas at Austin, Austin*
University of Texas at El Paso, El Paso*

Utah

Brigham Young University, Provo*
Family History Library, Salt Lake City
Salt Lake City Public Library*
University of Utah, Salt Lake City*

Vermont

Middlebury College, Middlebury
University of Vermont, Burlington*
Vermont Historical Society Library, Barre
Vermont State Archives, Montpelier

Virginia

Library of Virginia, Richmond*
United States Geological Survey Library, Reston
University of Virginia, Charlottesville*
Virginia Historical Society, Richmond
Virginia State Library, Richmond*
Virginia Tech University, Blacksburg

Washington

Central Washington State, Ellensburg*
Evergreen State College, Olympia
Seattle Public Library, Seattle*
Spokane Public Library
University of Washington, Seattle*
Washington State Library, Olympia
Washington State University, Pullman
Western Washington University, Bellingham

West Virginia

Archives and History Library, Charleston
West Virginia University, Morgantown*

Wisconsin

American Geographical Society Library, University of Wisconsin-
  Milwaukee, Milwaukee
Milwaukee Public Library*
Wisconsin Historical Society, Madison*
University of Wisconsin, Madison*
University of Wisconsin-Milwaukee, Milwaukee

Wyoming

Office of the State Engineer, Cheyenne
University of Wyoming, Laramie*

Index

A

Administrative Subdivisions of Countries, 55
Aerial photos, military, 168
African Americans, relocation of, 147
Alexandria Digital Library Gazetteer Server, The, 36
Aliquot parts, 125, 127
American Counties: Origins of County Names, Dates of Creation and Organization, Area, Population Including 1980 Census Figures, Historical Data, and Published Sources, 52
American FactFinder, 40
American Indian
    land, 131
    place-names, 16
    relocation, 147
    trails, 150
American Memory Web site, 82-83
American Reference Books Annual, 29
Ancestry's Red Book: American State, County & Town Sources, 28, 46, 48-49, 54
Atlases, 3, 32, 51, 54, 133
    citing, 90-93
    Commercial Atlas & Marketing Guide, 31, 54, 133
    county, 135-142
    county, locating, 140
    electronic, 114
    hachures on, 101
    Historical Atlas of United States Congressional Districts, The, 51
    history of, 84
    landownership, 140-141
    migration trail, 147
    road, 17
    surnames in, 140-142
Atlas of American Migration, 147
Atlas of Congressional Roll Calls, 51

B

Bar scale, 81-82
Baseline, principal, 124
Bibliographies, place-name, 28-30
    See also Citations, map and atlas
Bibliography of American County Histories, A, 48
Bird's-eye maps, 184-187
Blueprinting, 183-184

Books in Print, 29
Boundaries
    changes to, 5, 27
    county, 21, 42-55, 61, 63 (*see also* Counties)
Boundaries, jurisdictional, 10-11, 27, 41-63
    boroughs, 42, 46-47
    city-county, consolidated, 47
    See also Cities, independent; Counties; Precincts; Townships; Ward maps
Bureau of Land Management
    maps, 107
    records, 129

C

California in the Fifties: Fifty Views of Cities and Mining Towns in California and the West, 187
Cambridge Gazetteer of the United States and Canada, The, 30
Cambridge World Gazetteer: A Geographical Dictionary, 30
Cardinal points, 80-81
Cartofact, defined, 5
Cartographic Citations: A Style Guide, 90
Cemeteries, 78, 110
    mapping, 202-203
Census Bureau, 52-53
    U.S. Gazetteer: 2000 and 1990, 38-39
Censuses, 49-50, 56, 62, 141
    maps of, 49, 59-61
See also Enumeration districts; Precincts; Ward maps
Censuses, resources about
    Century of Population Growth, from the First Census of the United States to the Twelfth, 1790-1900, A, 56-57
    Descriptions of Census Enumeration Districts, 1830-1890 and 1910–1950, 57
    Map Guide to the U.S. Federal Censuses, 49, 147
    1930 Census: A Reference and Research Guide, The, 60-61
    1930 Census Microfilm Locator, 61
    Records of the Bureau of the Census, 59
    Your Guide to the Federal Census, 57
Checklist of Printed Maps of the Middle

West to 1900, 151
Citations, map and atlas, 90-94
Cities, independent, 47, 51
Cities, references about
    *Early Maps of Some of the Cities of
    the United States, ca. 1850–1877,*
    62
    *Handy Guide to Record-Searching in
    the Larger Cities of the United
    States, A,* 62
City-county, consolidated, 47
City directories, 62-63
City maps, 62
Coasts and islands, maps of, 108, 164
Collections, map, by state, 210-218
*Columbia Gazetteer of North America,
    The,* 30-31
Columbia Gazetteer of the World, The,
    31
*Columbia Lippincott Gazetteer of the
    World, The,* 31
Compass, using a, 80
    See also Triangulation
Coordinates, location, 17, 40, 71, 77,
    200-202, 206-207, 209
Coordinate systems, 69, 71, 76-78
    converting, 94
Counties
    boundaries for, changes to, 42, 48-53,
      147
    boundaries for, locating, 54-55, 61,
      104
    extinct, 47-48
    histories of, 137-140
    "Old Boundary Line Blues, The," 43
    resources about, 48-53, 56
Counties, formation of, 42-55, 61, 63
    boundaries, 21
    exceptions to, 42
    gerrymandering, 43
    land speculation, 43
    New York, 45-46
    Pennsylvania, 46
    Virginia, 44
Counties, formation of, models for,
    43-46
    mixed, 43, 45-46
    New England, 43, 45
    New York, 45-46
    Southern, 43-44
Countries, foreign, 55
County maps, 12, 107, 135-142
County rule, exceptions to, 44, 46-47
Culture, researching, 7-8, 10
    features of, on maps, 97, 128
Cyndi's List: Maps, Gazetteers & Geo-
    graphical Information, 35

D
Deeds, platting, 122-123
Descriptions, legal, 41
Dictionaries
    geographical, 30-31
    place-name, 17-18, 29
    topographical, 17-18
Division of Territory in Society, The, 43

E
Earth Science Information Centers,
    111-112
Enumeration districts, 55-62
    descriptions of, 57-59, 61
    *Enumeration District Maps for the Fif-
      teenth Census of the United States,
      1930,* 59
    *Index to Selected City Streets and Enu-
      meration Districts, 1930 Census,*
      60
    maps of, 55-57, 59-61
Ethnic groups, migration of, 146,
    152-153
*Evidence! Citation & Analysis for the
    Family Historian,* 90-91

F
Family History Library, 33-35
*Family Tree Resource Book for Genealo-
    gists, The,* 28, 48-49, 54
*Field Notes from Selected General Land
    Office Township Surveys,* 130
Fire insurance maps, 183-195
    revisions to, 191-192
    Sanborn Map Company, 189-194
    scale of, 188, 191
    sources of, 192-195, 210
"Fire Insurance Maps as Primary Historic
    Records," 189
*Fire Insurance Maps in the Library of
    Congress,* 192

G
Gazetteers, 16-20, 24-25
    features of, geographic, 18
    major, 30-32
    Newsman's Interpreter, The, 19
    on road maps, 76
    U.S. Board on Geographic Names, 20,
      26-27
    worldwide, 36-37
Gazetteers, locating, 28-30, 35-40
    bibliographies, 28-30
    CDs, 39
    Family History Library, 33-35
    foreign, 33
    online, 34-40

resources for, 32-35
resources for, government, 32-33, 37-39
search tips for, 26-27
Genealogical and Local History Books in Print, 30
"Genealogical Geography: Place Identification in the Map Library," 25
GenealogyTools.net, 122
General Land Office, 53
  field notes, 130
  plats, 129, 131
  records, 132
  surveys, special, 131
Geographer's line, 124
Geographical Imagination in America, 1880–1950, The, 84
Geographic Names and the Federal Government: A Bibliography, 33
Geographic Names Information System, 30
"Geographic Tools: Maps, Atlases, and Gazetteers," 28, 146
Geography
  "About Geography," Web site, 94
  features of, in gazetteers, 18
  hundreds, defined, 44
  speculative, 146
Getty Thesaurus of Geographic Names Online, 36
Global Gazetteer: Directory of Cities and Towns in World, 36
Global Positioning Systems, 17, 77, 196-209
  accuracy of, 198-200
  cemetery mapping, 201-203
  and compasses, 205
  coordinates for, 17, 77, 200-202, 206-207, 209
  datum for, 206-207, 209
  dithering, 198
  genealogical use of, 199-203
  geocaching, 208
  multipath error, 198
  references about, 203, 208-209
  selective availability, 197
  software for, 17, 114-115, 201, 204-205
  traveling with, 204-205
  use advice, 205-208
  waypoints, 197, 201-202, 205, 207
Graves, military, 166-167
  See also Cemeteries
Guide to Cartographic Records in the National Archives, 176
Guide to Federal Records in the National Archives of the United States, 32, 51
Guide to Reference Books, 29

H
Handybook for Genealogists, The, 28, 49, 54, 147-148
Heavens-Above, database, place-name, 36-37
Historical Atlas and Chronology of County Boundaries 1788-1980, 49-51
How Tis Done: A Through Ventilation of the Numerous Schemes Conducted by Wandering Canvassers, Together with the Various Advertising Dodges for the Swindling of the Public, 138

I
Isobaths, 108

J
"Jewish Cemetery in Rozhnyatov," 203
Jewish heritage, 31-32
Jurisdiction. *See* Boundaries, jurisdictional

L
Land & Property Research in the United States, 118, 129
Land, division of, 116-142
  arpents, 118
  butts and bounds, 119-120
  calls, 120-122
  expedientes, 119
  French, 118
  headright farms, 120
  indiscriminate location, 117
  measurement conversions, 120, 123, 125
  metes and bounds, 117-123
  Locating Your Roots: Discover Your Ancestors Using Land Records, 120-122, 125, 127
  Spanish, 118-119
  systematic, 117-118
  understanding, 130-131
  vara, 119
Landforms, maps of, 108
Land grants
  online, 132
  Spanish and Mexican, 119
Legal patent descriptions, 132-133
"Legal Terms in Land Records," 125
Library of Congress
  fire insurance maps, 192

map collection of, 113
searching, 62-63
Locality file, creating a, 9, 27, 88
Longitude and latitude, 17, 40, 69, 71, 76-78, 200-202, 206
defined, 82
"Recording Longitudes and Latitudes," 77
See also Coordinates, location

M

Magnetic north, 80
Map Appreciation, 66
Map Index to Topographic Quadrangles of the United States, 1882–1940, 112
Map Link, vendor, of military maps, 181-182
Mapping, 15, 94
online, 39-40
Mapping the Transmississippi West, 1540-1861, 151
MapQuest, 14, 78, 94
Maps
accuracy of, 75
analyzing, 88-90
analyzing, references about, 88
citing, 90-94
collecting, 9
collections of, 75, 113
collections of, by state, 210-218
mother, 96
quadrangle, 70, 82 (see also Quadrangles)
references about, 94-95
thematic, 108
Web sites about, 94
worksheet, 89
See also specific map
Maps, elements of, 68-85, 89
cartouche, 71
collar, 69, 71-73, 76
color, 83-84
coordinate system, 69, 71, 76-78 (see also Coordinates, location)
date, 69, 71, 73-75
insets, 69, 82-83
legend, 69, 75-76
maker and publisher, 69-70, 75, 91-93
neat line, 71
orientation, 69, 79-81
place-names, 69, 84-85
projection, 69, 78-79
reliability diagrams, 73
scale, 3, 69, 75, 81-84, 188, 191
symbols, 69, 75-76, 83-84
title, 69-70, 75

Maps for America, 105, 110
Maps, reading, 64-95
accessibility, 68
connectivity, 68
distance, 67-69
distance, psychological, 68
features, physical, 67
graphicacy, 66, 94-95
location, absolute, 67
location, relative, 67
longitude and latitude, 17, 30, 40, 67, 76-78 (see also Coordinates, location)
spatial interaction, 67-69
Maps, types of
coasts and islands, 108, 164
precinct, 55-56
pubic works, 63
road, 72-74, 76-77, 85
road department, 63
state transportation offices, 63
strip, 86
ward, 42, 55-56, 61-62
See also Censuses, maps of; City maps; County maps; Fire insurance maps; Migration maps; Military maps; Railroads, maps; Topographic maps; War maps
Maptech Historical Maps, 113
Measuring America: How the United States Was Shaped by the Greatest Land Sale in History, 129
Memorials and monuments, military, 167, 169
Meridians, 78, 124, 128, 133, 206
Migration, 5-7, 143-157
barriers to, 5-7, 145
"Cyndi's List: Migration Routes, Roads & Trails," 148
"Historical American Migration & Settlement Patterns: A Selected Bibliography," 148
"Locating Colonial Wagon Roads on a Modern Map," 147
Map Guide to American Migration Routes, 147
Migration maps, 144, 146-147, 150-151
emigrant and traveler, 144, 151-154
internal improvement, 144, 148, 150-151
See also Railroads, maps
Military graves, 166-167
Military Grid Reference System, 77
Military mapping, timeline of, 160-162
Military maps, 73, 107, 158-182
in newspapers, 170-171
obtaining, 180-182

vendors of, 181-182
Military maps, sources of
    libraries and archives, 173-176
    online, 168-169, 172-173
    war-specific, 169, 172-182
Military maps, types of, 159, 162, 168
    aeronautical charts, 164-165
    battle-related, 164-166
    forts and training centers, 164
    in history books, 165-166
    navigational charts, 164
    order-of-battle, 166
    panoramic, 163-164
    post-war, 166
    topographic, 159, 162
Mother Maps of the United States, The,
    96
Mug books, 137

N

Names. *See* Place-names
National Archives, records of the, 32, 51,
    150, 176
National Geographic Society, 84-85
National Geologic Map Database, 37-38
National Geospatial-Intelligence Agency:
    GEOnet Names Server, 36
Nature of Maps: Essays Toward Under-
    standing Maps and Mapping, The,
    15
Newspaper maps, 170-171
North
    finding, 87
    magnetic, 80
North American Datum, 206
Numbering, boustrophedonical, 124

O

Oddens' Bookmarks, gazetteers at, list of,
    35
Omni Gazetteer of the United States of
    America, 30
Omni Resources, vendor, military maps,
    182
Oxford Dictionary of the World, The, 32

P

Panoramic maps, 184-187
"Panoramic Maps 1847–1929," 186
Panoramic Maps of Cities in the United
    States and Canada," 186-187
Parallels, 124, 128
Parishes, 42, 51
Photo-Auto Guides, 72
Photogrammetry, 105
Place-names, 16-40, 128
    American Indian, 16

changes, 5, 16, 20, 25, 50
common, most, 21-22
creep in, 25
Heavens-Above, database, 36-37
historic, 153
locations, multiple, 21, 24
problems, 20-24
spelling, 20-21, 26-27
standardization, 19, 32
Place-names, resources about, 21-23
    atlases, 32 (*see also* Atlases)
    bibliographies, 28-30
    "Common Placenames," 21
    dictionaries, 17-18, 29, 31-32
    gazetteers, 16-20, 24-40 (*see also*
        Gazetteers)
    online, 23, 26, 34-40
    "Town Names of Colonial New En-
        gland in the West," 21
Plains and the Rockies: A Critical Bibli-
    ography of Exploration, Adven-
    ture, and Travel in the American
    West, 1800–1865, The, 153
Plat books, 135
Pocket maps, 152
Precincts, 42
    maps of, 55-56, 62
ProQuest Information & Learning, map
    collection of, 192-193
Public land states, 127

Q

Quadrangles, 97-99, 102, 104, 106-108
    scale systems for, 106-107, 109-110

R

Railroads
    lines, 11, 110
    maps, 154-157
    towns, 186
Rand McNally, 85
    atlas, 133
    map, railroad and county, 154
    maps, road, historic, 72
Range lines, 124
Records
    tracking, 10
    vital, locations of, 42-43, 45-47
Religious groups, migration of, 152-154
Road Map Collectors Association, 71
Road maps, 17, 63, 72-74, 76-77, 85

S

Sanborn Map Company, 189-194
Satellite imagery, 168
Scale, map
    fire insurance, 188, 191

topographic, 97-98, 102, 106-110
See also Maps, elements of, scale
Slaves, African, 147
Software, 17
AniMap Plus 2.5, 39, 52, 148
citing, 91
and coordinates, 17, 77
DeedMapper 3.0, 122
Legacy Family Tree, 77
map, 114
Master Genealogist, The, 77
place-name evaluation, 28
Terrain Navigator Pro, 114-115, 201
Topo!, 114, 201, 205
U.S. Cities Galore, 28
World Place Advisor, 28
See also Global Positioning System, software for
State land states, 127
Subject Guide to Books in Print, 29
Surnames, mapping, 10
Surveys, cadastral, 124, 135
See also U.S. Public Land Survey

T
Tiger Map Service, 39-40
Topographic maps, 91, 96-115
accuracy of, 109-110
on CD, 114-115
contour intervals, 102
online, 112-114
p-, 104-105
plan view format, 102
pre-1879, 97
provisional, 104-105
quadrangles, 97-99, 102, 104, 106-110, 112
raised relief, 108
revisions, 98-99, 105-106
revisions, photo, 73-75, 105-106
series of, 106-110
sources of, 111-115
U.S. Geological Survey, 97-100, 102, 104-115
using, 110-111
Topographic maps, elements of
altitude-tint, 100
color, 100, 104-106
dates, 73-75, 99
drainage courses, 104, 106
elevations, spot, 102
features, cultural, 105, 128
features, relief, 105
features, water, 105
hachures, 100-101
hypsometric, 100
legend, 84

lines, concave, 102-104
lines, contour, 100-104
lines, convex, 102-104
scale, 97-98, 102, 106-110
symbols, 99, 104-105
title blocks, 99
Topographic Maps of the United States, 112
Topographic Map Symbols, 105
Topography, dictionaries of, 17-18
TopoZone, Web site, 133-135
Towns, land grant, 156
Township and Range System, 124, 131
See also U.S. Public Land Survey
Township Atlas of the United States, 54, 133
Township lines, 124
Townships, 42, 53-54
boundaries, 54
civil, 53-54
congressional, 124
geographic, 53-54
sectioning of, 124-127
survey, 124
Trail West: A Bibliography-Index to Western American Trails, The, 153
Transportation in Nineteenth-Century America: A Survey of Cartographic Records in the National Archives of the United States, 150
Triangulation, 87, 90

U
U.S. Army Map Service, map series, 107-108
U.S. Board on Geographic Names, records, 32
USGenWeb Project, about counties, 52
U.S. GeoGen Project, database, of geographic coordinates, 78, 202
U.S. Geological Survey, 14, 97-100, 102, 104-115
Geographical Names Information System, 37-39
history of, 98
National Atlas Web site, 104
U.S. Public Land Survey, 53-54, 123-129
bearing tree, 126
boundaries, determination of, 125-126
forty acres and a mule, explained, 125
land descriptions, reading and mapping, 131-133
mistakes, 128
surveys, locating, 129
survey tracts, description of, 124
townships, sectioning of, 124-127

Universal Transverse Mercator, 77, 200-201
Urban maps, 184-195
  bird's-eye, 184-187
  fire insurance, 183-184
  in municipal offices, archives and courts, 194-195
  panoramic, 184-187
"Using Maps in Genealogy," 14

V

Views and Viewmakers of Urban America: Lithographs of Towns and Cities in the United States and Canada, 187

W

Wall maps, 135, 137
Ward maps, 42, 55-56, 61-62
Ward Maps of United States Cities, 61-62

War maps
  Civil, 178-179
  Cold, 180
  Colonial, 176
  Indian, 177
  Indochina, 180
  Korean, 180
  Mexican, 178
  Philippine Insurrection, 179
  Revolutionary, 177
  Spanish-American, 179-180
  Vietnam, 180
  War of 1812, 177-178
  World War I, 179
  World War II, 179-180
  See also Military maps
Where Once We Walked: A Guide to the Jewish Communities Destroyed in the Holocaust, 31-32
Wind rose, 80-81
World Mapping Today, 159, 162